From Landscapes to Cityscapes

Towards a Poetics of Dwelling in Modern Irish Verse

Marjan Shokouhi

PETER LANG
Lausanne - Berlin - Bruxelles - Chennai - New York - Oxford

Bibliographic information published by the Deutsche Nationalbibliothek. The German National Library lists this publication in the German National Bibliography; detailed bibliographic data is available on the Internet at http://dnb.d-nb.de.

A catalogue record for this book is available from the British Library.

Library of Congress Cataloging-in-Publication Data
Names: Shokouhi, Marjan, 1985- author.
Title: From landscapes to cityscapes: towards a poetics of dwelling in
     modern Irish verse / Marjan Shokouhi.
Description: Oxford; New York: Peter Lang, 2023. | Series: Reimagining
     ireland, 16629094; vol. 125 | Includes bibliographical references and
     index.
Identifiers: LCCN 2023028008 (print) | LCCN 2023028009 (ebook) | ISBN
     9781800798700 (paperback) | ISBN 9781800798717 (ebook) | ISBN
     9781800798724 (epub)
Subjects: LCSH: English poetry--Irish authors--History and criticism. |
     English poetry--20th century--History and criticism. | Place
     (Philosophy) in literature. | Ecocriticism--Ireland. | National
     characteristics, Irish, in literature. | Ireland--In literature. |
     LCGFT: Literary criticism.
Classification: LCC PR8771. S56 2023 (print) | LCC PR8771 (ebook) | DDC
     821/.91099417--dc23/eng/20230718
LC record available at https://lccn.loc.gov/2023028008
LC ebook record available at https://lccn.loc.gov/2023028009

Cover image: Granada Landscape, 2022 (etching) by Alejandro Pérez Clotilde.
Cover design by Peter Lang Group AG

ISSN 1662-9094
ISBN 978-1-80079-870-0 (print)
ISBN 978-1-80079-871-7 (ePDF)
ISBN 978-1-80079-872-4 (ePub)
DOI 10.3726/b19714

© 2023 Peter Lang Group AG, Lausanne
Published by Peter Lang Ltd, Oxford, United Kingdom
info@peterlang.com - www.peterlang.com

Marjan Shokouhi has asserted her right under the Copyright, Designs and Patents Act, 1988, to be identified as Author of this Work.

All rights reserved.
All parts of this publication are protected by copyright.
Any utilisation outside the strict limits of the copyright law,
without the permission of the publisher, is forbidden and liable to prosecution.
This applies in particular to reproductions, translations, microfilming,
and storage and processing in electronic retrieval systems.

This publication has been peer reviewed.

Contents

Acknowledgements — vii

Introduction: Irish Studies and a Continuing Commitment to
Environmentality — 1

CHAPTER 1
Wilderness Narratives: De-spirited Forests, Deforested Landscapes — 13

CHAPTER 2
The Land/Mindscape of Yeats's Ireland — 41

CHAPTER 3
Countryside Narratives: Rural Ireland in Irish Revival Literature — 81

CHAPTER 4
Towards a Poetics of Dwelling: Patrick Kavanagh and the
Countryside — 111

CHAPTER 5
City Narratives: An Urban Sense of Place in Modern Irish Literature — 143

CHAPTER 6
Patrick Kavanagh in Dublin: The Irish *Flâneur* and the Big City — 161

CHAPTER 7
Louis MacNeice's North: The 'Incorrigibly Plural' Sense of Place
in Modern Irish Poetry — 183

vi   *Contents*

Conclusion   207

Bibliography   213

Index   229

Acknowledgements

A few good years have passed since my first academic engagement with Irish Studies. I have had the opportunity to know great people along the way and across the continents, friends who inspired me to write and colleagues who encouraged me to pursue my research. I have been incredibly lucky to have had the support of my loving family back home, especially my parents who will forever remain my first and greatest teachers. I am grateful to Prof Farideh Pourgiv, Dr Alison O'Malley-Younger, Prof John Strachan, Dr Geoff Nash, Dr Pilar Villar-Argáiz, Dr José Ruiz Mas, Dr Eroulla Demetriou, Dr Audrey Robitaillié and Dr Eamon Maher, the Reimagining Ireland series editor. I would like to extend my gratitude to Alejandro Pérez Clotilde for his original engraving of La Fundación Rodríguez-Acosta in Granada, which appears on the cover of this book.

The initial research for this book was supported by The North East Culture Beacon at the University of Sunderland, without whose generous support I would not have been able to undertake this project. Hereby I acknowledge that all quotations from the writings of Patrick Kavanagh are by kind permission of the Trustees of the Estate of the late Katherine B. Kavanagh, through the Jonathan Williams Literary Agency. I would also like to mention that parts of Chapter 1, 4, 5 and 6 were previously published under 'Despirited Forests, Deforested Landscapes: The Historical Loss of Irish Woodlands', *Études Irlandeses*, 44/1 (2019), 17–30, 'Towards a Poetics of Dwelling: Patrick Kavanagh's Countryside', *Estudios Irlandeses*, 14 (2019), 146–59, and '"If Ever You Go to Dublin Town": Kavanagh's Urban *Flânerie* and the Irish Capital', *Journal of Franco-Irish Studies*, 3/1 (2013), 131–42.

Granada, April 2023

Introduction: Irish Studies and a Continuing Commitment to Environmentality

Despite a critical lag in the introduction of ecocriticism in the field of Irish Studies, the last two decades have witnessed a growing interest in the study of Irish literature and culture in dialogue with environmental discourse. Gerry Smyth's 'Shite and Sheep: An Ecocritical Perspective on Two Recent Irish Novels' (2000), Tim Wenzell's *Emerald Green: An Ecocritical Study of Irish Literature* (2009), Christine Cusick's *Out of the Earth: An Ecocritical Reading of Irish Texts* (2010) and Eamonn Wall's *Writing the Irish West: Ecologies and Traditions* (2011) constitute the first body of an ecocritical scholarship in Ireland. Smyth heralded the emergence of an Irish ecocriticism as a 'ready' option 'to surpass the *particularism* which has fed discourses of domination and division' in Ireland and to discuss the country's 'wider fortune' in a global context.[1] Wenzell highlighted the importance of ecocritical studies in preserving Ireland's natural history and landscape as well as its rich literary tradition.[2] The collection of essays contained in *Out of the Earth* offered analyses of a number of canonical and contemporary Irish texts from a range of theories, including ecopoetics, ecofeminism and environmental ethics. Wall, on the other hand, explored the possibility of a comparative environmental approach in the Irish and American literary traditions based on the 'Western-ness' of their landscapes.[3]

Just as the first generation of ecocritics felt the urge to establish the relevance of ecocriticism as a valid critical approach in literary and cultural

---

1   Gerry Smyth, 'Shite and Sheep: An Ecocritical Perspective on Two Recent Irish Novels', *Irish University Review*, 30/1 (2000), 163; *original emphasis*.
2   Tim Wenzell, *Emerald Green: An Ecocritical Study of Irish Literature* (Newcastle upon Tyne: Cambridge Scholars Publishing, 2009), 1–2.
3   Eamonn Wall, *Writing the Irish West: Ecologies and Traditions* (Indiana: University of Notre Dame Press, 2011), xiii–xiv.

studies, the majority of the early ecocritical publications in and about Ireland included an apology to justify the place of an Irish ecocriticism in the wider spectrum of Irish scholarship. However, as Malcolm Sen in *A History of Irish Literature and the Environment* (2022) has pointed out, such meditations often rely on 'ideological certainties and nationalist exceptionalism', which simplify the rich and complex interplay of nature and culture, further segregating rather than considering them as part of an interrelated system.[4] Moreover, the exclusivism and particularism of these narratives are counterintuitive to widening the scope of Irish Studies beyond nationalist, insular concerns. Today, Irish ecocriticism engages with concepts as diverse as political ecology, transnationalism, famine and ecology, climate narratives, travel literature, deforestation and animal rights amongst others.

In the field of ecocriticism, what was once considered a lack of a robust methodological approach can now be celebrated as its dynamic compass, enabling a varied critical discourse that extends beyond the field's primary literary and textual practices. In the case of Irish Studies, an ecocritical approach can provide a fresh perspective into the often politicized and historicist interpretations of place and identity. *From Landscapes to Cityscapes: Towards a Poetics of Dwelling in Modern Irish Verse* continues with the current environmental debates in Irish scholarship, with a particular focus on the works of three major Irish poets of the modern period: William Butler Yeats, Patrick Kavanagh and Louis MacNeice.

The study of place and place attachments

Ireland is a rewarding country for ecocritical studies due to the attraction of its natural history and landscape, the island's unique ecological and geographical situation in Western Europe and its rich literary tradition concerned with place and place attachments. Despite the late blooming of Irish ecocriticism, there is not a lack of precedent when it comes to

---

4 Malcolm Sen, 'Introduction', in Malcolm Sen, ed., *A History of Irish Literature and the Environment* (Cambridge: Cambridge University Press, 2022), 1.

Introduction

the study of place and place attachments in Ireland, evident from the plethora of interdisciplinary publications that in one way or another address questions that are very much relevant to or inspire environmental conversations. As Gerry Smyth has pointed out in *Space and Irish Cultural Imagination*, '[g]eographical peculiarity and historical discontinuity produced a situation in Ireland in which questions concerning space, landscape, locality, gender, urban and rural experience, nature, and so on became central to both the cultural and the critical imagination.'[5]

Historically, Ireland has been a contested territory with unstable sociopolitical boundaries. With time as the dynamic variant in historical narratives, place has often been taken for granted as unchanging and stable. In the words of the eminent historian James Camlin Beckett, '[w]e have in Ireland an element of stability – the land, and an element of instability – the people. It is to the stable element that we must look for continuity.'[6] Beckett's conviction was shared by the majority of the writers, scholars and politician of the Celtic Revival out of a 'desperate hope'[7] to restore stability and continuity to a nation of diverse ethnic, religious and political backgrounds amidst the country's continuous struggle for independence. Geographically, Ireland's diverse landscape and changing environmental conditions do not correspond to the notion of land as a stable and dehistoricized entity. The regional diversity of Ireland, portrayed by the likes of geographers Emyr Estyn Evans and Tom Jones Hughes, has been at odds with 'the monolithic nature of traditional nationalist historiography', responsible for legitimizing the idea that 'Ulster alone is the separate or different region in Ireland'.[8] Eamon de Valera's utopian vision of Ireland in his St. Patrick Day's radio address in 1943 was an example of ignoring the

---

5   Gerry Smyth, *Space and Irish Cultural Imagination* (Hampshire: Palgrave, 2001), 10–11.

6   James Camlin Becket; cited in Seamus Heaney, *Preoccupations: Selected Prose, 1968–1978* (New York: Farrar, Straus, and Giroux, 1989), 149.

7   Patrick Sheeran, 'The Narrative Creation of Place: Yeats and West of Ireland Landscapes', in Anne Buttimer and Luke Wallin, eds, *Nature and Identity in Cross-Cultural Perspective* (The Netherlands: Kluwer Academic Publishers, 1999), 287.

8   Brian Graham, 'Ireland and Irishness: Place, Culture and Identity', in Brian Graham, ed., *In Search of Ireland* (London: Routledge, 1997), 11; *original emphasis*.

geographical, hence cultural heterogeneity of Ireland, which resonated in the ethos of the 1937 constitution, imposing 'a startling degree of manipulated cultural homogeneity upon the twenty-six counties'.[9]

The intricate yet often ignored relationship between cultural heterogeneity and regional diversity is crucial to understanding the connections between marginal identities and marginal landscapes. The study of Ireland's cultural landscapes in relation to the environment can reveal the links and discrepancies between cultural values and environmental actions in various regions and throughout history. It might also provide answers as to why a certain place is left in ruins while others are heavily protected. As such, (re)reading Ireland's literary heritage in the light of its dehistoricized and marginalized landscapes becomes part of an attempt to preserve its environment, just as the study of the human-environment interactions turns out to be part of a larger quest for (re)defining identity and sense of place.

Irish ecocritics thus join the array of scholars, historians and geographers who have challenged the monolithic narratives of Irish identity popularized during the Irish Literary Revival. Declan Kiberd's *Inventing Ireland* (1995), Fintan O'Toole's *The Lie of the Land* (1997), Brian Graham's *In Search of Ireland* (1997) and Colin Graham's *Deconstructing Ireland* (2001) are examples of earlier academic scholarship that strongly criticized the portrayal of a certain identity type as a definitive version of Irishness due to its inability to encompass the multiplicity of experience on the island of Ireland. Brian Graham, for instance, addressed the multifaceted question of Irish identity from a 'geographer's concern with place', linking the confusions and contestations of identity in the North and South to 'the manipulation of cultural landscape' in the literary and non-literary texts.[10] O'Toole emphasized the importance of arriving at a new understanding of Irishness that integrates Ireland's multiple cultural experiences at home and abroad.[11] Colin Graham, on the other hand, questioned the 'boundary markers' of Irish Studies based on 'political commitment' and 'assumptions

9 Graham, 'Ireland and Irishness', 8.
10 Graham, 'Ireland and Irishness', 2–3.
11 Fintan O'Toole, *The Lie of the Land: Irish Identities* (London: Verso, 1997), 12–13.

Introduction   5

of authenticity' which underlie the dominant critical discourse.[12] Declan Kiberd similarly criticized the limited scope of both nationalist and revisionist accounts of the Irish past and envisioned the future of Irish Studies as moving towards the acceptance of multi-coloured and heterogeneous varieties of Irishness, 'all beautiful, all distinct, yet all connected too'.[13]

Ecocriticism provides an interdisciplinary perspective that allows for a consideration of place from a more comprehensive approach that marries the local to the global. As Wenzell in his pioneer study *Emerald Green* has remarked, the solution to the exclusivity of Irish literary studies is to redraw the lines 'from an ecocritical perspective'.[14] An ecocritical perspective, as Lawrence Buell has noted, is issue-driven, which refers to the acknowledgement of a commitment to environmentality rather than pursuing a strict methodology.[15] Clark, on the other hand, posits that for an ecocritic, 'every account of a natural, semi-natural or urban landscape must represent an implicit engagement with what nature means or could mean'.[16] Following this premise, *From Landscapes to Cityscapes* encourages a more integrated version of ecocriticism by adopting a thematic structure that starts with a consideration of more natural landscapes and continues with the study of semi-urban and urban environments in order to arrive at a more comprehensive understanding of how senses of place are formed, contested and reformed throughout time.

12   Colin Graham, *Deconstructing Ireland: Identity, Theory, Culture* (Edinburgh: Edinburgh University Press, 2001), xi.

13   Declan Kiberd, *Inventing Ireland: The Literature of the Modern Nation* (London: Vintage, 1995), 653.

14   Wenzell, *Emerald Green*, 5.

15   Lawrence Buell, *The Environmental Imagination: Thoreau, Nature Writing, and the Formation of American Culture* (London: Belknap, 1996), 430.

16   Timothy Clark, *The Cambridge Introduction to Literature and the Environment* (Cambridge: Cambridge University Press, 2011), 6.

6   INTRODUCTION

The play of the nature/culture dichotomy

In *The Cambridge Introduction to Literature and the Environment*, Timothy Clark refers to the environment as a term that functions 'to name what there is once the older term *nature* seems inadequate, sentimental or anachronistic'.[17] Nature as a pristine landscape is more or less a non-existent entity, a concept that exists outside humankind's daily experience, symbolized in the so-called 'nature preserves' protected from human interference for scientific purposes.[18] Modern technology has mapped almost every corner of the planet, affecting the way we perceive the environment today. As access to technology and new ways of exploiting the planet increase, nature becomes more of an alien and problematic vocabulary. When addressing environmental protection schemes, it is worth asking whose environment we are trying to protect since what surrounds us today bears little similarity to the 'endangered' environment in question. The term 'environment' is often used interchangeably with 'nature', which is in turn perceived as a fragile landscape in need of protection, a romantic notion of a wild scapeland,[19] a tourist destination, a *National Geographic* picture, a BBC documentary – the list is endless. These images place nature somewhere out *there*, as opposed to the now and here of the urban/suburban human experience. Nature no longer surrounds us (non-environ); it has become the idea of a 'primordial, pristine, untouched' place, 'inspired by wilderness before the onslaughts of modern technology'.[20] It is the sum of images that reflect a non-reality, a *simulacrum*. As such, it is alien, hence *other*, to modern human beings.

17   Clark, *The Cambridge Introduction to Literature and the Environment*, 6.
18   Clarence Glacken, 'Reflections on the History of Western Attitudes to Nature', in Anne Buttimer and Luke Wallin, eds, *Nature and Identity in Cross-Cultural Perspectives* (Dordrecht: Kluwer Academic Publishers, 1999), 11.
19   Scapeland, an inverted form of the term 'landscape', is borrowed from Lyotard's reference to the individual's feeling of dislocation (*dépaysement*) from the environment, hence the inversion.
20   Glacken, 'Reflections on the History of Western Attitudes to Nature', 11.

Introduction 7

To the British anthropologist Tim Ingold, 'the distinction between environment and nature corresponds to the difference in perspective between seeing ourselves as beings *within* a world and as beings *without* it.'[21] In fact, 'the world can exist as nature only for a being that does not belong there', and as long as we view the environment from a distance, it is 'easy to connive in the illusion that it is unaffected' by our presence.[22] In reality, we are situated along with other organisms in a world where the distinction between nature and culture is, more often than not, arbitrary and conflicting.

Gary Snyder's interpretation of nature in *The Practice of the Wild* also challenges the nature/culture dichotomy by offering a point of view that situates humankind and nature in close contact. For Snyder, 'Nature is not a place to visit, it is *home* – and within that home territory there are more familiar and less familiar places.'[23] While human beings have gradually moved away from the proximity of wild open landscapes towards the technology-oriented cityscapes of the modern world, some form of nature seems to be surrounding human beings at all times. In other words, nature is not 'limited to the 2 percent official wilderness areas'. It exists everywhere, from the 'ineradicable populations of fungi, moss, mold, yeasts and such that surround and inhabit us' to 'the visible hardy stalks and stems of vacant lots and railroads' and the bacteria 'in the loam of our yogurt'.[24] Synder's interpretation of nature, as remarked by Eamonn Wall, is more cultural than geographical, implying 'the location of nature can be as fluid as the meaning of the words: rural, urban, remote, internal'.[25]

This interpretation is particularly relevant to how 'nature' has been in constant negotiation with various socio-political and cultural forces involved in major historical narratives in Ireland, such as deforestation, colonization, industrialization and urbanization. Wenzell has referred to the gradual change of nature as a source of divine power and livelihood in

---

21 Tim Ingold, *The Perception of the Environment: Essays on Livelihood, Dwelling and Skill* (London: Routledge, 2010), 10; *original emphasis*.

22 Ingold, *The Perception of the Environment*, 20.

23 Gary Snyder, *Practice of the Wild* (San Francisco: North Point Press, 1990), 7; *original emphasis*.

24 Snyder, *Practice of the Wild*, 14–15.

25 Wall, *Writing the Irish West*, 17–18.

pre-Christian Ireland to 'an unnecessary threat' in industrial Ireland as a reason behind the country's environmental crisis.[26] According to him, the twentieth-century triumph of the industrial North and the booming of the Republic's economic growth during the Celtic Tiger era were examples of a strategic move against nature. Tracing the representations of this benign or threatening presence in the Irish literary and cultural repertoire reflects the progress, conflicts and attachments of a people whose identity is built upon their personal and social relationships with the land.

Joy Kennedy-O'Neill pinpoints the ambivalent portrayal of nature as both provider and destroyer as a result of the 'uneasy sense of place' in Irish culture.[27] A sense of place, often interpreted as one's attachment to a particular locale, has been a defining feature of Irish identity and often employed as an equivalent for the equally contested concept of 'Irishness'. F. S. L. Lyons and R. F. Foster, for instance, have referred to the 'unequivocal' Irishness of the 'Anglo-Irish type [as] the man or woman in whom love of place transcended divisions based on origins, religion, or politics'.[28] Such definitive interpretations of Irishness are often based on hegemonic narratives that exclude other types of identities and relationships, such as exile, detachment or alienation from one's local environment. There also seems to be an underlying assumption that a sense of place necessarily brings about a higher degree of environmental awareness and protection. Not to mention that such an assumption is often based on interpreting a sense of place in relation to wide open spaces as opposed to the urban *loci*, which happens to be the type of environment that most of us know and interact with on a daily basis.

In her remarkable article on Elizabeth Bowen in *Out of the Earth* (2010), Joanna Tapp Pierce questioned the traditional association of sense

26 Wenzell, *Emerald Green*, 103.
27 Joy Kennedy-O'Neill, 'Sympathy between Man and Nature: Landscape and Loss in Synge's Riders to the Sea', in Christine Cusick, ed., *Out of the Earth: Ecocritical Readings of Irish Texts* (Cork: Cork University Press, 2010), 36.
28 Francis Stewart Leland Lyons, *Culture and Anarchy in Ireland 1890–1939* (Oxford: Oxford University Press, 1979), 105; Robert Fitzroy Foster, 'Varieties of Irishness', in Maurna Crozier, ed., *Cultural Tradition in Northern Ireland* (Belfast: Institute of Irish Studies, 1989), 14.

Introduction 9

of place in Ireland with an attachment to the wild and rural landscapes of the West. Bowen's place-conscious narratives, including her short auto-biography *Seven Winters*, showcase the possibility of developing a sense of place in cities. According to Pierce, 'Bowen is able to find through her memories connections that shaped her identity, proving that, at least for her, in that place and time, Dublin offered enough opportunities for attachment to place, even if only for a little while.'[29]

Chapter synopsis

Starting with wilderness narratives, the first chapter offers an ecocritical perspective into the historical loss of Irish woodlands from the early medieval period to the present time. Reading samples of Irish poetry from hermit and bardic traditions, the chapter explores the philosophical implication of place as dwelling from a Heideggerian standpoint. The dwelling relationship between humankind and the environment in early Irish culture, exemplified in the etymology of Irish placenames, the building of *raths* and forts and the cultural traditions of druidry and bardry as well as the pre-Conquest legal system known as the Brehon laws, is set against the view of the land as raw material for exploitation in the hands of the Norman and English colonizers.

Chapter 2 continues with representations of wild open spaces in the early poetry of William Butler Yeats. The extensive use of natural imagery, folklore and mythology created a sense of place that was primarily linked to the natural and the metaphysical. Irishness was, therefore, first and foremost linked to the idea of recuperating Ireland's ancient heritage through a connection with the more natural landscape of the rural Sligo region, with which Yeats had a connection through childhood memories. Yeats's sense of place later evolved to encompass the Anglo-Irish tradition present

29 Joanna Tapp Pierce, '"Nothing can happen Nowhere": Elizabeth Bowen's Figures in Landscape', in Christine Cusick, ed., *Out of the Earth: Ecocritical Readings of Irish Texts* (Cork: Cork University Press, 2010), 54.

in the more cultural landscape of the Anglo-Irish demesne, namely that of the Big House and the cultivated gardens. Moving from the 'natural' to the 'cultural', Yeats's narrative construction of place underwent stages of development that ultimately legitimized his sense of belonging to Ireland as a dweller in the landscape.

Moving from the wilderness to the country, the third chapter questions the persistent perception of 'rural' Ireland as 'real' Ireland in both literary and enviro-political narratives. After providing a general overview of the Irish countryside in connection to environmental issues and policies, the chapter looks at some of the major representations of the countryside in the Irish Revival literature, finishing with a short analysis of W. B. Yeats's figure of the peasant bard. The next chapter continues with the country-side narratives, yet from the perspective of Patrick Kavanagh, the so-called 'peasant bard' of the Irish Literary Revival, who nevertheless challenged the stereotypical representations of rural Ireland in his mature work.

Whereas revivalist narratives often presented a romanticized or out-dated view of the countryside and the rural community, Kavanagh's rural poetics presented a more complex system of interaction between rural dwellers and their surroundings. Chapter 4 highlights how the country-side appears as both repressive and liberating to the personae of Kavanagh's poetry and fiction. To the poet-farmer Kavanagh, the land signified labour and inspiration at the same time. Exploring a sense of place beyond attach-ment and territoriality, Kavanagh's work breaks with the metanarrative of Irishness and helps to create a sense of identity that is as much about love and attachment as it is about detachment, conflict and change.

Moving from the country to the city, Chapter 5 considers the Irish sense of place in relation to the urban *loci*. Highlighting the importance of an urban ecocriticism, the discussion revolves around the representation of the city, or its lack thereof, in revivalist narratives. Viewed as an antidote to the country, the city – mostly Dublin – was considered unnatural and inauthentic, thereby, unIrish. This is while cities such as Dublin and Belfast, which accommodated the majority of the literary class, demanded a new mode of representation, one that integrated the city's dynamic flow and modern pace with the emergence of new voices and identities, who con-tributed to a new narrative of Irishness in the newly independent nation.

Introduction

Chapter 6 returns to Kavanagh's urban poetry and reviews his memorable accounts of Dublin, which helped liberate the 'countrified' narratives of Irishness by choosing the city as a subject matter for poetry at the cusp of the Second World War. Caught between the poet's adoration and detestation, Dublin emerges as Kavanagh's second parish, where his *flâneuresque* portrayal of the city streets, canals and banks suggest the possibility of developing a sense of place in cities. Similarly for MacNeice, the city was a site of exploration. The MacNeicean persona, often a traveller on board of a train, provides a panoramic vista of the land/cityscape in movement. Chapter 7, thus, addresses how movement and change characterize the modern city while emphasizing the modern Irish experience as being first and foremost related to the urban rather than rural space. The urban conditions of ennui, movement and displacement become manifest as indispensable aspects of modern Irish identity, crystallized in Kavanagh's Dublin and MacNeice's Belfast. Furthermore, the socio-environmental injustice suffered by the poorer, marginalized Catholic communities of the North, as reflected in MacNeice's Irish poems, show how poverty, inequality, segregation, violence and pollution are the outcome of a system of injustice and discrimination that affects both the environment and the people who inhabit it.

CHAPTER I

Wilderness Narratives: De-spirited Forests, Deforested Landscapes

Introduction

Forests have a wide range of definitions derived from their importance and use in human culture. In official documents, a forest is often defined in terms of parameters that indicate density, area and biodiversity variables of a piece of land not used by urban and semi-urban practices. For instance, according to the *Forest Resources Assessment Working Paper*, a forest is a piece of land 'spanning more than 0.5 hectares with trees higher than 5 meters and a canopy cover of more than 10 percent or trees able to reach these thresholds *in situ*'.[1] The United Nations Framework Convention on Climate Change (UNFCCC) Marrakesh Accords, on the other hand, provides a more detailed definition which deals with legal, international debates regarding land use, gas emission, forest stock, etc.[2] In scientific jargon, forests are a vital part of the earth's biosphere, regulating the climate, preventing floods and purifying water. Being home to more than 80 per cent of the earth's biodiversity, the study of forests invites an entire array of disciplines and specializations regarding soil, water, plants, animals and even human populations.

---

1   *FRA 2015 – Terms and Definitions*, 3, <https://www.fao.org/3/ap862e/ap862e.pdf>, accessed 12 January 2023.
2   'UNFCCC Marrakesh Accords', 2001, <https://unfccc.int/resource/docs/cop7/13a01.pdf>, accessed 12 January 2023.

The role that forests have played in human civilization and the extent that mankind depends on them as shelter, clothing, food and timber cannot be solely expressed via empirical scientific criteria. The various uses and representations of forests in human culture throughout history indicate the complex nature of the human-environment relationship. Eoin Neeson points out the importance of studying the relationship between humans and trees as 'two living organisms [...] no less complex and intimate than the relationship between man and animals'.[3] What brings this intricate relationship to the forefront of modern environmental discourse is the millennia-old process of deforestation. The human-tree relationship has changed significantly since humans were predominantly hunter-gatherers. Whereas early human civilizations, such as those during the Mesolithic period, cut down trees to make boats and build houses, later civilizations cleared forests for other purposes, including farming and industry. The economic value of forests in the form of timber reservoirs led to an increasing rate of deforestation, reducing the human-tree relationship to humans as exploiters and trees as raw material. In western metaphysics dichotomy of self versus other, the exploiter/raw material binary underlies the view that separates human beings from their surrounding environment and regards forests as *other*.

The history of human civilization is often synonymous with the history of deforestation, and Ireland is no exception in this case. Surveying the loss of Irish woodlands from an ecocritical perspective brings us closer to understanding the interconnectivity of environmental and cultural phenomena. In other words, an environmental timescape of Irish forests and their gradual annihilation is also a timeline of the country's turbulent history. The aim of this chapter is to understand how the island of Ireland, once known for its dense woodlands, became almost entirely denuded of tree cover by the end of the nineteenth century and continues to be among the least forested regions in Europe.

---

3 Eoin Neeson, 'Woodland in History and Culture', in John Wilson Foster and Helena C. Chesney, eds, *Nature in Ireland: A Scientific and Cultural History* (Dublin: Lilliput Press, 1997), 133.

The historical loss of Irish woodlands

Once considered one of the most heavily forested regions in Europe, the Republic of Ireland now lies at the bottom of the European forest cover index with 11.6 per cent of its total land area under forest cover.[4] Northern Ireland, with about 9 per cent coverage, is also the least forested region of the United Kingdom, compared to 10 per cent forest cover in England, 15 per cent in Wales and 19 per cent in Scotland.[5] Yet as the commemorative epithets of 'The Isle of Wood' and 'Emerald Green' imply, the memory of Ireland as a country densely covered in woodlands persists in Irish placenames that owe their existence to the once significant relationship between people and trees in ancient Ireland. Derry, for example, is taken from Doire, signifying an oak grove. The prefix 'Kill/ Kil/ Cill', common in Irish placenames such as Kilcommon, Kilcolman, Kildare and Kilkenny, derives from the Irish word Coill, which means a wood. MacCuill, son of hazel, MacCairthin, son of rowan, MacIbair, son of yew, and MacCuilin, son of holly are examples of Irish names related to trees.

The philosophical implication of 'naming' as an act of presencing (*Anwesen*) in Heideggerian philosophy points to the human language as a *clearing* with the ability to bring forth 'the growing things of nature as well as whatever is completed through the crafts and the art [...] at any given time to their appearance'; in other words, to bring something 'out of concealment into unconcealment'.[6] A proper investigation of the significance of trees in Irish placenames calls for a linguistic study of the Irish language. My purpose here is to focus on the human-tree relationship in

---

4   'Ireland's National Inventory Report', *EPA* 2022, <https://www.epa.ie/publicati ons/monitoring--assessment/climate-change/air-emissions/Ireland-NIR-2022_ %Merge_v2..pdf>, accessed 27 December 2022.

5   'Provisional Woodland Statistics 2022', 6, <https://www.forestresearch.gov. uk/tools-and-resources/statistics/statistics-by-topic/woodland-tatistics/ #:~:text=Key%20findings,and%209%25%20in%20Northern%20Ireland>, accessed 27 December 2022.

6   Martin Heidegger, *Basic Writings* (London: Routledge, 1993), 317.

16   CHAPTER I

Ireland under the more general theme of human relationship with the environment in the form of wilderness.

Trees are interpreted as '"charismatic" mega flora and fauna',[7] which play an important role in evoking feelings of geopiety among people as well as environmental and regional groups. Coined by J. K. Wright in 1947, geopiety denotes 'the sense of piety felt by humans in relation to both the natural world and the geographical space'.[8] In Ireland, feelings of geopiety as well as regional and national identity have often evolved around trees, such as oak, hazel, holly and ash, which carry strong cultural implications. In Celtic cultures '[e]very tree, mountain, rock and spring possessed its own spirit or numen' with a power to 'both foster and destroy living things'.[9] Trees were venerated by Irish Celts as a source of spirituality and power.[10] Along with herbs, they were used as medicine or associated with keeping off bad spirits or bringing good luck. Also included in the ancient legal code of Ireland known as Brehon laws, trees were considered communal property, and cutting or mutilating them was a serious offence.

Despite this early culture of tree veneration, the human-tree relationship in Ireland underwent significant changes under the impact of consequent arrivals and departures, among which the advent of Christianity around AD 400, the Anglo-Norman invasion of the twelfth century and the Tudor conquest in the sixteenth century left a permanent mark on both the Irish landscape and culture. The gradual loss of Irish forests from the early medieval period up to the nineteenth century is a long and tedious story that coincides with the history of colonization in Ireland, where the subjugation of the wilderness paralleled the subjugation of man. What follows is a short historical outline of the major events that played an

---

7   Carl J. Griffin, 'Space and Place – Popular Perceptions of Forests', in Eva Ritter & Dainis Dauksta, eds, *New Perspectives on People and Forests* (Dordrecht: Springer, 2011), 143.

8   Griffin, 'Space and Place', 143.

9   Miranda Green, *Animals in Celtic Life and Myth* (London: Routledge, 1992), 1–2.

10   See Charles Squire, *Celtic Myth and Legend: Poetry and Romance* (London: Gresham Publishing Company, 1905); Miranda Green, *Animals in Celtic Life and Myth* (London: Routledge, 1992); Neeson, 'Woodland in History and Culture', 133-56.

Wilderness Narratives

important role in the deforestation of the Irish landscape and a selective reading of a number of early medieval literary texts.

Deforestation: A timeline of arrivals and departures

Trees are believed to have recolonized Ireland at the end of the glacial period around 10,000 years ago. Analysis of pollen from the peat bogs shows that once about 80 per cent of the Irish land surface was covered in forests.[11] The interaction of man and woodlands in Ireland may have begun with the arrival of Mesolithic people, who were primarily fishers and hunter-gatherers. Timber was used to make boats and houses. The settlement of Neolithic farmers around five to six thousand years ago and the development of the blanket bog resulted in the earliest clearance of forests, which mostly affected the West and Midlands.[12]

The next group of settlers were the Celtic tribes who arrived in Ireland around 800 BC. The Celts started a new phase of interaction with the wooded environment commonly known as tree veneration. Hazel meant wisdom; ash, yew and oak were considered sacred; and birch was associated with love. In the ancient Brehon laws, trees stood for a certain social order according to their size, use and fruit type. In contrast to the Norman forest laws which gave absolute ownership to an individual, the woodland laws in the Irish legal system were part of the common laws where one piece of land with its natural resources was allocated to an individual of a high rank in trust, to be transferred to the next patron, who was not necessarily a direct inheritor. Communal ownership gave way to the rise of feudalism after the Norman Conquest. Medieval ownership, the development of the

11   Fraser J. G. Mitchell, 'The Dynamics of Irish Post-Glacial Forests', in J. R. Pilcher and S. S. Mac an T-Saoir, eds, *Wood, Trees and Forests* (Dublin: Royal Irish Academy, 1995); cited in 'Ireland's Forests – Annual Statistics', 2019, <https://www.teagasc.ie/media/website/crops/forestry/advice/Forest-Statistics-Ireland-2020.pdf>, accessed 28 December 2022.

12   Neeson, 'Woodland in History and Culture'.

blanket bog and farming resulted in what could be regarded as the first major period of deforestation during the twelfth and thirteenth centuries.

The felling of the forests and the change of land use accelerated in the sixteenth century when Ireland officially became a British colony. The industrial development of the fuel-hungry British Isle, the growing demand for cheap timber used for shipbuilding purposes and the inefficient and corrupt system of forest administration in Tudor England put the pressure on Ireland as a suitable target for invasion, both strategically and economically. The vast clearance of forests for agricultural purposes continued during the plantation period. '[S]ystematic plantation on a vast scale' by the English, Welsh and Scottish landlords from 1556 to 1690 subdued the inhabitants whose defence capabilities were dependent on forests as shelter and ambush.[13] The seventeenth-century plantation, which had started in the southern Midlands, spread through the entire country, leaving 1.5 out of 2 million acres of Irish landscape under plantation.[14]

After the Tudors, deforestation continued during the Stuart and Commonwealth periods, decreasing wildlife biodiversity and gradually alienating the native inhabitants who relied on the woods as shelter, dwelling and source of livelihood. In less than a hundred years the social and environmental impact of deforestation was already visible in Ireland. Native species such as wolves, eagles, birds of prey and wild cats dwindled as a result of losing their natural habitats. The Irish people, on the other hand, underwent immense pressure from the British colonizers who had not only bereft them of their shelter and source of income but also alienated them from their dwellings in the proximity of the woods. This was worsened in the aftermath of the Act of Union (1800) and the absentee landlordism, which severely affected the countryside under the increasing demand for food and shelter as a result of the population growth from 1700 to 1840. Nature, which had remained a source of livelihood and spirituality for centuries, gradually turned into an awe-inspiring, threatening

13   Neeson, 'Woodland in History and Culture', 140–1.
14   'History of Forestry in Ireland', *An Roinn*, Department of Agriculture, Fisheries and Food 2008, <http://www.agriculture.gov.ie/media/migration/forestry/fore stservicegeneralinformation/abouttheforestservice/IrishForestryAbriefhistory200 810.pdf>, accessed 23 June 2013.

Wilderness Narratives 19

presence. This shift in attitude was apparent in the reaction to the early reforestation schemes that planned to improve the rapidly dwindling Irish forests in the eighteenth century.

Reforestation by the gentry, who were direct descendants of the planters, started in 1765. The schemes were 'insufficient' and 'clearly elitist', not paying the least attention to the local population and the negative impact of colonization in poor rural areas. The Irish, who already regarded landowners as 'foreigners' and 'grabbers',[15] became more hostile towards both the owners and the land. The continuing hostility persisted for well over a century in the shape of mutilating and cutting trees as a sign of political protest. The reforestation scheme continued until 1845, regardless of the deplorable situation of the famine-stricken farmers who were denied all sources of income during the minor periods of famine in the nineteenth century. Ultimately *an Gorta Mór*, the Great Irish Famine, which resulted in the death of more than one million people and the emigration of another million from 1845 to 1852, proved the indifference of the formerly 'benign' nature to the suffering of millions of poor farmers whose only means of survival was the land. In other words, the Famine carved a line of demarcation between the pre-Famine reverential attitude towards nature and the post-Famine distrust of nature.

The last but not least major cause of deforestation was the Land Acts of 1881 and 1885, implemented for the purpose of transferring land ownership to farmers. The former landowners 'were forced to fell their tree stocks prior to the sale of estate lands', and the tenants who bought the demesne uprooted what was left.[16] Furthermore, farmers exploited the remaining woodlands in search of tillage and grazing. When state forestry began replanting trees in 1903, only 69,000 hectares of Ireland's ancient and long-established forests were left, that is, 1 to 1.5 per cent of the total land area.[17]

---

15 Neeson, 'Woodland in History and Culture', 146.

16 Terence Reeves-Smyth, 'The Natural History of Demesnes', in John Wilson Foster and Helena. C. Chesney, eds, *Nature in Ireland: A Scientific and Cultural History* (Dublin: Lilliput Press, 1997), 556.

17 'History of Forestry in Ireland', Forest Service Department of Agriculture, Fisheries and Food, 2008, 3, <https://www.agriculture.gov.ie/media/migration/forestry/forestservicegeneralinformation/abouttheforestservice/IrishForestryAbriefhistory200810.pdf>, accessed 23 June 2013.

State forestry stopped during the decades that led to the independence of Ireland from Britain. The newly independent state had other priorities on the agenda; hence, reforestation disappeared in the background for some time. The increased demand for timber and fuel during the First World War led to a further reduction of Ireland's forests, while the Second World War hindered state afforestation to a considerable extent until the Forestry Act of 1946, which accelerated the process of planting trees by up to 10,000 acres per annum. Furthermore, Ireland's entry in the European Economic Community (now the European Union) in 1973 encouraged afforestation through the privatization of Ireland's forestry.[18]

The European funds, including European Commission grants, resulted in 'eliminating the sheep/tree conflict' among the farmers who had joined the reforestation scheme to plant trees in marginal farmlands. By 1979 Ireland had 'the largest and most rapidly expanding forest area per capita in Europe'.[19] Yet this acceleration was to be hindered once again as the country entered a new phase of economic prosperity during the Celtic Tiger period. Among other factors, the growth of urban sprawl led to an increasing demand for building roads that connected the countryside to cities, which at times required vast clearance of wooded regions. Furthermore, the popularity of Ireland as a tourist destination since the last decades of the twentieth century has acted as a double-edged sword. While cultural tourism led to the preservation of certain areas such as Lough Gill in County Sligo or Coole Park in Galway, the increasing human interference with the landscape as a result of insufficient management, frequent visits, road construction, traffic and pollution has had adverse effects on the environment. Today, Irish forests receive over 29 million visits per annum, which equals to an estimated value of €179 million in forest recreation.[20]

Afforestation, the creation of new forests, is still at the top of Ireland's environmental agenda, targeting 1.2 million hectares to be covered by 2030,

18 'History of Forestry in Ireland', 3.
19 Neeson, 'Woodland in History and Culture', 154.
20 ECOVALUE: Valuing the Ecosystem Services of Irish Forests, 2015. Teagasc; cited in 'Ireland's Forests – Statistics 2020', <https://www.teagasc.ie/media/website/crops/forestry/advice/Forest-Statistics-Ireland-2020.pdf>, accessed 28 December 2022.

Wilderness Narratives

that is, 17 per cent of the total land use.[21] As a result of the continuing process of reviving Ireland's woodlands during the last century, the forest cover has increased to 808,848 ha (11.6 per cent) of the total land area, which is the highest record in over 350 years.[22] Nevertheless, Ireland still lies at the lower end of the spectrum compared to the European average of 35.5 per cent.[23] Afforestation is now subject to strict environmental regulations due to biodiversity considerations. Planting the wrong species of trees or cultivating the wrong area would endanger the balance of the ecosystem, which would in turn lead to the extinction of more vulnerable species and the multiplication of others. The EU-funded schemes to stop further agricultural land use by planting trees in marginal farmlands during the 1980s was one instance that caused a serious threat to bogland biodiversity. Instead of planting trees on marginal farmlands, farmers who were given a grant to avoid further land use planted coniferous evergreen trees such as pine and spruce in large areas of peat bogs.

The non-native species of Sitka spruce, Norway spruce, Lodgepole pine and Japanese larch make up a total of 60 per cent of Ireland's forest area compared to an average of 25 per cent coverage by native species like oak, with a growth period of 120–150 years.[24] Sitka spruce species alone covers 45 per cent of the total forest area in Ireland.[25] This type of conifer takes between 35 to 55 years to mature and is considered a dominant and renewable source of timber despite its lower wood quality. On a cultural level, conifers lack the symbolic significance of oaks as emblems of nationhood

---

21   Richard O'Hanlon, 'Forestry in Ireland: The Reforestation of a Deforested Country', *The Forestry Source*, 2012, 7, <http://www.rohanlon.org/downloads/O'Hanlon%20Forestry%20Source%20June%202012.pdf>, accessed 17 February 2013.

22   National Forest Inventory 2022, <https://www.gov.ie/en/collection/15b56-forest-statistics-and-mapping/#annual-forest-sector-statistics>, accessed 28 December 2022.

23   'Ireland's Environment – An Assessment, 2016', Environmental Protection Agency, <https:// epaweb app.epa.ie/ ebo oks/ soe2 016/ files/ ass ets/ basic- html/ page-1.html#>, accessed 2 February 2018.

24   O'Hanlon, 'Forestry in Ireland: The Reforestation of a Deforested Country', 7.

25   Forest Statistics 2022, <https://www.gov.ie/en/collection/15b56-forest-statistics-and-mapping/#annual-forest-sector-statistics>, accessed 28 December 2022.

and spirituality and might as well carry 'further political and ideological discourses' as in the case of the British dislike of conifers.[26]

Today, more than half of the Irish forests are in private ownership and less than thirty years of age. The Republic of Ireland is one of the largest exporters of wood to the United Kingdom.[27] The growing interest in Irish forestry as in many parts of the world falls back on multiple incentives among which economic gain seems to overshadow environmental concerns. Forestry continues to be a growing industry in Ireland with a total economic value of €2.3 billion in 2012, equivalent to € 1,096.5 million in terms of GVA (Gross Value Added).[28] Since then, the total value of economic activity in the forestry and wood product sectors has increased by 375 per cent and 120 per cent, respectively. In 2020, the GVA at basic prices from the forestry and logging sector was €38 million, while the GVA from the wood products sector (except furniture) reached €282 million.[29] Moreover, the forestry sector has been a source of employment, especially in rural areas. In 2020, the forestry and related sectors generated about 9,500 full-time employment positions.[30] Forest recreational areas have also been contributing to the Irish economy significantly.[31] More recently, the impact of the COVID-19 pandemic and Brexit on the number of annual visits, employment, import and export of wood products in Ireland as well as the

26   Owain Jones, 'Materiality and Identity – Forests, Trees and Senses of Belonging', in Eva Ritter & Dainis Dauksta, eds, *New Perspectives on People and Forests* (Dordrecht: Springer, 2011), 168.

27   'Annual Review and Outlook for Agriculture, Food and the Marine 2019', *Department of Agriculture, Food, and the Marine, Forest Statistics*, 41, <https://assets. gov.ie/97198/bed066d2-194c-4645-81cd-8e7ba2a3448e.pdf>, accessed 28 December 2022.

28   'Forest Statistics Ireland 2020', 58, <https://www.teagasc.ie/media/website/crops/ forestry/advice/Forest-Statistics-Ireland-2020.pdf, accessed 28 December 2022.

29   'Forest Statistics Ireland 2020', 58.

30   'Ireland's Forests – Statistics 2022', 60, <https://www.teagasc.ie/media/website/ crops/forestry/advice/Forest-Statistics-Ireland-2022.pdf>, accessed 28 December 2022.

31   'Forest Statistics Ireland 2020', 54.

Wilderness Narratives

work of the Forest Health Section through 2021[32] has offered new data, which is currently under investigation by environmental and other experts.

***

Deforestation is a long and continuous narrative in Ireland, a narrative that links the colonization of land to the colonization of man and speaks of the changing relationship between humans and their living environment. As Eoin Neeson concludes in his study of 'Woodland in History and Culture', the Irish history of deforestation covers a 'full circle, from a country very largely covered by natural woodland, through one virtually denuded of tree cover, to one in which virtually all woodlands are cultivated as a crop and in which forestry is tree farming'.[33] Having briefly mentioned the outline of major incidents in the history of Irish woodland, the rest of this chapter focuses on the advent of Christianity and the arrival of the Anglo-Normans as two major events that altered not only the actual shape and form of the landscape but also changed people's understanding of their surrounding environment and consequently their relationship with it.

The arrival of colonizers

The constant arrival of the neighbouring tribes and the turbulent history of conquests and exploitations alongside periods of climate change and natural disasters transformed the Irish environment in parallel with the Irish culture. From the arrival of the first Christian missionaries in the fifth century AD to the Norman Conquest of Ireland in the twelfth Century and from the introduction of feudalism to the later British rule,

32   'Irish Forests – Annual Statistics 2019', <https://www.teagasc.ie/media/website/crops/forestry/advice/Forest-Statistics-Ireland-2022.pdf>, accessed 28 December 2022.
33   Neeson, 'Woodland in History and Culture', 155.

the land appears to have been the first target of transformation in Ireland. The anonymous writer of 'Ireland's Lost Glory' in *Birds and All Nature* (1900) refers to 'the gradual rise of English supremacy in the land' as the most important factor that led to the destruction of Ireland's forests. The English landlords destroyed large areas of woodland 'to increase the amount of arable land, to deprive the natives of shelter, to provide fuel, and to open out the country for military purposes'.[34] The writer further refers to the increasing value of timber and the continual destruction of the wooded landscape from the seventeenth century to the nineteenth, leaving Ireland with only one-eightieth of its forested landscape in 1900.

At first glance, economic gain seems to be the primary motivation behind the exploitation of forests as well as the cultivation of land and town building. Unlike the native Gaels, who showed little interest in landscaping and farming, the Norman and English settlers had an eye for the hidden profit in the development of an agricultural system and using Ireland's dense forests in the form of timber reservoirs. In 1183, Giraldus Cambrensis or Gerald of Wales, who had travelled to Ireland 'partly to join the Norman Conquest, partly to see and explore the country',[35] found the Irish lack of interest in farming and husbandry as a sign of barbarity. In the tenth chapter of *Topographia Hibernica*, which is considered one of the 'most influential accounts of the role of the environment in colonialist discourse of empire',[36] he describes the character, customs and habits of the Irish people as barbarous and slothful:

> The Irish are a rude people, subsisting on the produce of their cattle only, and living themselves like beasts – a people that has not yet departed from the primitive habits of pastoral life. [...] their pastures are short of herbage; cultivation is very rare, and there is scarcely any land sown. [...] The whole habits of the people are contrary to agricultural pursuits.[37]

34 Anonymous, 'Ireland's Lost Glory', *Birds and All Nature*, 7/4 (1900), 188.
35 Annette Jocelyn Otway-Ruthven, *A History of Medieval Ireland* (London: E. Benn, 1968), 1.
36 Amy C. Mulligan, 'Landscape and Literature in Medieval Ireland', in Malcolm Sen, ed., *A History of Irish Literature and the Environment* (Cambridge: Cambridge University Press, 2022), 36.
37 Giraldus Cambrensis, *The Topography of Ireland* (Cambridge: In parentheses, 2000), 70.

Wilderness Narratives

Dependent on fishing, hunting and gathering as well as keeping cattle, the Gaelic civilization before the Conquest was automatically considered inferior by the Normans and later on by the English whose comparatively developed system of agriculture had enabled them to draw benefit from the land. For Gerald of Wales, who described the movement from 'the forest to the field, from the field to the town' a natural course from barbarity to civilization,[38] the Irish way of life and customs were indeed a sign of incivility and lack of industry. Interestingly, it was not the uncultivated land per se that was subject to negative portrayal; more often than not, the description of the natives' appearance matched the hostile description of their surrounding landscape as 'truly barbarous':

> This people, then, is truly barbarous, being not only barbarous in their dress, but suffering their hair and beard (*barbis*) to grow enormously in an uncouth manner [...] indeed all their habits are barbarism. [Barbarism] sticks to them like a second nature.[39]

Remembered less as a naturalist and more for his anti-Irish rhetoric, Gerald of Wales provided – through his detailed and scientific accounts of the Irish environment, its flora and fauna, fish and fowl – an anti-Irish 'landscape-based rhetorics' whereby the English stewardship of the Irish soil was deftly justified. In fact, he considered both his *Topographia* and *Expugnatio* as examples of environmental practices, where 'writing the Irish landscape was conceived of as a way of "working the land" and, in so doing, appropriating it'.[40] His Muse, described as 'untrained' in *Expugnatio Hibernica*, should learn by way of hard work and practice in a field that is 'confined and arid, rough and untilled' and 'may yet be cultivated with the aid of my pen'.[41]

The derogatory portrayal of the Irish people became a common reference in the later colonial period, when the English found the colonized 'the perfect foil to set off their virtues'.[42] Edmund Spenser's description of

---

38 Cambrensis, *The Topography of Ireland*, 70.
39 Cambrensis, *The Topography of Ireland*, 70.
40 Mulligan, 'Landscape and Literature in Medieval Ireland', 49.
41 Giraldus Cambrensis, *Expugnatio Hibernica*, 25; cited in Mulligan, 'Landscape and Literature in Medieval Ireland', 49.
42 Declan Kiberd, *Inventing Ireland: The Literature of the Modern Nation* (London: Vintage, 1996), 9.

the Irish people in *A View of the Present State of Ireland* (1596) resembles that of Gerald of Wales in attributing characteristics such as wildness, barbarity, sloth and disorder to the native inhabitants. In a dialogue between Eudoxus and Irenius, the latter, who has recently returned from a trip to Ireland and appears to be an expert on Irish matters, explains the native laws, religion and customs as why 'so goodly and commodious a soyle' has not turned 'to good uses, and reducing that salvage nation to better goverment and civillity'.[43] The term salvage (obsolete for savage) is a derivative of sylva, Latin for wood, which explains the association of the natives with their wooded landscape from a negative perspective. What is seen in both Gerald of Wales and Spenser's narratives is a colonial point of view that ultimately justifies the exploitation of the neighbouring land. Like Gerald of Wales, the poet-planter Spenser points to the agricultural potential of the Irish soil, yet goes a step further by asserting his colonial perspective on subjugating the people. Cultivating the land was not only to put the Irish soil to 'good' use but to bring the so-called 'savage nation' under control and civilization. While describing the local Brehon laws to Eudoxus and explaining why the English rule had not yet tamed the natives, Irenius reduces the Irish people to animals left on their own, in need of a bridle:

> so were this people at first well handled, and wisely brought to acknowledg allegiance to the King of England: but being straight left unto them selves, and ther owne inordinate life and manners, they eftsones forgot what before they were taught, and so sone as they were out of sight by them selves, shooke of their bridles, and began to colt anew, more licensiously than before.[44]

The colonial narrative clearly functions on a dichotomous axis where the colonized are stigmatized as wild, barbarous and uncultivated; in one word, as *other*. According to Oona Frawley, aligning 'the uncultivated state that the Irish were believed to live in' with 'the uncultivated state of the land' implied that taming the landscape would result in taming

---

43   Edmund Spenser, *A View of the Present State of Ireland* (Oregon: University of Oregon Press, 1997), 2.

44   Spenser, *A View of the Present State of Ireland*, 5.

the people.[45] Hence, the notoriety of the bogs and woodlands was not only a result of the hidden military threat from the Irish; rather, the negative attitude towards the wilderness and the association of the inhabitants with the wild landscape of their surroundings justified a reform policy to tame the landscape. In the words of William Cronon, the negative attitude towards a landscape is prerequisite to transforming it: 'the most basic requirement of [exploiting the land] is that the earlier form of that landscape must either be neutral or negative in value. It must *deserve* to be transformed'.[46] The Irish landscape was seen as *terra nullius,* nobody's land; as such, the arboreal Irish landscape became part of what Jane Jacobs has termed the 'geography of desire', which mapped the colonizers' harnessing of the Irish environment for colonialist uses.[47]

Viewed from an ecocritical perspective, the colonized/colonizer binary also reinforces the negative attitude towards nature in the nature/culture dichotomy, justifying the modification and transformation of the physical environment. While referring to the rather unsuccessful project of subjugating the natives via the practice of Tudor laws under Henry VIII and a further suppression of the Irish people during the reign of the 'Faerie Queene', Queen Elizabeth I, Spenser's derogatory portrayal of the Irish system of law, religion and customs can be studied under the English superior stance not only towards the Irish people but also towards nature. Man as the master of the universe, placed at the uppermost level in the Great Chain of Being – the fruit of Christian and Scholastic philosophies – was still a popular ideology during the Renaissance. This antagonistic view turned into physicophobia, defined as the 'alienated, hostile reaction to the natural world',[48] which the likes of Descartes and Hobbes promoted during the Enlightenment.

45 Oona Frawley, *Irish Pastoral: Nostalgia and Twentieth-Century Irish Literature* (London: Irish Academic Press, 2005), 26.
46 William Cronon, 'A Place for Stories: Nature, History, and Narrative', in Anne Buttimer and Luke Wallin, eds, *Nature and Identity in Cross-Cultural Perspectives* (Dordrecht: Kluwer Academic Publishers, 1999), 209.
47 Jane Jacobs; cited in Mulligan, 'Landscape and Literature in Medieval Ireland', 46.
48 Roy Jackson, 'Overcoming Physicophobia – Forests as Sacred Source of Our Human Origins', in Eva Ritter and Dainis Dauksta, eds, *New Perspectives on People and Forests*, 29.

Whereas the negative attitude towards the landscape was a key strategy for transforming it, the potential economic benefit of the Irish soil reinforced the colonial narrative of progress based on cultivation and manipulation of the land. Hence, the density of the woods 'was to be deplored but also welcomed' – deplored for the fear of the unknown harboured in the Irish wilderness and welcomed for the potential economic benefit of its soil,[49] described by Spenser as 'goodly and commodious'.[50] Cultivation was to bring the maximum energies of the land to the surface, releasing the hidden profit by taming the wilderness. Spenser's investors were powerful New Englanders such as Richard Boyle and Walter Raleigh. Boyle had made a fortune from mills, mines and timber, and Releigh, to whom Spenser dedicated *The Faerie Queene*, was 'one of the first New English settlers to develop the timber trade in Ireland'.[51] No wonder Spenser's narrative of the wooded landscape 'gestures toward a plantation economy of timber industry',[52] based on intervention and exploitation.

One can see in the unprecedented felling of the forests during the colonial period in Ireland – be it for the purpose of transforming woodlands to agricultural land or for the myriad uses of timber – a view that reduces the forests and the entire landscape into what Heidegger calls *Bestand*; that is, a massive 'standing-reserve [...] on call for a further ordering'.[53] Such a perspective is an antidote to the comparatively less intervening role of early Irish culture, regarded by the Norman and English invaders as uncivilized. The relationship between the colonizers and the Irish landscape can further be explained via the Heideggerian notion of *Anwesen* (presencing), which implies the disclosure and 'bringing-forth' of an entity

49 John Wilson Foster, 'Encountering Traditions', in John Wilson Foster and Helena C. Chesney, eds, *Nature in Ireland: A Scientific and Cultural History* (Dublin: Lilliput Press, 1997), 26.

50 Spenser, *A View of the Present State of Ireland*, 2.

51 Thomas Herron, '"Goodly Woods": Irish Forests, Georgic Trees in Books 1 and 4 of Edmund Spenser's *Faerie Queene*', *Quidditas: Journal of the Rocky Mountain Medieval and Renaissance Association*, 19 (1998), 118.

52 Anna Pilz, 'Narratives of Arboreal Landscapes', in Malcolm Sen, ed., *A History of Irish Literature and the Environment* (Cambridge: Cambridge University Press, 2022), 36.

53 Heidegger, *Basic Writings*, 322.

Wilderness Narratives

through unconcealment.[54] The colonizers' manipulation of the landscape, on the other hand, represents what Heidegger calls *Herausfordern*, which means challenging or forcing an entity toward 'furthering something else'.[55] Rather than 'setting-in-order' (presencing), *Herausfordern* 'sets upon nature'. Hence, it is an expedition in two ways: 'It expedites in that it unlocks and exposes. Yet that expediting is always itself directed from the beginning toward furthering something else, i.e. towards driving on to the maximum yield at the minimum expense.'[56] This is reflected in Spenser's reference to making good use of the Irish soil.

Viewing the landscape from a standing-reserve perspective is an ecological hindrance to establishing a land community based on a mutual interaction between humans and the environment, a notion that constitutes the central feature of Aldo Leopold's land ethics. The Leopoldian concept of 'land community' expands the definition of community to include not only humans, but 'soils, waters, plants, and animals' or what he 'collectively' calls 'the land'.[57] One can possibly argue that a notion of land ethics or geopiety was present in Irish society before the Norman Conquest. As mentioned earlier, the land was a communally owned property in Brehon laws. The very fact that cutting or destroying trees was consequent with paying fines is proof of a higher degree of environmental ethics in precolonial era Ireland.

Linked to the notion of land ethics, the human-environment interaction in early Irish culture can also be interpreted as a form of *dwelling*. In 'Building Dwelling Thinking', Heidegger pursues the links between dwelling and being through the act of building: 'The Old English and High German word for building, *buan*, means to dwell. This signifies: to remain, to stay in a place.'[58] The German terms for building (*Bauen*) and neighbour (*Nachbar*) originate from 'buri, büren, beuren, beuron', which

54   Heidegger, *Basic Writings*, 317.
55   Heidegger, *Basic Writings*, 321.
56   Heidegger, *Basic Writings*, 321.
57   Aldo Leopold, *A Sand County Almanac* (New York: Oxford University Press, 1949), 204.
58   Martin Heidegger, *Poetry, Language, Thought* (New York: Harper & Row, 1975), 144.

signify 'dwelling, the abode, the place of dwelling'. Heidegger continues digging up the root of the verb *bauen* (to build), only to arrive at the verb *bin* (to be). Therefore, *ich bin* and *du bist* (I am and you are) mean 'I dwell, you dwell. The way in which you are and I am, the manner in which we humans are on the earth, is *Buan*, dwelling'.[59] It is from building to being (both derived from the verb 'to be') that mankind's relationship with the environment takes the shape of dwelling, which in return leads to 'preserving and sparing'; that is, the fundamental characteristics of dwelling.[60] Building is not 'merely a means' to an end nor 'a way toward dwelling', per se. Building and dwelling are not two separate concepts or activities; rather, 'to build is in itself already to dwell' and to dwell means to be at peace, 'to spare, to preserve'.[61] However, as Heidegger reminds us, the essential meaning of building as dwelling 'has been lost to us'.[62] In other words, having lost our most basic relationship with our environment, we are no longer dwellers.

An interesting example of the Heideggerian dwelling in early Irish culture can be seen in the circular fortifications called *raths*. Also known as forts or ringforts, they were built in the first millennium AD and remained in use until the twelfth century.[63] A prototype of an Irish dwelling-place in proximity of the natural landscape, *raths* along with *duns*, *cathairs* (*cahirs*) and other fortifications were first abandoned or destroyed in the Christian period.

The advent of Christianity

Among the poems preserved from the early medieval period in Ireland is the trio of fragments from the sixth century AD with which Thomas Kinsella

---

59 Heidegger, *Poetry, Language, Thought*, 145.
60 Heidegger, *Poetry, Language, Thought*, 147.
61 Heidegger, *Poetry, Language, Thought*, 148.
62 Heidegger, *Poetry, Language, Thought*, 144.
63 Bruce Proudfoot, 'The Economy of the Irish Rath', *Medieval Archaeology*, 5/1 (1961), 94.

Wilderness Narratives

opened *The New Oxford Book of Irish Verse*. The three fragments read together as a whole act as a premonition of how the arrival of the *other* – the Christian missionaries – disrupted the so-called 'natural' order of the pagan world in which the relationship between man and the environment could be described as *dwelling*:

The rath in front of the oak wood

belonged to Bruidge, and Cathal,

belonged to Aedh, and Ailill,

belonged to Conaing, and Cuilíne

and to MaelDúin before them

– all kings in their turn.

The rath survives, the kings

are covered in clay.

***

Three rounded flanks I loved

and never will see again:

the flank of Tara, the flank of Tailtiu

and the flank of Aed Mac Ainmirech.

***

He is coming, Adzed-Head,

on the wild-heade sea

with cloak hollow-headed

and curve-headed staff.

He will chant false religion

at a bench facing East

and his people will answer

32   CHAPTER I

'Amen, amen.'[64]

The first fragment starts with 'The rath in front of the oak wood' which had survived despite the death of the kings who were once owners of the rath. The construction of these dwelling places next to the groves, especially the oak tree which was considered sacred, sanctified the *raths* and placed man and nature in close proximity, making the words 'environment' and 'nature' truly interchangeable.

Dwelling was not restricted to *raths*; rather the entire landscape environing these fortifications was considered a dwelling-place by the early inhabitants. In the second fragment, the anonymous poet regrets that he would never see the 'Three rounded flanks' of Tara, Tailtiu and Aed Mac Ainmirech again. As the fragment cuts short, the reason behind the poet's sense of loss remains unknown. Yet, given the increasing power of Christianity in the sixth century, foreseen in the next fragment, the poet must have anticipated the imminent destruction of the sites. The sudden announcement of the arrival of the 'Adzed-Head' in the first line of the last fragment – 'He is coming' – is the harbinger of a sense of doom arriving from the East. Chanting his 'false religion', the man with the 'cloak' was on his way to change the course of Irish history by *desacralizing* the groves, bereaving the landscape from its protecting deity (*genius loci*) and disconnecting the native population from their surrounding environment.

The Christian missionaries also played a fundamental role in the later abolishment of the native traditions of druidry and bardry and the destruction of assembly hills, inauguration sites, *raths* and forts; that is, all that was associated with the pagan order of Gaelic society. An early example is the prologue from the ninth-century poem called 'The Calendar of Oengus' in which the destruction of the ancient dwelling places is hailed by the anonymous Christian poet:

Tara's great palace perished

with the fall of its princes

64   Thomas Kinsella, *The New Oxford Book of Irish Verse* (Oxford: Oxford University Press, 1989), 3.

Wilderness Narratives 33

while great Armagh remains

with all its worthy choirs.

[...]

The Faith has spread

and will last till the Day of Doom

while evil pagans are borne off

and their raths deserted.

[...]

The dún of Emain is vanished,

only its stones remain,

while thronged Gleann Dá Loch

is the monastery of the western world.

[...]

The Pagans' ancient cahirs

not permitted to last long

– they are wastes without worship now

like the place of Lugaid –[65]

The poet portrays the *dúns*, *raths* and *cahirs* as deserted and the pagan sites vanished along with their kings. He compares the glory and majesty of the newly 'crowded shrines' and monasteries to the deserted and destroyed dwelling places and worship sites of the pagan order. The destruction of the sites was equal to dislocating people from their dwelling places next to the forests; hence, distancing man from nature and bringing an end to an age when nature was synonymous with the term environment, a place that environs. Referring to Heidegger's definition of dwelling, Patrick Sheeran argued that 'the Irish, apart from the rath-dwellers, have never truly dwelt in Ireland any more than the aborigines have dwelt in

65   Kinsella, *The New Oxford Book of Irish Verse*, 38.

34 CHAPTER I

Australia'.[66] With the loss of status as *dwelling* and the distancing of man from nature, the forests and groves became a periphery, which nevertheless prepared the grounds for the felling of the trees during the colonial period.

The role of Christianity in Irish cultural history is double-sided. On the one hand, it prepared the grounds for the further destruction of the forests and the annihilation of earlier customs and traditions; on the other, it led to the preservation of some of the finest examples of Irish oral tradition, such as that of early Irish nature writing where Christianity remains a 'dominant element'.[67] However, as Kinsella noted, the majority of the poems between the sixth and fourteenth centuries share 'a "pagan" purity of view which gives the lyrics of the early Christian hermits their extraordinary directness and force'.[68] 'Pangur Bán' and 'The Hermit Marbán' are famous examples from this period, where the God of Christianity is seen in nature and Christian hermits bewail the loss of an earlier connection to nature.

Overall, there seems to be little unanimity as to whether it was the Norman Conquest or the Tudor colonization of Ireland that brought an end to early Irish nature writing. While Christianity desacralized the groves and the Norman Conquest opened the country to foreign exploitation, the decline of Ireland's native traditions, including the genre of nature writing, accelerated under the reign of Tudor monarchs, exemplified in the following stanzas from a late sixteenth-century poem by the Monaghan poet Laoiseach Mac AnBháird:

A fond greeting, hillock there,

though I'm cheerless at your decline:

a source of sorrow your brown thorn,

the smooth stem we knew at your top.

---

66 Patrick Sheeran, 'The Narrative Creation of Place: Yeats and West of Ireland Landscapes', in Anne Buttimer and Luke Wallin, eds, *Nature and Identity in Cross-Cultural Perspective* (The Netherlands: Kluwer Academic Publishers, 1999).
67 Kinsella, *The New Oxford Book of Irish Verse*, xxiii.
68 Kinsella, *The New Oxford Book of Irish Verse*, xxiii.

Wilderness Narratives

A grief to all, the gathering bush
we knew as our assembly place:
its boughs broken – a dismal day.
The land is meaner now it's gone.

[...]

The assembly hill – it troubles the schools –
today in stranger's hands.
I am in sorrow for its slopes,
the fair hill that held my love.[69]

According to the poet, the cutting of the 'beloved' tree and the decline of the hillock itself, which had been an inauguration site, had happened in the hands of the 'stranger'; that is, the English, who were also responsible for the decline of the bardic schools. By the end of the sixteenth century, bardic poetry was on the wane as the continuous state of war and conflict in Ireland resulted in the banishment of the earls from their native lands, which put an end to the Irish patronage system. The final blow was the Flight of the Northern Earls Tyrone and Tyrconnell in 1607, which led to the plantation of Ulster and the rising of 1641.

The story of Christianity in Ireland is no less complicated than the history of colonization and its impact on the environment. Regardless of its subtler effect, Christianity's role in Irish deforestation was rather fundamental. By devaluing the landscape, revered by the Irish, the Christian missionaries set the ground for the expedition and exploitation of the land at the hands of the Norman and English colonizers. In other words, depriving the land of its former status as *dwelling*, Christianity brought about the earliest form of cultural mutation in Celtic Ireland, that is, desacralization of the landscape. Very soon, what was left of Ireland's despirited forests turned into a deforested landscape; the desacralization of the natural world prepared the ground for destroying acres of forests and

---

69 Kinsella, *The New Oxford Book of Irish Verse*, 149–50.

dense wooded landscape of which Mac AnBháird's well-beloved and sacred hillock was but an example.

The nostalgia invoked in early Irish poems, exemplified above, recurs throughout the width and breadth of Irish history. Smith interprets nostalgia as 'an essential ingredient of ethnicity [which] embodies the desire to return to a mythic, simple "golden age"'.[70] In Irish literature, nostalgia serves as a 'safety mechanism designed to bridge past and present' in order to cope with the continual experience of change and trauma.[71] The recurrence of similar narratives in later periods is closely connected to a shared cultural anxiety which associated the loss of Ireland's cultural tradition to the loss of its natural landscape under the threat from the *other*.

An early form of this nostalgia can be seen in Irish hermits' seclusion in the woods and the creation of a body of literature that speaks of a desire to return to a former way of life, when humans were not isolated from the rest of the environment. The hermit's 'hut' in the anonymous medieval poem 'The Hermit Marbán' is an example of a post-Christian dwelling which invokes a sense of place that is predominantly nostalgic. By choosing a temporary dwelling in the woods, Hermit Marbán wishes to restore the human-nature relation to its former state of harmony, yet from a Christian perspective aligned – rather than conflicted – with the former beliefs in the sanctity of nature in pre-Christian Ireland.

Nature as periphery

The seclusion of the hermit poets in the woods and the abundance of nature writing in the form of monastic poems in the medieval period can be interpreted in light of the loss of an earlier tradition and the nostalgia to renew the connection between man and nature. While gradually abolishing the cult of nature worship and pagan traditions in Irish forests

---

70 Cited in Eva Ritter and Dainis Dauksta, eds, *New Perspectives on People and Forests* (Dordrecht: Springer, 2011), 7.

71 Frawley, *Irish Pastoral*, 3.

Wilderness Narratives

and groves, Christianity was the major reason Irish oral tradition exists in print form today. The survival of some of the finest poems of the Gaelic tradition is due to the literacy of the Christian scribes who undertook the task of compiling the non-Christian oral literature in monasteries. The same period that produced 'The Calendar of Oengus', compiled in the monastery of Tallaght in the ninth century, was the age of monastic poems such as 'Pangur Bán' and 'The Hermit Marbán', where the line between the old and new orders of the Irish society almost fades.

'The Hermit Marbán' is a conversation between King Guaire and his brother Marbán, which probably served as a model for William Butler Yeats's 'Fergus and the Druid', where Fergus, 'king of the proud Red Branch kings', desires to 'Be no more a king / But follow the dreaming wisdom' that belongs to the druid.[72] Hermit Marbán is not a druid but a Christian hermit who seems to have taken the same path trodden by the pre-Christian druids whose vocation was inseparable from the very environment (e.g. groves) the abolishment of which brought an end to their practice.

The poem starts with King Guaire asking: 'Hermit, Marbán, / why can't you sleep in your bed? / You spend your nights so often / with your tonsured head on the fir-grove ground'.[73] The King's reference to Marbán's 'bed' outside the grove and the fact that he 'often' chooses to sleep 'on the fir-grove ground' refer to Marbán's hut in Druim Rolach as a temporary dwelling, itself indicative of the concept of nature as periphery or wilderness as *other.* Marbán describes his hut as a hidden place in the woods, where 'An ash tree one side is its wall, / the other a hazel, a great *rath* tree'.[74] Both ash and hazel were considered sacred and a source of love and wisdom in Celtic culture. The hut is not an enclosed space in the same fashion that houses are confined by walls. Instead, the forest's open ground is Marbán's dwelling: 'It is a humble, hidden house / – but the path-filled forest is mine'.[75] The forest is an 'enclosure' in that it encloses the 'quarrel / or noise

---

72 William Butler Yeats, 'Fergus and the Druid', in Peter Allt and Russell K. Alspach, eds, *The Variorum Edition of the Poems of W. B. Yeats* (New York: Macmillan, 1966), 103.

73 Kinsella, *The New Oxford Book of Irish Verse*, 32.

74 Kinsella, *The New Oxford Book of Irish Verse*, 32.

75 Kinsella, *The New Oxford Book of Irish Verse*, 33.

or clamour'[76] of the world of man, separated from nature, as Marbán later refers to King Guaire's palace. Marbán's knowledge of the food and fruits in season, the type of trees in the vicinity, the wild and tame animals, and birds and insects in the forest is the result of a close relationship with the environment, one in which Marbán is at home. The wind, the clouds, and the river communicate with Marbán who describes 'The voice of the wind' and 'the river rapid / babbling on rocks' as 'lovely music'.[77] The gifts of nature – the fruit of the trees, the berries, 'the eggs / nuts, onion and honey' – are called 'the gift of God'; yet, Marbán's 'Lord' is no different from Mother Nature. As Tim Wenzell has noted, the hermits' desire to 're-treat into the shrinking forests of Ireland' was a vital part of understanding God in early Christian society of Ireland'.[78]

The former Christian view of forest as a place of sin, where man loses himself and his connection to God, is replaced with a new belief in the existence of Divine Providence in nature. According to Oona Frawley, Christianity 'brought to Ireland its own image for the archetype of a perfect existence in nature in the story of Eden, and in the idea of God as the creator of the world'.[79] As such, Druim Rolach is Marbán's Eden and Mother Nature his Lord. There seems to be no discrepancy between the old and the new religions as the hermit awaits the *Samain* Eve – a pagan antecedent of the later Christian All Saints' Night. The poem's ending is another indication of a way of life long lost but still alive in the collective memory of Ireland, a way of life for which King Guaire is ready to give his 'ample kingdom'[80] and the share of the kingly birth right to Marbán – a life in unison with nature and divinity.

'The Hermit Marbán' is a counter-narrative to Christianity's conflicting relationship with a spirited landscape discussed in earlier poems. While nature, central to the hermit's solitary and spiritual way of life, remained peripheral to the changing Irish society under foreign invasions,

---

76   Kinsella, *The New Oxford Book of Irish Verse*, 36.
77   Kinsella, *The New Oxford Book of Irish Verse*, 35.
78   Tim Wenzell, *Emerald Green: An Ecocritical Study of Irish Literature* (Newcastle upon Tyne: Cambridge Scholars, 2009), 10.
79   Frawley, *Irish Pastoral*, 8.
80   Kinsella, *The New Oxford Book of Irish Verse*, 36.

Wilderness Narratives

the pastoral aspects of a Celtic relationship with nature continued in the form of a romantic nostalgia in later periods, namely the Romantic and Revival periods, which are the subject of inquiry in the following chapters. The poetry of early medieval Irish hermits and monks provided a model of behaviour and dwelling that later nature writers strived to teach us. As Amy Mulligan mentions, it is them who taught us 'how to dwell, how to pause and listen, within a wooded environment', and perhaps in their devotion to the world as a work of divine creation, these Christian scribes established a link that connects the word to the world; in other words, they created a 'complex model for the intertwining of language and environment'.[81]

81   Mulligan, 'Landscape and Literature in Medieval Ireland', 36.

CHAPTER 2

The Land/Mindscape of Yeats's Ireland

After the gradual decline of nature writing, a new interest in nature was triggered by the European Romantic movement that reached Ireland in the turbulent years which led to the Rebellion of 1798[1] and the Act of Union (1800). Besides the antiquarian focus on reviving old Irish traditions such as Gaelic bardic poetry, which had close ties with the natural world, rural Ireland's sublime and picturesque landscapes were celebrated in Irish topographical verse. Charlotte Brook's *Repiques of Irish Poetry* (1789), Thomas Moore's *Irish Melodies* (1807) and Mary Tighe and Mary Leadbeater's volumes of verse are fine examples. At the same time, Irish novelists including Sydney Owenson (Lady Morgan), Maria Edgeworth and Charles Thomas Maturin dealt with questions of identity and nationhood in narratives that shifted from melancholy and nostalgia to Gothic trauma and horror.

Despite the awakened interest in nature and the recurring dominance of natural imagery in works ranging from Oliver Goldsmith's 'The Deserted Village', where the first signs of nostalgia over the loss of a natural environment was manifest, to the early pastoral and topographical poems of William Butler Yeats, there seems to be little interest in nature for and in itself. More often than not, nature is a cultural construct, a symbol, a backdrop to a more urgent political or national agenda. According to J. W. Foster, '[t]here are no Irish poets of the time to whom we might refer to as "nature poets" in the way we might refer to Wordsworth and

---

[1] Claire Connolly in the new *Cambridge History of Irish Literature* observes: 'Ireland entered the period of Romanticism scorched by what Quaker writer Mary Leadbeater called the "ruthless fires" of the 1798 rebellion.' Claire Connolly, 'Irish Romanticism, 1800–1830', in Margaret Kelleher and Philip O'Leary, eds, *The Cambridge History of Irish Literature* (Cambridge: Cambridge University Press, 2006), 407.

Clare.'[2] Yet, we should not forget that when we talk about 'nature' in Irish Romanticism, we do not deal with the peaceful pastoral surroundings of an English countryside under threat by urban encroachment; nor is the poet an exalted, philosophical figure musing over the sublime and picturesque setting of a Mont Blanc or Scottish Highlands landscape. When Irish poets wrote about the picturesque landscapes of places such as Killarney in County Kerry or Glendalough in County Wicklow, they dealt with an environment under imminent threat from both Irish insurgency and the yeomanry. Aware of the horror of violence behind the actual landscape, the Irish Romantic poets often faced the challenge of either smoothing over or acknowledging the morbid terror of local violence and military occupation. In the words of Jim Kelly, if there exists a metanarrative to Irish poetry in this period, 'it involves the attempt to accommodate sentimental literature to brutal historical experience'.[3]

Overall, Irish Romantic literature is a literature preoccupied with questions of national identity and representation in post-Union Ireland. While there is an obvious return to the nostalgic mode over the loss of nature and an insistence on restoring the quintessential Romantic ideals of individuality and authenticity, there is a competition for narrative space between 'Ireland's natural beauties and economic decay' as seen in the novels of the period.[4] Equally, nineteenth-century Irish poetry, regardless of its refined Romantic sensibility and appreciation of the natural landscape, is deeply engaged with political issues of its time, including religious sectarianism, violence and the struggle for Catholic emancipation. This is why Kelly deems the scholarly separation of Irish Studies from Romantic Studies in the twentieth century due to the 'irreducibly political character of Irish literature' in the nineteenth century.[5]

2   John Wilson Foster and Helena C. Chesney, eds, *Nature in Ireland: A Scientific and Cultural History* (Dublin: The Lilliput Press, 1997), 411–12.
3   Jim Kelly, 'Ireland and Union', in David Duff, ed., *The Oxford Handbook of British Romanticism* (Oxford: Oxford University Press, 2018), 150.
4   Claire Connolly, *A Cultural History of the Irish Novel, 1790–1829* (Cambridge: Cambridge University Press, 2011), 41.
5   Kelly, 'Ireland and Union', 139.

The Land/Mindscape of Yeats's Ireland

Returning to the topic of nature writing in Irish literature, there is a keyword that distinguishes eighteenth- and nineteenth-century Irish nature poetry from earlier examples: the term 'landscape' with its overriding symbolist value. Derived from the Middle Dutch 'lantscap' and closely associated with Renaissance landscape paintings, the English term 'landscape' has 'incorporated notions of *locus amoenus* (pleasant prospect), Arcadia, the Golden Age, the sublime, the beautiful, the picturesque, wilderness or parkland, home or homeland according to taste or politics'.[6] Similarly, the notion of landscape in Irish Romantic and, later on, Revival poetry denotes a poetic landscape whose relationship with the actual environment is usually symbolic or esoteric. Insistence on nature in the form of primitive, ruined or abandoned landscapes throughout the period created an interest in the pre-Conquest Irish culture associated with all that was noble, natural and authentic. The past and its heroic values, the mystery of the woods and bogs and the folkloric and supernatural appeal of the landscape stood in sharp contrast to the post-Conquest Irish culture embedded in the cultivated gardens of the Anglo-Irish demesne, which signified the presence of a foreign imperial culture, i.e. the English.

Rooted in the Roman and English cultures, hence considered a nonnative influence, and with focus on cultivating the land for the purpose of improving growth, the gardens were seen as a cultural artefact, designed to be pleasing to the eye from the interior of the big house, 'the center of the estate, and to the lord and lady, center of civilized life in the country'.[7] Despite the shift in aesthetic and cultural priority of the demesne from the seventeenth century, focused on subduing nature and showcasing the grandeur of the big house and its owner, to the eighteenth-century appropriation of a more 'natural' model of landscaping, which gave the gardens the appearance of a natural parkland, to the 'wild garden' aesthetic of the

---

6   Dainis Dauksta, 'Landscape Painting and the Forest – The Influence of Cultural Factors in the Depiction of Trees and Forests', in Eva Ritter and Dainis Dauksta, eds, *New Perspectives on People and Forests* (Dordrecht: Springer, 2011), 125.

7   Ruth Glancy, *Thematic Guide to British Poetry* (Connecticut: Greenwood Press, 2002), 168.

44 CHAPTER 2

late nineteenth century,[8] the Anglo-Irish demesne remained a highly problematic space in the Irish cultural imagination.

Up until the beginning of the decline of the Anglo-Irish demesne in 1870, there were more than 4,000 big-house estates, of which only fifty remain in the ownership of their original families today.[9] The Big House was laden with Protestant guilt over the Catholic dispossession of the very land upon which such estates were built. The cultivated gardens were also a reminder of the tangled history of foreign invasions, plantation and deforestation. No wonder young W. B. Yeats evaded any mention of the gardens or Lady Gregory's Coole House in his first volumes and focused instead on the more 'natural' and ancient landscape of the seven woods.

Abundant in wild natural imagery and symbolism, the early poems of W. B. Yeats conveyed a sense of loss and nostalgia that was characteristic of Irish Romanticism while echoing the long-lost nostalgic tunes of an earlier tradition of Irish nature writing, exemplified in the bardic and hermit poetry. For the Irish historians who trace the beginning of Irish Romanticism – with almost half-a-century delay – in the works of James Clarence Mangan and Thomas Davis, the early poetry of W. B. Yeats is considered the fruition of the movement in Ireland. Under the influence of Thomas O'Grady and the Celtic Revival of Thomas Moore, the young poet was intent on creating a sense of place – hence of Irishness – through a connection to the landscape. Moving from a more 'natural' to a more 'cultural' landscape throughout his poetic trajectory, Yeats's narrative construction of place engages with various forms and shapes of dwelling, which is worth scrutiny from an ecocritical perspective.

---

8   Kelly Sullivan, 'The Ecology of the Irish Big House, 1900–1950', in Malcolm Sen, ed., *A History of Irish Literature and the Environment* (Cambridge: Cambridge University Press, 2022), 177.
9   Sullivan, 'The Ecology of the Irish Big House, 1900–1950', 173.

The narrative construction of place

The early poetry of William Butler Yeats insists on the 'natural' side in the play of the nature/culture dichotomy, representing Irishness in connection to the woods, waters, mountains and valleys. The woods, particularly, make up the dominant imagery. Oisin follows Niamh to a 'bare and woody land';[10] *Crossways* starts with nostalgia over the loss of Arcady: 'The woods of Arcady are gone';[11] the Indian temple in 'Anashuya and Vijaya' is surrounded by a garden inside a forest; King Goll wanders in the woods where the leaves flutter around him; the 'leafy island' where the faeries take the 'stolen' child is somewhere in 'Sleuth Wood',[12] and so on and so forth.

In contrast to the gardens, the woods are a place of natural growth. They embody a wide range of significations, from joy to madness, from spiritual revelation to fear and darkness and from the natural to the supernatural. Yet, despite the dominant role of natural imagery in these poems, there seems to be 'a striking lack of interest in nature or landscape per se'.[13] Similar to the symbolic or nationalist constructions of 'nature' in Irish Romanticism, the rivers, hills, woods and valleys in Yeats's wilderness are often represented not 'so much for their intrinsic or even aesthetic value but insofar as they can be made to symbolise a world elsewhere or because they are connected with a particular incident'.[14] The woods and valleys are where the supernatural happens, as exemplified in two of Yeats's most popular songs: 'The Stolen Child' and 'The Song of Wandering Aengus'. Lakes and rivers are mostly associated with esoteric and theosophical concepts, such

---

10   William Butler Yeats, *The Wanderings of Oisin*, in Peter Allt and Russell K. Alspach, eds, *The Variorum Edition of the Poems of W. B. Yeats* (New York: The Macmillan Company, 1957), 15.

11   Yeats, 'The Song of the Happy Shepherd', in *The Variorum Edition of the Poems,* 64.

12   Yeats, 'The Stolen Child', in *The Variorum Edition of the Poems,* 86.

13   Patrick Sheeran, 'The Narrative Creation of Place: Yeats and West-of-Ireland Landscapes', in Anne Buttimer and Luke Wallin, eds, *Nature and Identity in Cross-Cultural Perspective* (Dordrecht: Kluwer Academic Publishers, 1999), 292.

14   Sheeran, 'The Narrative Creation of Places', 292.

as in 'I Walked among the Seven Woods' and 'Coole and Ballylee, 1931'. Birds, animals and flowers are poetic ornamentations or symbols, such as in *The Wanderings of Oisin*, the 'Rose' poems and 'Two Songs of a Fool'.

Patrick Sheeran pointed out the importance of considering the Irish landscape in relation to the narrative approach to place and place-making.[15] Just as Yeats's 'nature' – representing his early notion of Ireland – was inseparable from the literary and cultural narratives interwoven in the Irish West, the actual landscapes of Lough Gill in County Sligo or Coole Park in County Galway, for instance, became indivisible from the Yeatsian mindscapes of Innisfree, Coole, Sligo, Leitrim, etc. To paraphrase Sheeran, it is impossible not to think of Hamlet when at Elsinore or of Yeats when on Innisfree.[16] Indeed, Yeats's narrative construction of place has become part of the very landscape, tangled with its flora and fauna.

In relating stories to place and invoking a sense of place in terms of topophilia and attachment, Yeats's early poetry can be read as a modern example of *dinnseanchas*, where places turn into potent cultural constructs by conjuring up layers of myth, history and memory. Considered as one of the most assiduous studies that led to the creation of a large body of literature, *dinnseanchas*, or 'the lore of high places', served as 'a kind of Dictionary of National Topography' in the early medieval period.[17] John Montague translated *dinnseanchas* as 'place wisdom', which implies a 'sense of the historical layers and legends which give character to an area, a local piety deeper than the topographical'.[18]

The *Temair Breg* poem, translated by Edward J. Gwynn, is a fine example of early *dinnseanchas*, which renders a topographical account of the Hill of Tara. The historical significance of Tara goes back to Celtic and in some documents to pre-Celtic and Neolithic periods in Irish history, where the Hill is believed to have been the seat of high kings and *Tuatha Dé Danaan* (the tribe of goddess Danu), the gods and goddesses of ancient Ireland dwarfed into faeries in Christian Ireland.

15   Sheeran, 'The Narrative Creation of Place', 292.
16   Sheeran, 'The Narrative Creation of Place', 290.
17   Robin Flower, *The Irish Tradition* (Oxford: Clarendon Press, 1966), 1.
18   John Montague, *The Figure in the Case and Other Essays* (New York: Syracuse University Press, 1989), 56.

The Land/Mindscape of Yeats's Ireland   47

Located near the river Boyne in County Meath, the Hill of Tara is among Ireland's most popular heritage sites and an example of the Irish *genius loci* turned into *genius fabulae*, when stories about a place replace the place itself, leaving it to 'wrack and ruin'.[19] The construction of the M3 motorway near the site in 2007, which led to widespread protests asking for a rerouting of the motorway to save the Valley of Tara, is among the incidents that point to 'the Irish failure to cultivate, cherish or enhance place in any material way'.[20] In other words, the sense of local piety, characteristic of *dinnseanchas* and other Irish topographical traditions, does not always parallel an equal sense of awareness, care and responsibility towards the actual environment. Topophilia or a knowledge of one's place may be a prerequisite for protecting a certain locale or region, yet to assume that topophilia alone leads to protection is an oversimplification that does not take into consideration the complex nature of human relationship with place and how social, political, and regional factors – amongst many others – shape, reshape or even destroy places.

In *Temair Breg*, the bard Fintan pursues the history of Tara from 'a time when it was a pleasant hazel-wood / in the days of the noble son of Ollcan / until the tangled wood was cut down / by Liath son of Laigne Lethanglas'.[21] Here is an excerpt from the third poem of the *Temair* narrative where Fintan's topography is merged with historiography and mythology:

Eastward from Rath Grainde in the glen

is the Marsh of strong Temair;

east of the Marsh there are

RathNessa and RathConchobair.

The Measure of the Head of grim Cuchullin

lies north-east from Rath Conchobair;

19   Sheeran, 'The Narrative Creation of Place', 291.
20   Sheeran, 'The Narrative Creation of Place', 291.
21   Edward John Gwynn, *The Metrical Dindshenchas* (Dublin: Hodges, Figgis, and Co.; London: William and Noegate, 1924), 3, <http://archive.org/stream/met ricaldindsenco4royauoft/metricaldindsenco4royauoft_djvu.txt>, accessed 12 April 2013.

48 CHAPTER 2

> the dimension of his Shield under its Boss
>
> is wonderful and huge.[22]

The poet follows the bloodline of every king and warrior whose history was once interwoven with the history of Temair. Each *rath* invokes one layer of a historical or mythical cycle, bringing back to life other narratives associated with it. The reference to Rath Conchobair, for instance, relates to the history of Conor mac Nessa, the famous king of the Ulster Cycle and also revives the memory of Cuchulain, the legendary hero of *The Tain* and his gigantic shield. Fintan reads Tara as a text related to previous texts, as each *rath* embodies a certain narrative. In other words, the poet communicates through intertextuality which, as Sheeran noted, is 'the way to grasp a topographical tradition.'[23]

The intertextuality of the topographical tradition goes in parallel with the intertextuality of the landscape in general. Barnes and Duncan mention places as 'intertextual sites because various texts and discursive practices based on previous texts are deeply inscribed in their landscapes and institutions.'[24] In the *Temair* poem, it is the invocation of the same mythic histories, chronicles and memories associated with a certain locale – the hill of Tara – that defines the poet's sense of identity and belonging to Ireland. Early in the poem, Fintan refers to his fame as an Irish bard by exalting Temair as a place of memory and heroism: 'I am Fintan the poet, / I am a salmon not of one stream; / it is there I was exalted with fame, / on the sod-built stead, Temair.'[25] As Heaney wrote, '[o]ne half of one's sensibility is in a cast of mind that comes from belonging to a place, an ancestry, a history, a culture,'[26] and Tara provides that background for the poet and those writing of Tara and Ireland thereafter.

---

22 Gwynn, *The Metrical Dindshenchas*, 18.
23 Sheeran, 'The Narrative Creation of Place', 299.
24 Trevor J. Barnes and James S. Duncan, eds, Writing Worlds: Discourse, Text and Metaphor in the Representation of Landscape (London: Routledge, 1992), 7–8.
25 Gwynn, *The Metrical Dindshenchas*, 5.
26 Seamus Heaney, *Preoccupations: Selected Prose, 1968–1978* (New York: Farrar, Straus, and Giroux, 1989), 35.

Fintan's testimonial reference to his vocation as an Irish bard was a popular practice in what was known as the Contention of the Bards in the Middle Ages, where a bard's position among his peers depended on his knowledge of the landscape in its historical and topographical contexts. The poets of the north and south often legitimized their sense of belonging to Ireland by appealing to a sense of place. This early invocation turned into an anxiety to create a hegemonic understanding of place in later colonial period when the necessity of challenging British stereotyping created a linear narrative of Irish identity known as Irishness. Often understood as two sides of the same coin, Irishness and sense of place are among the most frequent issues discussed in the field of Irish Studies. As Sheeran noted, '[i]t is well-nigh a truism that Irishness and a sense of place go together.'[27] Edward Estyn Evan in *The Personality of Ireland* (1973), Seamus Heaney in *Preoccupations* (1980) and Oliver MacDonagh in *States of Mind* (1983) equally acknowledged the interchangeability of sense of place and Irishness.

A sense of place is most commonly described as one's affinity with a particular region in terms of topophilia or love of place. There are, perhaps, as many definitions of sense of place as there are various types of relationships between individuals and places. Right of birth, personal and community attachments to a particular region, emotional and psychological affiliations and religious and historical narratives are among factors that influence one's sense of belonging to a place or region. On the other hand, one could also make the case that there is a negative association with place that marks out this concept – Auschwitz being an obvious example with its marking of the Jewish literary practice since the Holocaust. A sense of place, therefore, conveys a wide range of relations from attachment and affinity to trauma and displacement, exemplified by the poems written in the years of the 1798 rebellion and the 1800 Act of Union. The problematic experiences of detachment, alienation, inbetweenness and placelessness equally describe a type of connection with place which can still be categorized under a sense of place and, for that matter, a sense of one's identity, both individual and collective.

---

27   Patrick Sheeran, '*Genius Fabulae*: The Irish Sense of Place', *Irish University Review*, 18/2 (1988), 192.

In Ireland, the sense of place has primarily been a question of one's relationship with land. 'Throughout the length and breadth of Ireland, setting aside great towns, the main interest of life for all classes is the possession of land', and this knowledge, writes Stephen Gwynn in *Irish Books and Irish People* (1919), is an essential requirement for a writer concerned with Irish life.[28] Gwynn's statement continues with the hyperbolic, yet somewhat true, assertion about the peasantry's peculiar relationship with land: 'Irish peasants seldom marry for love, they never murder for love; but they marry and they murder for land.'[29] These commentaries reflect the inevitable presence of land issues in narratives of Irish life, including the painful history of class division and land struggle while pointing to the exclusion of cities from these narratives.

The complicated and conflicting relationship of the peasantry with land can be explained under John Brinckerhoff Jackson's definition of sense of place as a sense of 'recurring events'.[30] For Jackson, 'a sense of place is something that we ourselves create in the course of time; it is the result of habit or custom' rather than 'our response to features which are already there [...], natural or man-made.'[31] The continuous history of land agitations, heightened by the application of the Penal Code which prevented the Catholics from owning land and property, the absentee landlordism of the following years, the Catholic Emancipation of 1829 and the resulting conflicts that continued up to the mid-nineteenth century summarize the sense of place in Ireland as a sense of recurring land conflicts for the Catholic majority, who were often living in impoverished conditions. This sense of place, built on the continuing discrimination and class struggle, starvation, death and emigration, was buried under the increasingly popularized load of narratives that promoted a hegemonic understanding of place under the illusion of a shared sense of place and aimed at appealing to a middle-class audience in Dublin and abroad. Not surprisingly, the majority of these narratives were written by a minority of Anglo-Irish writers who had held

28   Stephen Gwynn, *Irish Books and Irish People* (Dublin: Talbot Press, 1919), 10.
29   Gwynn, Irish Books and Irish People, 10.
30   John Brinckerhoff Jackson, *A Sense of Place, A Sense of Time* (New Haven: Yale University Press, 1994), 151.
31   Jackson, *A Sense of Place*, 151.

The Land/Mindscape of Yeats's Ireland

a prominent position in the literary/political scene since the eighteenth century. Interestingly, while the Anglo-Irish minority, whose story of involvement with land went back to the seventeenth-century plantation and the rise of the Protestant Ascendency, experienced a different side to the ongoing narratives of possession and dispossession of land, their sense of place was also tied to the land.

The rhetoric of compensation and the myth of place in Anglo-Irish narratives

Despite their diminishing socio-political influence under the Act of Union (1800) and the series of Land Acts (1870–1909), which gradually dispossessed the landed class of their previously owned estates, the Anglo-Irish minority continued to play a dominant role in the Irish literary scene. Maria Edgeworth and Sydney Owenson, for instance, attracted a large readership at home and abroad. Following the Celtic revival in Europe and the increasing demand for an Irish version of Romanticism, the market for the selling of materials dealing with the matter of Ireland flourished in Dublin, London and New York. According to James Camlin Beckett, the popularity of these narratives was a result of their superior literary merit in comparison to the novels written by the Catholic writers. We may not be able to neglect the rather one-dimensional representation of Irish life from the Ascendency point of view, which was often 'weakened by an air of artificiality and make-believe'; yet, the image they represented 'was misleading only because it was not balanced by any companion price'. In Beckett's view, from the mid-nineteenth century 'to the early decades of the twentieth, Catholic Ireland failed to produce any novelist of sufficient ability to catch and keep the attention of the English-speaking world'.[32]

---

32 James Camlin Beckett, *The Anglo-Irish Tradition* (London: Faber and Faber, 1976), 141–2.

Besides responding to the literary market inside and outside Ireland, the Anglo-Irish writers were concerned with regaining their sense of belonging by establishing a spiritual connection with land in place of their former relationship based on ownership. The struggle for a spiritual repossession of land has been a characteristic of postcolonial cultures. In Ireland, the strategy was 'to move from the brute fact of conquest to a claim of spiritual inheritance, which retrospectively legitimates possession'.[33] The interest in topographical narratives such as the Gaelic tradition of *dinnseanchas* among the Protestant writers, including Yeats, was part of a rhetoric of compensation where place-as-the-stable-element replaced the recent history of discrimination, political unrest, and famine. In the words of Declan Kiberd, '[w]hile the majority of the writers of the Catholic Irish background seemed obsessed with the history of their land', the Protestant writers 'turned to geography in the attempt at patriotization.'[34] Irishness, therefore, addressed a notion of a shared historical consciousness embedded in the landscape. This forged notion of identity was meant to surpass ethnic, religious and socio-political differences which were but a source of dispute between the Catholics and Protestants since the rise of the Ascendency. The myth of place was thus offered as an 'assuagement both for the guilt of the possessors and the grief of the dispossessed'.[35]

Along with the myth of place came the 'proprietorial interest in fairies' which, besides 'the discovery of antiquarianism, archaeology, topography, and history', aimed at satisfying the Ascendency's impulse to belong to an 'authentic' version of Irish culture.[36] The Irish fiction written after the Catholic Emancipation often employs 'supernatural stratagems as a way of responding to history'.[37] Supernatural elements and landscapes cover almost the entire length of the Revival period up to the early twentieth century where the supernatural, most notably the belief in the existence of

33 Sheeran, 'The Narrative Creation of Place', 287.
34 Declan Kiberd, *Inventing Ireland: The Literature of the Modern Nation* (London: Vintage, 1996), 107.
35 Sheeran, 'The Narrative Creation of Place', 287.
36 Robert Fitzroy Foster, *Words Alone: Yeats and His Inheritances* (Oxford: Oxford University Press, 2011), 115.
37 Foster, *Words Alone*, 95.

The Land/Mindscape of Yeats's Ireland

the *Sidhe*, dominated Irish Gothic fiction, the Big House novels, national ballads and topographical poetry. Books such as Thomas Crofton Croker's seminal work on Irish folklore *Fairy Legends and Traditions of the South of Ireland* (1825) influenced the revivalists who incorporated the fairylore existent in Irish rural culture 'into the rediscovery and assertion of an individual national identity'.[38]

The majority of these writers, including Charles Maturin, Sheridan Le Fanu, Bram Stoker and later on Elizabeth Bowen and W. B. Yeats had emerged from Protestant families whose habit of living in England had created a sense of loss and nostalgia, mirrored in their engagement with the occult and supernatural. In their attempts at defining their country and identity, the Anglo-Irish writers created an Ireland that was 'auto-exotic';[39] that is, exotic and other even to themselves. In a way, auto-exoticization enabled them to explore the 'otherness' of their own country.[40] As a result, Irish history was 'traced back to mythical, fictional but colourful roots', and Irish life was 'reduced to its un-English aspects',[41] and what could possibly be more exotic, natural and Irish than the past?

Indeed, the Revival's fascination with all things Irish had become equivalent with all things past. Constant reference to the past as a golden age inflicted representations of Ireland with a growing sense of nostalgia. By pushing the hands of the clock backward in time, the Anglo-Irish writers meant to create a point of reference in history where the past was no longer a reminder of famine, discrimination, poverty and death, but a kind of utopia which represented tradition, virtue, chivalry and victory. Ironically, what this auto-exoticization and emphasis on the supernatural and occult delivered was a sense *not* of place, but of placelessness. According to Roy Foster, the revivalists' occult preoccupations 'mirror a sense of displacement, a loss of social and psychological integration, and an escapism motivated by

---

38   Foster, *Words Alone*, 102.

39   Joseph Theodoor Leerssen, *Remembrance and Imagination: Patterns in the Historical and Literary Representation of Ireland in the Nineteenth Century* (Indiana: University of Notre Dame Press, 1997).

40   Foster, *Words Alone*, 124.

41   Leerssen, *Remembrance and Imagination*, 225.

54   CHAPTER 2

the threat of a takeover by the Catholic middle classes'.[42] This sense of displacement is particularly evident in Yeats's early poetry where the personae keep wandering in landscapes that are simultaneously real and imaginary, natural and supernatural, welcoming and threatening. Despite the symbolic and esoteric references to landscape in most poems, the inextricable link between Yeats's representations of place and the development of his various poetic personae can still be viewed from the vantage point of ecocriticism. In particular, the narrative construction of place with emphasis on rootedness relates to the Heideggerian notion of dwelling.

Between landscapes: The evolution of the Yeatsian personae

If one thing connects W. B. Yeats's poetry to the long-established tradition of nature writing in Ireland, it is the elaborate description of the Irish landscape. The landscape, whether in its physical or mental shapes (mindscape), is not just a setting for the final development of a particular theme or persona; rather, in many cases, the landscape constitutes the main element in the poem. It is impossible to imagine 'The Stolen Child' without the dreamlike scenery of Sleuth Wood or to think of Lady Gregory's house outside the context of the seven woods of Coole.

The trio of the 'Indian' poems in *Crossways*, 'Anashuya and Vijaya', 'The Indian upon God' and 'The Indian to His Love', is an example of the organic relationship between the Yeatsian personae and their surrounding landscapes. The first poem, titled 'Jealousy' in the 1895 version, 'was meant to be the first scene of a play about a man loved by two women', according to a note which dates back to 1925 in Yeats's commentary in *Collected Poems*.[43] The name Anashuya was taken 'from Kalidasa's play *Sakuntala*', which Yeats had read in the translation of Monier Williams.[44] What connects the poem

42   Foster, *Words Alone*, 115.
43   William Butler Yeats, *The Collected Poems of W. B. Yeats* (London: Macmillan, 1967), 523.
44   Alexander Norman Jeffares, *A Commentary on the Collected Poems of W. B. Yeats* (London: Macmillan, 1968), 6.

The Land/Mindscape of Yeats's Ireland

to the pastoral theme of Yeats's early poetry is not exactly the love triangle or the idea of 'two people with one soul' which was developed later,[45] but the theme of nature veneration, reflected in the close relationship between the personae and the landscape. The setting is described as a 'little Indian temple in the Golden Age', surrounded by a garden 'around which is *the forest*'.[46] Yeats incarnates the image of the poet as the nature lover and pantheist in the persona of Anashuya, the young Brahman priestess who offers 'prayers for the land' and prayers for her beloved on the same score:

> Send peace on all the lands and flickering corn. –
>
> O may tranquillity walk by his elbow
>
> When wandering in the forest, if he love
>
> No other. – Hear, and may the indolent flocks
>
> Be plentiful.[47]

All parts of nature are deemed equally valuable as the priestess prays for the land. The flocks, 'the flies below the leaves', 'the young mice / In the tree roots', and 'all the sacred flocks / Of red flamingos'[48] are blessed in Anashuya's prayer before she says a blessing for her lover Vijaya. The blessings in the context of the wooded scenery recall the Celtic veneration of nature in early Irish poetry. Nature veneration, as mentioned in the previous chapter, implies the existence of a land community where an egalitarian view is to be seen 'on the part of humans not only toward all members of the ecosphere, but even toward all identifiable entities or forms in the ecosphere'.[49]

---

45 Yeats, *The Collected Poems*, 523.

46 Yeats, 'Anashuya and Vijaya', in Peter Allt and Russell K. Alspach, eds, *The Variorum Edition of the Poems of W. B. Yeats* (New York: The Macmillan Company, 1957), 70; *original emphasis*.

47 Yeats, 'Anashuya and Vijaya', 71.

48 Yeats, 'Anashuya and Vijaya', 75.

49 George Sessions, ed., *Deep Ecology for the Twenty-First Century: Readings on the Philosophy and Practice of the New Environmentalism* (London: Shambhala, 1995), 270.

Young Yeats had probably chosen the scene because of his acquaintance with Indian culture and philosophy through Mohini Chatterjee at the age of twenty-two. Certain elements in predominantly rural Indian culture might have fascinated the young poet keen on reviving the ancient cultural tradition of his own country. Anashuya's prayer brings to mind the pre-Christian Gaelic culture where blessings and fertility sacrifices were common ingredients in bardic and druidic rituals amidst the groves. On the other hand, the pre-modern relationship between the Indian peasants and their land might have inspired Yeats who was intent on depicting the character of the Irish peasantry and subsequently their relationship with land, a theme to which I will return in the following chapters.

The elaborate and dreamlike descriptions of landscape in these three poems incorporate the Indian scene to the general theme of *Crossways* (1889), which contains Yeats's early pastoral poetry. *Crossways* introduces the personae in a perpetual quest for finding the lost Arcadia of ancient Ireland – a place of 'traditional sanctity and loveliness',[50] to quote a line from Yeats's poem 'Coole and Ballylee, 1931'. As the title of the volume suggests, *Crossways* is a hint to the wandering state of the personae in a landscape between other landscapes, a place of passing rather than dwelling. The boundaries often merge between the natural and supernatural, between reality and fantasy and between past and present. In other words, the actual landscape is often inseparable from the mental image/s the poet creates by projecting his own moods and thoughts onto the landscape, making the place a mixture of the 'natural' landscape and the 'poetic' mindscape.

The personae appear in many shapes; often, they are the reincarnation of earlier characters and/or reflect the poet's progressive characterization of his own masks and philosophies. As the druid in 'Fergus and the Druid' changes 'from shape to shape' – from being a raven, then a weasel, and finally a human being[51] – the Yeatsian personae manifest a constant state of transition from one land/mindscape to another. Oisin leaves the Fenians in search of *Tír na nÓg* and returns to Ireland three hundred years later

50   Yeats, poem 'Coole and Ballylee, 1931', *The Variorum Edition of the Poems*, 491.
51   William Butler Yeats, 'Fergus and the Druid', in *The Variorum Edition of the Poems of W. B. Yeats*, 102.

The Land/Mindscape of Yeats's Ireland 57

in search of the Fenians. King Goll is a stranger in the woods as the leaves flutter all around, dragging him into madness. The stolen child is allured by the fairies to the 'waters and the wild'.[52] Fergus, weary of 'drifting like a river from change to change', asks to 'be no more a king' and to 'learn the dreaming wisdom'[53] of the Druid; Aengus wanders in the 'hazel wood' in search of the 'glimmering girl / With apple blossoms in her hair'[54] until he grows old.

Whether in search of love, joy, wisdom or eternal life, these personae do not find consolation in a landscape to which they do not or cannot belong. This landscape may be described as a landscape of possession and dispossession, embodying the continuous history of arrivals and departures in Ireland. It also represents a nature that has been tamed and ravaged by man, sometimes dominating, sometimes dominated. In the early Yeatsian landscapes, the wilderness – the woods, seas, mountains, rivers, etc. – and the otherworld, which is often situated at close proximity to the natural world, appear as places of madness, wildness and loneliness. Man is but an estranged figure in the landscape, caught between the two worlds of reality and dream. This early manifestation and the intermediary position of the Yeatsian personae caught between the two worlds mirrored Yeats's status as an Anglo-Irish writer at a time where the struggle for independence was part of Ireland's immediate cultural and political concern. If we consider the landscape as a reflection of the poet's own 'mood', as in Yeats's reference to the surroundings of Thoor Ballylee,[55] the interaction between the personae and landscapes takes place in three major phases: wandering, settling down and returning after death.

Patrick Sheeran interpreted these three stages in relation to Yeats's 'perception of his own self and its various permutations. Yeats is by turn a druidic magus, a renaissance courtier, an Anglo-Irish squireen and a ghost who re-visits all these earlier incarnations.'[56] In other words, the Yeatsian

52   Yeats, 'The Stolen Child', 87.
53   Yeats, 'Fergus and the Druid', 103.
54   Yeats, 'The Song of the Wandering Aengus', *The Variorum Edition of the Poems*, 149–50.
55   Yeats, *The Variorum Edition of the Poems of W. B. Yeats*, ed. Peter Allt and Russell K. Alspach (New York: Macmillan, 1966), 490.
56   Sheeran, 'The Narrative Creation of Place', 292.

persona emerges as 'Wanderer', 'Dweller' and 'Revenant' in a mindscape that is often spatialized in the form of a 'natural' landscape, situated west of the River Shannon. Overall, Yeats's attempt at patriotization takes place through a connection with the land in the form of poetic dwelling. By creating a mythical topography under a rhetoric of compensation, Yeats confirms his rootedness – hence Irishness – in the very soil of Ireland.

The early poems and the 'wandering' personae

The occult and fairylore, derided by the likes of T. S. Eliot, W. H. Auden and F. R. Leavis, continued to haunt the Protestant imagination in Ireland, reaching what Roy Foster calls 'some kind of apotheosis in Yeats'.[57] In *Autobiographies*, the poet asks: 'Have not all races had their first unity from a mythology that marries them to rock and hill?'[58] The recurrence of fairylore in the early poems and stories, including those of the *Celtic Twilight* and *Mythologies,* was to reconnect the Ascendency to the land by means of a shared knowledge of the supernatural existent among the peasantry. The Revival defined the peasantry as 'the essence of an ancient, dignified Irish culture'; their 'supernatural folklore and imaginative wealth' were 'posed against the modern industrial and commercial British spirit'.[59] In this context, folklore and mythology gained even greater importance in the creation of Irish identity.

According to Harris, Yeats's 'historical myths of self-explanation' are 'myths of possession',[60] which originate from a quest for belonging or, as Yeats himself put it, a quest for 'original relations' to Ireland.[61] Fairies were associated with 'historical memories of dispossession and invasion and

---

57   Foster, *Words Alone,* 124.
58   William Butler Yeats, *Autobiographies* (London: MacMillan Press, 1973), 169.
59   Edward Hirsch, 'The Imaginary Irish Peasant', *PMLA,* 106/5 (1991), 1120.
60   Daniel A. Harris, *Yeats: Coole Park and Ballylee* (Baltimore: John Hopkins University Press, 1974), 9.
61   William Butler Yeats, *Essays and Introductions* (New York: MacMillan, 1961), 235.

The Land/Mindscape of Yeats's Ireland   59

long-ago battles'.[62] In Irish folklore, the *Tuatha Dé Danann* were the ancient inhabitants of the island of Ireland who were dispossessed of their land and driven to peripheries by the arrival of an Iberian tribe called the sons of *Míl Espáine*, the Milesians. These peripheries were believed to be situated deep in the forests or in the underground mounds across the western sea where they lived in a parallel world to human beings called *Tír na nÓg* (Land of Youth). It is to the invitation of Niamh of the Danann tribe that Yeats's first persona, Oisin, sets off on a journey to the otherworld.

The Wanderings of Oisin (1889) is a fine example of the poet's early fascination with Irish subject matters and his self-recognition in the persona of Oisin, the poet-warrior of Celtic Ireland, who had already appealed to a large audience as James Macpherson's Ossian. In his final revision, Yeats moved the poem from the 'Narrative and Dramatic' section of his *Collected Poems* to the beginning of the *Definitive Edition*, where Oisin's state of wandering sets the theme for the entire volume. Written in three parts, *The Wanderings of Oisin* is the story of Oisin's three-hundred-year sojourn in the isles of Joy, Victory and Forgetfulness, respectively. In a lengthy dialogue with St. Patrick, Oisin narrates the story of his seaward journey in the company of Niamh, the daughter of Aengus and Edain. He stays with the merry-making, everlasting young people of the Danann tribe for a hundred years, hunting, dancing and singing until the sight of a spade washed ashore reminds him of his days among the Fenian warriors of the south. The next journey takes Oisin and Niamh to an island where he fights with a demon for a hundred years in an abandoned castle that belongs to the sea-god Manannán. Tired of fighting, Oisin remembers the calm and repose that he was used to among the Fenians.

The journey then takes him to the third isle, which is the dwelling-place of slumbering giants who have grown tired of the world and shall sleep until the world comes to an end. They have slept for so long that owls have nested in their beards. Borrowing Niamh's horse, Oisin finally returns home to Ireland; yet, as Yeats later referred to his fate in 'The Circus Animal Desertion', Oisin passed from 'Vain gaiety, vain battle, vain repose'[63] only

62   Foster, *Words Alone*, 116.
63   Yeats, 'The Circus Animal Desertion', *The Variorum Edition of the Poems*, 629.

60   CHAPTER 2

to return to an Ireland that he no longer knew. Christian Ireland under
St. Patrick turns out to be another wandering image of an island where
Oisin finds himself a stranger. The Fenians are long dead and doomed to
a life in hell, as Patrick warns Oisin that a similar fate awaits him unless he
repents. While trying to help some men carrying a heavy sandbag, Oisin
falls from his horse and the three hundred years of wandering fall back on
his shoulders, turning him into what Patrick now describes as 'bent, and
bald, and blind, / With a heavy heart and a wandering mind'.[64] As Michael
Sidnell has pointed out, the Yeatsian personae often undergo 'many meta-
morphoses', which nevertheless lead to 'the same result'.[65] Similarly, Oisin
comes to the end of a journey where the lesson learned is but the poet's
famous remark in 'Under Ben Bulben': 'Horseman pass by!'[66]

What connects the persona's wandering state to the environment
wherein he undertakes the journey is the dreamlike wandering rendition of
the isles. The three isles of *Tír na nÓg*, Fear and Forgetfulness mentioned
in the poem are vaguely described. When Finn asks Niamh where her
country is, she replies: 'far / Beyond the tumbling of this tide', 'out from
the human lands', 'over the glossy sea'.[67] *Tír na nÓg* is further described as
a 'bare and woody land' through 'long and shadowy ways'; it is a 'lonely
land' with 'windless woods'.[68] Descriptions of the other isles are not any
clearer. The second island is represented with 'dark towers', which are also
referred to as 'seaweed-covered pillars' with 'Dark statues glimmered over
the pale tide / Upon dark thrones' in the middle of the slimy sea.[69] The last
island is a dense wood 'with dripping hazel and oak', where 'no live creatures lived',[70] and there is a deep valley where the slumbering bird-like giants
sleep. Through Oisin's narration, we learn that all the islands (including
Ireland, the land of the Fenians) are sea-bound and connected. The scenery

---

64   Yeats, *The Wanderings of Oisin*, 2.
65   Michael J. Sidnell, 'The Allegory of Yeats's "The Wanderings of Oisin"', *Colby
     Library Quarterly*, 15/2 (1979), 139–40.
66   Yeats, 'Under Ben Bulben', *The Variorum Edition of the Poems*, 640.
67   Yeats, *The Wanderings of Oisin*, 5, 10, 11.
68   Yeats, *The Wanderings of Oisin*, 15, 16, 21, 22.
69   Yeats, *The Wanderings of Oisin*, 30, 31.
70   Yeats, *The Wanderings of Oisin*, 47, 48.

The Land/Mindscape of Yeats's Ireland   61

is natural and supernatural at once, corresponding to the phantasmagorical representations of Ireland, merging the real and imaginary, which Yeats had probably drawn from Baudelaire, Rimbaud and Poe.[71]

The permeability of the isles through a seaward voyage and Oisin's placelessness in each of them suggests the wandering state of the Yeatsian character in a landscape to which he cannot belong. Perhaps no other word could have explained Yeats's image of Ireland and his position as an Anglo-Irish poet more robustly as the recurring term 'wandering', which in a way corresponded to the unstable and constantly changing Ireland young Yeats knew. The poem starts with reference to Oisin's 'wandering mind' and continues with images of 'wandering moon', 'wandering land breeze', 'wandering dances', 'wandering osprey sorrow', 'wandering ruby cars', 'wandering and milky smoke', 'wanderings seas', etc. Similarly, the poem ends with Niamh's reference to Oisin as a 'wandering' figure in the famous lines: 'O wandering Oisin, the strength of the bell branch is naught / For there moves alive in your fingers the fluttering sadness of earth.'[72]

Disconnected from both worlds of reality and imagination, caught between the natural and supernatural, Oisin becomes a wandering figure in a constant search which is meant to bring him contentment. His nostalgia for Ireland while in the company of Niamh and his sense of bereavement on his return to Ireland after three hundred years of wandering embody Yeats's preoccupation with defining Ireland in terms of loss and nostalgia, characteristic of his early Romantic aesthetics. Despite the stasis of the isles, which offer constant joy, constant victory, and constant forgetfulness, Oisin experiences constant sadness and loss as he keeps remembering the Ireland he had left behind. By the end of the second journey, he asks Niamh: 'And which of these is the Island of Content?' The answer is: 'None knows.'[73] Oisin's lack of contentment originates from the inability to dwell in either of the landscapes, a theme that continues throughout the majority of the poems in Yeats's early volumes.

---

71   Richard Ellmann, *Identity of Yeats* (London: Macmillan, 1954), 62.
72   Yeats, *The Wanderings of Oisin*, 2, 3, 13, 20, 22, 47, 50, 55.
73   Yeats, *The Wanderings of Oisin*, 46.

An interesting example is the frequently quoted 'Lake Isle of Innisfree', where the poet, weary with the 'pavements grey'[74] of London, dreams of going to Innisfree and building a cabin. The immediate ecocritical reading of the poem concerns the dichotomy of city life vs. life in proximity of nature as expressed in Henry David Thoreau's *Walden* with which Yeats had been familiar as a young boy. However, Yeats's sudden urge to 'rise and go'[75] poses other important issues. Patrick Sheeran, for instance, questioned Yeats's 'curious fantasy' to build a cabin on 'other people's islands: 'What inclined the young man in London to think that he could circumvent all rights of property and deeds of ownership and build a cabin on Innisfree without as much as by your leave from anybody?'[76]

We could perhaps reconsider this so-called 'curious fantasy' in the light of Yeats's early search for a landscape to which he *could* belong – the poetic landscape. Yeats's reference to building resonates Heidegger's reference to building as dwelling; however, his description of the cabin makes us wonder whether Innisfree is yet another Yeatsian mindscape where dwelling is possible only symbolically. The cabin, made of 'Wattles and Clay', reminds the reader of a familiar dwelling-place in *The Wanderings of Oisin*; that is, Aengus's cabin, made of 'wattles, clay, and skin', inaccessible to Oisin once he leaves *Tír na nÓg*. Whether or not the poet meant to build a real cabin, his urge to 'rise and go' to Innisfree is about creating another hyper-reality where he achieves poetic dwelling in a land/mindscape where the boundaries of reality and imagination merge. As Sheeran referred to Yeats's early fascination with the occult, the persona's quest is that of a search for a metaphysical realm rather than a physical retreat from city life:

> While the young Yeats was as appalled as his Pre-Raphaelite brethren by the conditions of modern urban life, his reaction took a more metaphysical turn. Where they retreated in a verse to wood or sea or walled garden to nourish their reveries, Yeats additionally explored other realms construed from his study of traditional folk belief and his experience of the occult.[77]

---

74   Yeats, 'Lake Isle of Innisfree', *The Variorum Edition of the Poems*, 117.
75   Yeats, 'Lake Isle of Innisfree', 117.
76   Sheeran, 'The Narrative Creation of Place', 291.
77   Sheeran, 'The Narrative Creation of Place', 293.

The Land/Mindscape of Yeats's Ireland

63

Yeats kept writing of Innisfree on several occasions, including in his reply to 'schoolgirls who had asked if Innisfree was a real island'.[78] He referred to living there as a childhood ambition formed in Sligo, the place that introduced the young boy to Celtic legends and myths. In *John Sherman* and 'The Danann Quicken Tree', Innisfree is closely associated with folklore and the supernatural. According to Yeats's note in the latter, '[i]t is said that an enchanted tree grew once on the little lake island of Innisfree, and that its berries were [...] the food of the *Tuatha de Danann* or faeries.'[79] Thus, Innisfree (the actual landscape) is connected to the mindscape of the early poems where dwelling becomes a temporary condition in the persona's passage from one land/mindscape to another. Such merging of the physical and metaphysical situates Yeats's sense of place between landscapes, somewhere in and outside Ireland at the same time, implying a sense of inbetweenness or placelessness.

What links these temporary poetic dwellings to the actual landscape is the proximity of natural and supernatural domains. The invocation of places where 'nature' and 'super-nature' merge is characteristic of Yeats's representation of both the wilderness and the countryside. Referring to Yeats's early poems, Thomas L. Byrd states that the world of the mortals (humans) and the world of the immortals (faeries) 'are really one and the same', and Yeats 'is describing a universe in which two worlds are really one world. Man, through the process of civilization, has lost the capacity to see the "other world"'.[80] While familiarizing the actual landscape with the inscription of Gaelic placenames in English, Yeats's representation of the fairyland as a domain in proximity of the countryside converts local places into mental landscapes. Innisfree, Innismurray, Knocknarea, Knocknashee, Tiraragh, Ballinafad and Colooney turn into places of imagination and fantasy similar to the isles in *The Wanderings of Oisin*. In other words, the absence of distance between the two domains makes the actual countryside as imaginary a place as *Tír na nÓg* while *Tír na nÓg* becomes as real and tangible as the actual landscape.

---

78 Cited in Jeffares, *A Commentary on the Collected Poems of W. B. Yeats*, 33.
79 Cited in Jeffares, *A Commentary on the Collected Poems of W. B. Yeats*, 34.
80 Thomas L. Byrd, *The Early Poetry of W. B. Yeats: The Poetic Quest* (New York: Kennikat Press, 1978), 11.

64   CHAPTER 2

Another example is 'The Stolen Child', where the 'leafy island' of the *Sidhe* by the 'the rocky highland / Of Sleuth Wood'[81] seems to be not far from Sligo. The domestic imagery of the 'calves on the warm hillside / Or the kettle on the hob',[82] set against the wild imagery of fairyland – the herons, water rats, and slumbering trout – marks the permeable boundary between the natural and supernatural landscapes as the child is lured from one to the other. Likewise, the fairyland of the poem 'The Man Who Dreamed of Faeryland' is close to 'Dromahair', 'Lissadell', 'Scanavin' and 'Lugnagall', where the wandering persona dreams, muses and finally ends up sleeping forever. The 'world-forgotten isle' of the fairyland is vaguely indicated somewhere 'to north or west or south' as the lug-worm sings with 'its gay and muddy mouth' in the poem,[83] but that is all we ever learn from the otherworld: The fairyland is near; it could be anywhere and nowhere; it is a place of placelessness, where the personae wander from one temporary state of dwelling to another, never reaching contentment.

From Kyle to Coole and from wandering to settling: Middle poems

There is a fine line between the wilderness and the country in Yeats's poetry. Much like the wandering isles of Oisin's adventures, the Yeatsian countryside is a place of multiple locations with merging boundaries. The reappearance of the natural/supernatural sceneries throughout Yeats's canon, in poems such as 'To an Isle in Water' and 'The Lake Isle of Innisfree' as well as the discarded play *The Island of Statues* and the omitted poem 'The Danann Quicken Tree', represents the countryside as a familiar place with a charm of the uncanny. Through compensation and auto-exoticization, Yeats creates a mindscape that turns the actual

81   Yeats, 'The Stolen Child', 86.
82   Yeats, 'The Stolen Child', 88.
83   Yeats, 'The Man Who Dreamed of Faeryland', *The Variorum Edition of the Poems*, 126–9.

landscape of the rural west into a timeless zone that hovers between the imaginary and the real. In other words, Yeats's sense of place becomes heterotopic, relying on illusion and compensation. In these poems, Yeats conjures a place that is *other* and exotic; it is here and there, simultaneously physical and mental.

The search for dwelling continues throughout the majority of the early volumes, where the personae wander between land/mindscapes of reality and imagination. According to Sheeran, the places of quest in Yeats's poetry are neither 'concrete locations' nor 'even the aesthetic space of the work of art but levels of consciousness which are presented in terms of a symbolic geography'.[84] It is not until midway in Yeats's poetic vocation that the personae settle down, and Yeats's search for metaphysical landscapes (mindscapes) turns into a celebration of the actual landscape, as reflected in his valorization of the Anglo-Irish Big House, namely Lady Gregory's estate in Coole Park and Yeats's tower Thoor Ballylee.

Coole Park, perhaps the most iconic Yeatsian mind/landscape, continues to attract a large number of tourists every year. Situated in Gort, Co. Galway, it is now part of the Coole-Garryland Complex Special Area of Conservation. In reality, the forest exceeds Yeats's seven woods and would have been much richer than he had portrayed them at the time. According to the Department of Arts, Heritage, and the Gaeltacht, 'the remnants of the natural forest cover and the disappearing lake and river are part of the finest turlough complex not merely in Ireland but in all the world.'[85] The river is home to a 'rare riverine habitat', characterized by Trifid Burmarigold, Red Goosefoot and species of Knotgrass. Every year, the woods attract various bird species, such as the Whooper Swan, Berwick Swan, Wigeon, Mallard, Pochard, Tufted Duck, Lapwing, Curlew and Dunlin. Although most of the area is covered with non-native coniferous species, some semi-natural deciduous woodlands still survive. The majority of the woods are managed or cultivated with hints of wild species in odd corners.

---

84   Sheeran, 'The Narrative Creation of Place', 292.
85   'Brief History of Coole Park', *An Roinn*, Department of Agriculture, Fisheries and Food, <http://coolepark.ie/location/index.html>, accessed 14 January 2013.

66   CHAPTER 2

Oak, ash, hazel, yew and elm are to be found in richer soils along with rich shrubs and species of otter and pine marten.[86]

Lady Gregory, who had come to live in Coole demesne after her marriage to Sir William Gregory, described the trees as well-beloved and cared for by herself and the generations before her: 'Their companionship had often brought me peace',[87] she wrote. Yet, this sense of belonging and affection did not come to Lady Gregory until after the birth of her son Robert Gregory and through the long years of widowed life that bound her to a land she did not originally belong to:

> Yet Roxborough [Lady Gregory's hometown] with its romance of river and hillsides came for a long time first in my imagination. It wasn't until my child's birth that I began to really care, looking before as well as after. And that love has grown through the long years of widowed life, when the woods especially became my occupation and delight.[88]

For Lady Gregory the sense of belonging to Coole was synonymous with tending the trees and taking care of the landscape: 'These woods have been well loved, well tended by some who came before me, and my affection has been no less than theirs. The generations of trees have been my care, my comforters.'[89] The Gregories were indeed good patrons of Coole. Many of the trees were planted by the first Robert Gregory, former governor of Ceylon, who had changed 'the face of the district',[90] as recorded in Lady Gregory's Journals.

Returning to Heidegger's description of the basic trait of dwelling as preservation, Coole became Lady Gregory's dwelling through conservation. She adopted Coole as her native land once she became the patron of the place. Michel Haar in *Songs of the Earth* describes the native as 'neither patriotic, nor political, nor purely geographic, nor linked to the singular charm

---

86   'Nature and Wildlife', *An Roinn*, Department of Agriculture, Fisheries and Food, <http://coolepark.ie/location/index.html>, accessed 14 January 2013.
87   Augusta Gregory, *Coole* (Dublin: The Cuala Press, 1931), 24.
88   Cited in Robert Todd Felton, *A Journey into Ireland's Literary Revival* (Sydney: ReadHowYouWant, 2007), 380.
89   Gregory, *Coole*, 24.
90   Cited in Harris, *Yeats: Coole Park and Ballylee*, 15.

The Land/Mindscape of Yeats's Ireland   67

of a place; it is the "home" which, though being completely spontaneously given, keeps asking to be chosen, adopted'.[91] Haar's description, drawn on Heidegger's concept of dwelling, also applies to Yeats's reconstruction of the Norman tower which became his iconic dwelling in later poems. Yeats's sense of attachment to Coole, however, outdated his residence in Thoor Ballylee, which was once owned by the Gregories. The young poet had come to appreciate the demesne through Lady Gregory in whose house he was a frequent visitor. Yet, he often saw himself as more than a visitor; in later descriptions of Thoor Ballylee, for example in 'Cool and Ballylee, 1931', Yeats insisted on the link between the tower and the demesne:

> Under my window-ledge the water race,
>
> Otters below and moor-hens on the top,
>
> Run for a mile undimmed in Heaven's face
>
> Then darkening through 'dark' Raftery's 'cellar' drop,
>
> Run underground, rise in a rocky place
>
> In Coole demesne, and there to finish up
>
> Spread to a lake and drop into a hole.[92]

But what had turned Coole into such an attractive landscape, especially in Yeats's middle poems? Based on what grounds did he regard himself a 'native' rather than a 'visitor' of the place? Yeats's earliest reference to Coole starts with 'I walked among the Seven Woods of Coole', which appeared as a dedication to Lady Gregory at the beginning of the dramatic poem *The Shadowy Waters* (1906). In this poem, Yeats introduces the woods as a place of tranquillity, ancientness and mystery. They are named one after another: Shan-walla (old wall), 'where a willow-bordered pond / Gathers the wild duck from the winter dawn'; Shady Kyle-dortha (dark Kyle) and sunnier Kyle-na-no (wood of the nuts), 'Where many hundreds of squirrels are happy'; Pairc-na-lee (field of the rock), 'Where hazel and ash and

---

91   Michel Haar, *The Song of the Earth: Heidegger and the Grounds of the History of Being* (Bloomington: Indiana University Press, 1993), 63.

92   Yeats, 'Coole and Ballylee, 1931', 490.

68   CHAPTER 2

privet blind the paths'; Dim pairc-na-carraig (field of the rock), 'where
the wild bees fling / Their sudden fragrances on the green air'; Dim Pairc-
na-tarav (field of the bull), 'where enchanted eyes / Have seen immortal,
mild, proud shadows walk'; and finally Dim Inchy wood (wood of the
islands) 'that hides badger and fox / And marten-cat, and borders that old
wood / Wise Biddy Early[93] called the wicked wood'.[94]

In his topographical account of Cool, the young bard discloses the
seven woods through naming and conjuring up their hidden layers of Celtic
myth and folklore. Naming is an act of dwelling in Heideggerian philosophy
and to disclose something means to bring it out of concealment into being.
Consequently, the namer is a dweller whose in-depth knowledge of the
landscape turns him into an active participant in negotiating the meaning
of the landscape.[95] It is true that Yeats was not a native speaker of Irish, and
his use of Gaelic placenames might come across as arbitrary if not for the
purpose of creating an air of Celticism and mystery in his early poems and
stories; yet, his affinity with the wooded landscape of Coole comes from a
close knowledge of and involvement with the region. In *Autobiographies*,
he refers to how he had come to know the whereabouts of the lake 'better
than any spot on earth':

> Coole House, though it has lost its great park full of ancient trees, is still set in the
> midst of a thick wood, which spreads out behind the house in two directions, in one
> along the edges of a lake, which, as there is no escape for its water except a narrow
> subterranean passage, double or trebles its size in winter. In later years I was to know
> the edges of that lake better than any spot on earth, to know it in all the changes of
> the seasons, to find there always some new beauty.[96]

Yeats's early interest in Coole remains with its woods and turloughs, and
he seems to be quite uninterested in the House and its gardens, which, as
mentioned earlier, was an act of deliberate avoidance of his Anglo-Irish

---

93   A famous witch (wise woman) in Co. Clare.
94   Yeats, 'I Walked among the Seven Woods of Coole', *The Variorum Edition of the
     Poems*, 217, 18.
95   See Martin Heidegger, *Basic Writings*. Rev. and expanded edn, ed. David F. Krell
     (London: Routledge, 1993), 317.
96   Yeats, *Autobiographies*, 260.

The Land/Mindscape of Yeats's Ireland 69

origins. Harris believes Yeats's disregard of Coole House in the early poems was a result of his inability to metamorphose the House into a domain of Celtic myth or add a Classical dimension to it, as he did in the short story 'Rosa Alchemica' (1896). Under the influence of Dante, Blake and Shelley, Yeats had learned to spurn 'all enemies of imagination' and would only acknowledge the influence of the eighteenth-century Anglo-Irish tradition after 'elaborate disguising'.[97] In 'Rosa Alchemica', the narrator's Augustan house in Dublin is transformed into an exotic realm of the occult. Similarly, the pictures on the walls are replaced with a picture of Madonna by the Renaissance painter Carlo Crivelli. The candlelight transmutes 'all neoclassical elements', as the narrator remembers Swift 'joking and railing' on the staircase.[98]

It is true that the Anglo-Irish influence inherent in Gregory's house was not the first thing that caught the attention of the young poet fascinated with Celtic mythologies; yet, we should not underestimate the natural beauty of the woods and turloughs and Coole's diverse flora and fauna, which would have possessed a far more romantic charm as a subject matter for poetry in comparison to the House that looked square and uninteresting on its own. In *Autobiographies*, Yeats remembers how his early lack of taste for the Anglo-Irish heritage in the House and his fascination with the 'mediaevalism of William Morris' had grown in him a dislike of the golden frames around the pictures and the ornaments in the drawing room. He wrote: '[Y]ears were to pass before I came to understand the earlier nineteenth and later eighteenth century, and to love that house more than all other houses.'[99] Indeed, some decades had to pass before Yeats gave up his early obsession with Celticism and saw himself as a member of the Anglo-Irish class. He had visited Lady Gregory in her Georgian estate in 1896; however, until 'Upon a House Shaken by Land Agitation' in 1906, Coole remained Kyle, the Celtic domain of Irish myth. The House with its Georgian architecture and Anglo-Irish decorations remained obscure compared to the surrounding woods and their mythologies. This, according

97   Harris, *Yeats: Coole Park and Ballylee*, 5.
98   Harris, *Yeats: Coole Park and Ballylee*, 5.
99   Yeats, *Autobiographies*, 389.

to Harris, places Yeats's early poems on Coole 'out of context',[100] a point of view which, in my opinion, fails to take into consideration the textual community that dominated the literary atmosphere in *fin de siècle* and early twentieth-century Ireland.

A textual community is composed of 'a group of people who have a common understanding of a text and who organise aspects of their lives as the playing out of script'.[101] The textual community around Coole Park, including George Russell and C. W. Leadbeater, 'held similar esoteric beliefs about the relation between the natural and the astral worlds'.[102] Therefore, while the poems seem to be out of context in regard to the demolition of many of the Anglo-Irish houses at the time and the decreasing influence of the Ascendency in Ireland, Yeats's search for a so-called 'higher' level of consciousness, one that was connected with the Celtic wisdom of ancient Ireland, places the Coole poems nowhere but in the context of the textual community of Coole at the time.

While the early poems on Coole confirmed Yeats's Irishness through an act of poetic dwelling, it was not until his later commemoration of the House itself and embracing the culture of the demesne that he became a dweller in the actual landscape. Dwelling in this period did not come from an act of naming; rather, it resulted from concretizing the world 'in buildings and things',[103] an act that brings about another level of attachment to place. It is not a coincidence that Yeats's celebration of the Anglo-Irish heritage was almost simultaneous with his celebration of Coole House and Thoor Ballylee. In 'Ireland 1921–1931', an essay originally published in *Spectator* on 20 June 1932, Yeats explicitly uttered his disappointment with the nationalist propaganda as well as his earlier obsession with Celticism:

> Freedom from obsession brought me a transformation akin to religious conversion. I had thought much of my fellow workers – Synge, Lady Gregory, Lane – but had seen nothing in Protestant Ireland as a whole but its faults, had carried through my

---

100 Harris, *Yeats: Coole Park and Ballylee*, 4.
101 Sheeran 'The Narrative Creation of Place', 294.
102 Sheeran 'The Narrative Creation of Place', 294.
103 Christian Norberg-Schulz, *Genius Loci: Towards a Phenomenology of Architecture* (New York: Rizzoli, 1980), 23.

The Land/Mindscape of Yeats's Ireland   71

projects in face of its opposition or its indifference, had fed my imagination upon the legend of the Catholic villages or upon Irish mediaeval poetry; but now my affection turned to my own people, to my own ancestors, to the books they had read.[104]

At this stage, even the earlier use of the term 'Celtic' is replaced with 'Irish'. What had originally been regarded as an emblem of unity was now to be avoided as a source of division between the Catholics and Protestants. The change of perspective is evident as the poet mentions his affection being turned towards his own people, to his ancestors who had descended from the same century that he had earlier called 'that hated century'.[105] Yeats's literary heritage went back to Swift, Berkeley, Burke, Goldsmith and Sheridan, who had made the eighteenth century a century of their own. These writers had stamped their influence on the Irish literary scene of the following centuries as the 'Great Century' had 'stamped its characters on Dublin, [...] given the provincial cities and towns most of their best buildings and [...] dotted the countryside with graceful houses, large and small.'[106] It is in the context of these graceful eighteenth-century estates that Yeats's sense of place in the middle poems becomes a matter of dwelling through building and cultivating.

The Big House: Building, dwelling, Irishness

Much has been written about the big houses and what they stood for. The cultivated gardens of the Anglo-Irish heritage, the absentee landlordism and the diminishing influence of the gentry are frequent topics when mentioning these estates. The early nineteenth-century representations of the Big House – such as in Maria Edgeworth's *Castle Rackrent* (1800), William Carleton's *Traits and Stories of the Irish Peasantry* (1834) and William Stuart Trench's report on Shirley Estate in Monaghan – have

104   William Butler Yeats, *Uncollected Prose*, ed. John. P. Frayne and Colton Johnson (London: Macmillan, 1975), 488–9.
105   Yeats, *Autobiographies*, 148.
106   Beckett, *The Anglo-Irish Tradition*, 46.

often been interpreted according to their prevailing elitist attitudes, which presented the Big House as an agent of stability in an impoverished and wild landscape.[107] As the Act of Union, Catholic Emancipation, the series of Land Acts and the socio-cultural consequences of the Famine lessened the influence of the Ascendency in Ireland, the later manifestations of the Big House delivered a different sense of place that, according to Patrick Duffy, cannot be simply called elitist or Anglo-Irish:

> Although late twentieth-century Ireland has claimed as its own its distinguished architectural and cultural inheritance of the big houses – a result of both the heritage industry and historical revisionism – some of the ambivalences in representations of the big house and its symbolism for Ireland remain.[108]

The exaggerated sense of guilt is one such ambivalence that is often projected onto the Anglo-Irish character. John Anster's journey to Limerick rectory is one interesting anecdote that serves as an example. Anster, the translator of *Faust* and one of the eminent writers of the *Dublin University Magazine*, was pursued by a crowd of angry peasants on his visit to the Le Fanu family in County Limerick's rectory at the time of unrest. Anster was completely ignorant of why the crowd was following him and had the impression that he had been cheered for his literary accomplishments. It did not occur to him 'that the local people saw the rector [Thomas Le Fanu, the father of the novelist Sheridan Le Fanu] as a bloodsucking exploiter – as they clearly did'.[109] In fact, as Foster points out, '[w]e may be more conscious of the Ascendency's need to feel guilt than they were.'[110]

Although the Anglo-Irish Big House stood as a symbol of discrimination and aristocratic extravagance during a time when the majority of the Irish peasants were living in impoverished conditions not far from the demesnes, one cannot deny the nurturing role that some of these estates played during the later Revival period. Lady Gregory's house in Coole, for

---

107 Patrick J. Duffy, 'Writing Ireland: Literature and Art in the Representation of Irish Place', in Brain Graham, ed., *In Search of Ireland: A Cultural Geography* (London: Routledge, 1997), 72.

108 Duffy, 'Writing Ireland', 74.

109 Foster, *Words Alone*, 112.

110 Foster, *Words Alone*, 112.

The Land/Mindscape of Yeats's Ireland

instance, was a centre of literary and cultural interchange where figures such as George Bernard Shaw, Hugh Lane, John Millington Synge and W. B. Yeats were frequent visitors. Coole Estate was built in 1768 by Robert Gregory, the great-grandfather of Sir William Henry Gregory whom Lady Gregory married in 1880. A typical country house, 'with a wine cellar, library, servant's hall, and gun room, in addition to bedrooms, drawing rooms, and rooms for entertaining',[111] Coole House was the most popular of the Anglo-Irish estates in Galway. Other Houses included Edward Martyn's Tullira Castle, Count de Basterot's Doorus House and Thoor Ballylee, all situated within miles of one another. What made Coole House different was its patron Lady Gregory, whom Yeats commemorated in various poems, such as in 'Coole Park, 1929':

> I meditate upon a swallow's flight
>
> Upon an aged woman and her house,
>
> A sycamore and lime-tree lost in night
>
> Although that western cloud is luminous
>
> Great works constructed there in nature's spite
>
> For scholars and for poets after us.[112]

The house represents a nest that accommodates scholars and poets – Hyde, Synge, Shaw, Taylor and Lane – whom Yeats calls 'swallows' kept to their 'intent' by Lady Gregory's 'powerful character'.[113] Decades after its demolition in 1941, Coole House is still remembered as a symbol of aristocratic excellence, support for art and poetic inspiration, as anticipated in the poem's ending stanza which heralds the near-destruction of the estate:

> Here, traveller, scholar, poet, take your stand
>
> When all those rooms and passages are gone,

---

111 Felton, *A Journey into Ireland's Literary Revival*, 41.
112 Yeats, 'Coole Park 1929', *The Variorum Edition of the Poems*, 488.
113 Yeats, 'Coole Park 1929', 489.

74   CHAPTER 2

> When nettles wave upon a shapeless mound
>
> And sapling root among the broken stone.[114]

The house stayed with the family until 1927, when it was sold to the Ministry of Lands and Agriculture. Lady Gregory continued living in the house as a tenant until her death in 1932, after which the estate was sold to building contractors for its stone value and finally demolished in 1941 by Land Forestry. The house turned into the shapeless mound of Yeats's poem; however, it continued to embody – ironically in its absence – the presence of a sense of place in the Anglo-Irish demesne that, according to Sheeran, connects the Ascendency to the land:

> In so far as there is any sense of place in the conventional meaning of that term to be found in our traditions it belongs, squarely, to those among the Anglo-Irish who cultivated their estates and who sought for an attachment to place that was less problematic than an attachment to people. To add one more paradox to the cairn of paradoxes raised above Irish culture, we might say that the Anglo-Irish dwelt in a land to which they did not belong and the Irish belonged to a land in which they did not dwell.[115]

Once again, we are reminded that it is not the passive state of attachment to place through right of birth or ancestry that determines one's ability to dwell in a place. Dwelling, as described earlier, is an active process of continuous interaction between humans and the environment, crystallized in this case in the very architecture of the house, the topography of the demesne and the Anglo-Irish history of the region. Sheeran's reference to the inability of the Irish people to dwell in a landscape to which they belonged explains the earlier state of 'wandering' in Yeats's first group of poems, focused on the idea of rootedness as prerequisite to Irishness. Yeats's early landscapes were not peopled landscapes; his sense of place was mostly built upon memories of a distant past and the mythological significance of the landscape, regardless of its present shape or more recent history. Hence, dwelling was achieved only poetically. The second group of poems, however, gave shape to dwelling

114   Yeats, 'Coole Park 1929', 490.
115   Nina Witoszek and Patrick Sheeran, *Talking to the Dead: A Study of Irish Funerary Tradition* (Amsterdam: Editions Rodopi, 1998), 78.

The Land/Mindscape of Yeats's Ireland   75

through the very acknowledgement of the unIrish elements in the landscape which, despite their lack of so-called authenticity, conveyed a sense of place that was immanent in the actual place.

'Coole and Ballylee, 1931' is another example where connection to the land is established through an invocation of a sense of place associated with a particular building and its surroundings. The poem begins with a description of the natural imagery below the castle's window-ledge. The scenery is unornamented and 'arrogantly poor': 'Nature's pulled her tragic buskin on', the wood is 'Now all dry sticks under a wintry sun' and the lake is flooded. Inside, however, 'Old marble heads' and 'old pictures' are everywhere.[116] From inheritor to inheritor, the house had been a dwelling of 'content and joy'.[117] Unlike Oisin's adventures in *Tir na nÓg* and the majority of the early poems where the personae, not having found contentment, keep wandering from landscape to landscape, the middle poems depict a period of settlement and repose in the actual landscape.

In other words, the house becomes an emblem of dwelling which binds together the built and natural elements in the environment. Cloke and Jones interpret dwelling as 'the rich intimate ongoing togetherness of beings and things which make up landscapes and places, and which bind together nature and culture over time'.[118] As Yeats shifted from the relatively natural exterior to the ornamented interior of the building, the old dichotomy of nature/culture, which he had presumably avoided in early poems, is now resolved. The house emerges as the very 'spot' where memories of 'marriages, alliances and families' link the 'ancestral trees' – representing 'nature' – to the gardens – representing 'culture':

A spot whereon the founders lived and died

Seemed once more dear than life, ancestral trees,

Or gardens rich in memory glorified

Marriages, alliances and families.[119]

116   Yeats, 'Coole and Ballylee, 1931', 490.
117   Yeats, 'Coole and Ballylee, 1931', 491.
118   Paul Cloke and Owain Jones, 'Dwelling, Place, and Landscape: An Orchard in Somerset', *Environment and Planning A: Economy and Space*, 33/4 (2011), 651.
119   Yeats, 'Coole and Ballylee, 1931', 491.

It is through this ritualistic union with nature – through 'marriages, alliances and families' – that the stone and mortar of the tower become one with the ancestral trees and surrounding landscape of the house. Such spots, marked by memory and ritual, provide a testimony 'to a possible fullness of life [however ephemeral] in a country in which one otherwise lived in a permanent state of crisis'.[120] These spots are also encrypted in the form of another ritual that connects one to the landscape beyond marriages and alliances.

Yeats's final invocation of a sense of place did not occur through an incident of birth or marriage, as in the attachment of Lady Gregory to Coole. Neither was it a purely metaphysical attachment sought in the early landscapes. What testifies Yeats's ultimate sense of belonging to the Irish landscape is the incident of death and the very act of burial that haunt the majority of the poems written in the last decade of Yeats's life. Based on the idea of attachment to the land, the last poems invoke a funerary sense of place where the Yeatsian persona confirms his sense of belonging to place by becoming part of its very soil and topography through death and burial.

The tomb and the final dwelling-place: Last poems

As early as the middle poems, the haunting presence of the dead warns of the temporariness of dwelling in a landscape saturated with a sense of loss and nostalgia. In the poem 'In Memory of Major Robert Gregory', the memory of the deceased, triggered by the death of Lady Gregory's son in the First World War, preoccupies the poet's mind, robbing him of a 'fitter welcome' to his newly reconstructed house, Thoor Ballylee. He repeats in various lines: 'All, all are in my thoughts to-night being dead'; 'all that come into my mind are dead'; 'a thought / Of that late death took all my heart for speech'.[121] There is a sense that the tower and its

---

120   Sheeran 'The Narrative Creation of Place', 296.
121   Yeats, 'In Memory of Major Robert Gregory', *The Variorum Edition of the Poems*, 324–8.

The Land/Mindscape of Yeats's Ireland

surrounding landscape are the dwelling-place not only of the living but also of the dead, as Yeats finds himself a dweller among shadows. On this occasion, however, the shadows are not from a mythological past such as Forgael and Dectora in 'I Walked among the Seven Woods of Coole'; rather, they are the familiar visitors of Coole House and Yeats's companions of youth: Lionel Johnson, John Millington Synge, George Pollexfen and Robert Gregory are among the shadows that haunt Yeats in what he claims to be his ancestral dwelling.

The act of settlement (dwelling) in the tower, mentioned in the first stanza, is replaced with disturbing thoughts of death. At this stage, Yeats does not see himself as a dead man who admonishes the future generation from his post-mortem presence in the countryside. The 'cold eye' which would be cast on life and death and bid the horseman 'pass by' is yet to come as Yeats gradually passes from denunciation of old age to acceptance of death in the final stage of his poetic career. In the short poem 'The Wheel', he writes, what 'disturbs our blood' is the 'longing for the tomb';[122] and not long after, 'the tomb' becomes the dwelling-place from which the Yeatsian persona communicates with future generations.

In *Last Poems* (1936–1939), Yeats no longer speaks from the vantage view of a persona surrounded by the memory of the dead; rather, he is one of them now, writing from a post-mortem perspective, as in 'Under Ben Bulben'. We come across this perspective earlier in poems such as 'The Tower' and 'Meditations in Time of Civil War'. In the latter, the stones of Thoor Ballylee, regardless of 'whatever flourish and decline',[123] remain *his* monument, his 'adopted' house even after death. In fact, he becomes the 'ancestral' figure of the earlier poems, who now occupies the house as a shadow. In other words, Yeats becomes the figure in the landscape, the landscape which in Tim Ingold's perspective is 'the world as known to those who *have* dwelt there, who *do* dwell here, and who *will* dwell here'.[124] In contrast to the nostalgia of the earlier landscapes, the past and

---

122 Yeats, 'The Wheel', *The Variorum Edition of the Poems*, 434.
123 Yeats, 'Meditations in Time of Civil War', *The Variorum Edition of the Poems*, 423.
124 Tim Ingold 1995; cited in Cloke and Jones, 'Dwelling, Place, and Landscape', 652; *original emphasis*.

78 CHAPTER 2

future are 'copresent with the present – through processes of memory and imagination'.[125]

In Sheeran's opinion, it is not that Yeats simply 'positions himself among the dead and speaks to us from beyond the grave'; rather, he 'is more intent on haunting, on being a definite presence in the countryside from whence he will build his reputation as a great admonisher'.[126] In connecting together place, death and identity, Yeats draws upon the funerary sense of place, which is part of the Irish topographical tradition; hence, it delivers a sense of place through intertextuality. Nina Witoszek deems the funerary sense of place found in the Irish preoccupation with death as 'the most evident hallmark of the Irishness of Irish culture'.[127] The great number of rituals surrounding death, funeral and burial in Ireland shows a continuous concern for death and burial traditions, a modern-period example of which is the omnipresent theme of death in the Joycean narratives of Irish life: *Dubliners, Ulysses, and Finnegan's Wake.*

Drawing on Montague, Murphy and Heaney's 'tribal necrologies', Sheeran referred to graveyards as 'focal points in the landscape', which 'function as inverse omphali, sacred places which link this world to the one above and below'.[128] In the famous lines from 'Under Ben Bulben', the graveyard in Drumcliff becomes the omphalos that connects Yeats to the past and future of Ireland:

> Under bare Ben Bulben's head
>
> In Drumcliff churchyard Yeats is laid.
>
> An ancestor was rector there
>
> Long years ago, a church stands near,
>
> By the road an ancient cross.
>
> No marble, no conventional phrase;
>
> On limestone quarried near the spot

---

125 Cloke and Jones, 'Dwelling, Place, and Landscape', 652.
126 Sheeran, The Narrative Creation of Places', 298.
127 Nina Witoszek, 'Ireland: A Funerary Culture', *Studies: An Irish Quarterly Review*, 76/302 (1987), 207.
128 Patrick Sheeran, '*Genius Fabulae*: The Irish Sense of Place', *Irish University Review*, 18/2 (1988), 203.

The Land/Mindscape of Yeats's Ireland 79

By his command these words are cut:

> Cast a cold eye
>
> On life, on death.
>
> Horseman, pass by![129]

Like Fintan in *Temair Breg* who testified his Irishness by interweaving the geography of Tara with the history of kings and warriors who had become part of Tara's environment, Yeats uses Ben Bulben as a text that connects him to the 'seven heroic centuries', to the peasantry, the aristocracy and to all of those he bids the future generation to sing to:

> Sing the peasantry, and then
>
> Hard-riding country gentlemen,
>
> The holiness of monks, and after
>
> Porter-drinkers' randy laughter;
>
> Sing the lords and ladies gay
>
> That were beaten into the clay
>
> Through seven heroic centuries;
>
> Cast your mind on other days
>
> That we in coming days may be
>
> Still the indomitable Irishry.[130]

Ben Bulben becomes Yeats's ultimate dwelling-place. The journey that had started with wandering in the mythical woods of supernatural domains ends with burial in the actual landscape. In other words, it is death that concretizes Yeats's sense of place and his right of belonging to Ireland as his body dissolves in the soil, becoming part of the Irish landscape. From the wanderer of the phantasmagoria of the early poems to the builder/dweller of the middle poems to the returning ghost of the final poems, the Yeatsian persona remains a constant figure in the landscape.

---

129   Yeats, 'Under Ben Bulben', 640.
130   Yeats, 'Under Ben Bulben', 639–40.

CHAPTER 3

Countryside Narratives: Rural Ireland in Irish Revival Literature

Introduction

Despite its manifold importance to Irish economy and culture, from farming to forestry and from literature to tourism, the countryside remained a rather disadvantaged, marginalized environment with uneven population growth, unemployment, high emigration rate and relative poverty up to 2000, when the narrative of rural Ireland changed from that of poverty to progress.[1] Referring to the centrality of rural life and traditions in Ireland's search for independence and unity, Fredrick Aalen once regretted the poor understanding of the Irish countryside, which despite enshrining 'so much of the island's history, seems to be so poorly understood, generally undervalued and persistently abused by private and public activities'.[2] While there has been visible socio-economic improvements in the last decades, Aalen's remark is still relevant today as rural Ireland continues to face serious challenges with regard to both its environment and local populations.

A comprehensive understanding of the Irish countryside would require a study of the volatile socio-economic and environmental changes

---

1 Mícheál Ó Fathartaigh, *Developing Rural Ireland: A History of the Irish Agricultural Advisory Services* (Dublin: Wordwell Books, 2022).

2 Fredrick Aalen, 'Imprint of the Past', in Desmond Gillmor, ed., *The Irish Countryside: Landscape, Wildlife, History, People* (New York: Barnes and Noble, 1989), 119.

that have transformed Ireland in the past century, including the implementation of new agricultural plans and policies under the European Union directives and the economic boom of the Celtic Tiger era and its aftermath. More recently, the 2008 recession, COVID-19 pandemic and Brexit have also left their mark on the Irish countryside. According to the latest report by the Government of Ireland in *Rural Development Policy 2021–2025*, rural and coastal regions have specifically suffered from the adverse effects of both the pandemic and Brexit. These are regions with sectors such as agro-business and tourism that rely on direct human interaction and investment from multinational companies.[3] The ageing population, unemployment, water and soil pollution are still among the top socio-environmental concerns in rural regions. According to the 2016 Census, 37 per cent of the Irish population live in rural areas of less than 1,500 people, a figure that rises to almost one half of the population if we also consider smaller towns and villages. Furthermore, Ireland's transitioning towards a carbon-neutral, climate resilient economy would certainly bring about new challenges for the Irish countryside.

Moving from the wilderness to the countryside, my aim in this chapter is to challenge the flawed perception of 'rural' Ireland as 'real' Ireland in the Revival literature and address the poor understanding of the countryside in both environmental and literary narratives. The first part of the chapter engages with some immediate ecological concerns in rural Ireland and argues for a recognition of local voices and the role of direct engagement when it comes to questions such as sustainability and preservation. The second part deals with the literary representations of the countryside and the peasantry, with a focus on W. B. Yeats's poetry.

---

3   'Our Rural Future: Rural Development Policy 2021–2025', <https://www.gov.ie/en/publication/4c236-our-rural-future-vision-and-policy-context/>, accessed 1 August 2022.

Countryside Narratives 83

From pastoral to agro-industrial: A short overview of the Irish countryside in progress/decline

Despite the lack of data on prehistoric landscapes during the Neolithic period (3500–1800 BC) and Bronze Age (1800–500 BC), pastoralism is believed to have been the dominant way of life on the island of Ireland for centuries. The moist climate of the island would have made it more suitable for keeping livestock than farming. The uplands are still a favourable place for herding and dairying practices. As mentioned in the previous chapter, the relative lack of agricultural activity before the Norman Conquest was recorded as a lack of civility and culture by the historians and travellers such as Gerald of Wales. The English who officially colonized Ireland in the sixteenth century had similar, if not more extreme, views. Despite the endorsement of Greek and Roman pastoral traditions in English Renaissance literature, a pastoral way of life was regarded as the least favourite English colonial enterprise. Edmund Spenser's antipastoral, colonial view of Irish civilization as debased and in need of government stood in contrast with his celebration of a pastoral way of life in such works as *The Faerie Queene* (1590–1596), *Colin Clouts Come Home Againe* (1595) and *Shepheardes Calender* (1579).

As pastoralism gave way to systematized and large-scale farming practices throughout the island, the human-environment relationship underwent significant changes. The land became the first target of colonization and thereby an effective tool for subjugating the natives. From 1600 to 1840, colonial Ireland entered a period of economic growth. Agricultural improvements and the introduction of new crops such as the potato led to a rapid population rise. Cities including Dublin, Cork, Waterford and Limerick grew in size and 'served as a stimulus to develop in this broad rural hinterland.'[4] Rural settlements grew primarily as a result of the modernized field system. Open-field structures like those of the old villages of the Pale and farm clusters in Gaelic areas disappeared gradually, as new farming methods and field systems proved more efficient in terms of economic

4   Aalen, 'Imprint of the Past', 101.

84   CHAPTER 3

profit. However, economic growth was neither even nor consistent in all areas. In fact, various periods of crop failure and famine, including the so-called 'Forgotten Famine' of the eighteenth century, following the Great Frost (1739–1741), proved the inefficiency of the single crop system as well as the unsuitability of the land for agricultural purposes, which, together with wanton and cruel British policies, culminated in the mid-nineteenth-century calamity of *an Gorta Mór* or The Great Hunger (1845–1851).

Famine narratives, from contemporary pamphlets, poems, novels, anecdotes and traveller's diaries to later literary and scholarly publications, have frequently examined the reasons and impacts of prolonged famine periods from the eighteenth century to the 1900s. These narratives fluctuate between attributing the famine to 'genocidal government intention (Britain's "famine plot"), religious providentialism ("God's famine"), and economic and social determinism (the consequences of a laissez-faire system)'.[5] Despite disagreements in historiographical accounts on theories of causation regarding the Famine, there still seems to be a common ground that views the crop failure, government neglect, hunger, disease and death as a mesh of interconnected social, political and environmental phenomena that affected Ireland at the time; in other words, a true ecological catastrophe.

By the end of the nineteenth century, Ireland entered a late period of industrialization, which extended the gap that already existed between the city and the country. The demographic map of nineteenth-century Ireland shows a country at the verge of a major transition: Ireland gradually transformed from a mainly rural country to the most urbanized state in Europe by the end of the century. Urban encroachment on rural land became a dominant 'feature of most towns and cities in Ireland'.[6] Urban sprawl continues to affect the rural environment in Ireland today.

---

5   Margaret Kelleher, 'Famine and Ecology, 1750–1900', in Malcolm Sen, ed., *A History of Irish Literature and the Environment* (Cambridge: Cambridge University Press, 2022), 128.

6   Mary Cawley, 'Rural People and Services', in Desmond Gillmor, ed., *The Irish Countryside: Landscape, Wildlife, History, People* (New York: Barnes and Noble Books, 1989), 198.

Countryside Narratives 85

Since the 1960s, a series of economic events, which culminated in the prosperous years of the Celtic Tiger (1994–2007), led to a renegotiation of the urban/rural dichotomy. The growth of the modern commuting system, which facilitated transportation between rural and urban Ireland, further permeated the boundaries of the city and country life. A large number of rural dwellers employed in cities had to commute to and from the countryside on a daily basis, while more and more urbanites tended to travel regularly to the countryside during the weekend and holiday season.

Technology has changed the way we perceive geographical and temporal distance; once the distance is erased or renegotiated, the country becomes the new suburbia. The recent pandemic has also challenged our perception of space and distance. On the one hand, there has been a reduced need for relocation and commuting due to an opportunity to work from home; on the other, the quarantine caused serious financial losses in the countryside due to the necessity of direct human engagement for most rural practices, especially smaller shops and firms which had to close during the pandemic. Focusing on creating new job opportunities in the countryside, the government of Ireland is now working towards reversing the country-city relocation for professional purposes. Nevertheless, communication and connectivity remain major challenges.

Tourism is another significant factor in the social and ecological state of the countryside. Modern tourism, which is among the most labour intensive, indigenous sectors in the Irish economy, was badly hit by the COVID-19 pandemic. Before the pandemic, 260,000 people were employed in the tourism industry across Ireland, with the sector generating over €9 billion from international and domestic tourism. Since the pandemic, however, up to 180,000 of these jobs were either lost or jeopardized. Ruth Andrew, the Chairperson of Tourism Recovery Taskforce, has referred to the impact of the pandemic as 'existential'.[7] Building a sustainable tourism industry is first on the list of Ireland's Tourism Recovery Plan 2020–2023.

---

7   Cited in 'Tourism Recovery Plan 2020–2023', prepared by the Tourism Recovery Taskforce (2020), 5, <https://www.gov.ie/pdf/?file=https://assets.gov.ie/90006/80801fc3-a69b-4faf-843b-be9bff4d6a0f.pdf#page=null>, accessed 21 March 2023.

As a scattered activity at the beginning of the twentieth century, tourism did not bear much impact on the environment. Modern tourism, on the other hand, as much as being a major contributor to the Irish economy, has had serious repercussions in the region. What was once considered a 'small-scale, almost passive [...] activity' in the past has turned into 'post mass tourism' as a result of Ireland's globalized economy and position in the Eurozone.[8] While tourism has contributed to the preservation of certain iconic landscapes, generated revenue and created job opportunities in the countryside, it has also led to 'a decline in the scenic and amenity value of landscapes and seascapes [...], a decline in water quality [...], and a loss of historic character in cities, towns, and villages'.[9]

The building of holiday houses in the countryside in the last couple of decades serves as an example of how tourism can impact the rural environment. These private and modern-built residences often 'lack sympathy with the immediate environment in terms of design, siting and building materials'.[10] The less numerous 'architect-designed' buildings, for instance, reflect borrowings from foreign cultures – 'Tudor half-timbering', 'curb roofs' and 'Spanish arches' being the most popular. Despite their individual aesthetics, these houses lack compatibility, both in terms of the landscape and their host culture, hence threatening 'the historic character' of Irish villages and towns.[11] The disregard for harmony in modern housing reflects the general lack of knowledge about the history of the countryside and its complex socio-environmental structure.

To the urban dweller, the countryside provides 'a feeling of belonging' and 'face-to-face relations'.[12] The urbanite who seeks a sense of community

8   Ruth McAreavey et al., 'Conflicts to Consensus: Contested Notions of Sustainable Rural Tourism on the Island of Ireland', in John McDonagh, et al., eds, *A Living Countryside? The Politics of Sustainable Development in Rural Ireland* (Surrey: Ashgate, 2009), 219–20.
9   'Tourism and the Environment', *Fáilte Ireland's Environmental Action Plan 2007–2009*, 9, <https://discomap.eea.europa.eu/map/Data/Milieu/OURCOAST_103_IE/OURCOAST_103_IE_Doc6_EnvironmentTourism.pdf>, accessed 1 April 2023.
10   Cawley, 'Rural People and Services', 205.
11   Cawley, 'Rural People and Services', 205–6.
12   Cawley, 'Rural People and Services', 198.

Countryside Narratives   87

by purchasing a holiday home in rural areas or taking up 'hobby farming'[13] as a way of experiencing rural practices and indulging in a so-called bucolic way of life often perceives the place as a cultural construct that at its best signifies community attachments or simply clean air and water. However, this sense of community, much sought after, is rather a product of intuition, combined with experience and active engagement with the land, as Tim Ingold reminds us in *The Perception of the Environment*.

For the rural dweller, the land is not only a social construct but also a physical environment, the perception of which is part of his or her identity. To dwell is not only to inhabit but also to interact with all the animate and inanimate phenomena that mutually dwell in an ecosystem and whose existence is interrelated with that of one another. In other words, it is the dwelling perspective that differentiates the perception of the countryside from inside and outside. For the majority of rural visitors, the land is first and foremost appreciated in terms of scenery and aesthetics. Their information of the region's flora and fauna, its soil type, ecosystems and communities is certainly limited and usually mediated through science, media or other cultural lenses. Temporary residence in the countryside, though possibly enriching the visitors' personal experience, often falls short of developing into a more serious engagement with land. Even for those who indulge in hobby farming, the land remains a source of recreation or at most a temporary experiment that does not quite summarize the experience of living *off* the land or interacting with the rural community from a local perspective.

Urban sprawl, rural housing, the building of factories and infrastructures in rural areas and, above all, the growth of rural tourism have rendered a new face of the countryside. What we face in rural Ireland today is the 'new' countryside, a place where 'traditional practices of production are being replaced by consumption practices',[14] as exemplified in the central role of globalized, post-mass tourism in the twenty-first-century Irish economy. In fact, when we refer to the countryside, we are addressing a

---

13   Desmond Gillmor, 'Land, Work and Recreation', in Desmond Gillmor, ed., *The Irish Countryside: Landscape, Wildlife, History, People* (New York: Barnes and Noble, 1989), 168.

14   McAreavey et al., 'Conflicts to Consensus', 219–20.

complex matrix of social, political and economic variants that are at work in the form of organizations, groups and institutions. Consequently, environmental campaigns in the countryside are involved with issues as diverse as biodiversity, rural housing, land use, chemical disposals, water pollution, forestry management, infrastructures, industrialized farming and tourism. These factors, as unrelated as they might seem at first glance, are highly interdependent, and the consideration of one often demands a proper understanding of others. The following section on sustainable development will show how structural deficiencies, lack of governmental support, political influences, as well as the failure to address local communities have led to the near failure of many environmental campaigns and movements in Ireland. The rather 'unsuccessful' project of sustainable development is proof that 'rurality' is still subject to misunderstanding not only in popular culture but also among major decision makers and actors of environmental laws in Ireland.

Rural Ireland and sustainable development: A short review

During his address at the launch of the Northern strategy in 2006, Jonathan Porritt famously characterized sustainable development in Northern Ireland as a 'constipated process',[15] a remark that more or less extends to the slow and inefficient process of environmental policy development and implementation in the Republic. Indeed, the latest Environmental Protection Agency report, EPA 2020, points out the lack of an integral plan especially with regard to sustainable development. When it comes to environmental decision making and implementation in both jurisdictions, environmental laws remain as what Scannell and Turner have described as 'a creature of "soft law" – more akin to a policy or political

---

15   Cited in Yvonne Scannell and Sharon Turner, 'A Legal Framework for Sustainable Development in Rural Areas of the Republic of Ireland and Northern Ireland', in John McDonagh et al., eds, *A Living Countryside? The Politics of Sustainable Development in Rural Ireland*, 29.

Countryside Narratives   89

commitment than an obligation or objective with legal force'.[16] In other words, until recently there has been no strict governmental commitment with regard to sustainable development in both regions. More often than not, environmental laws remain 'a discrete "policy area" with little or no connection to mainstream policy'.[17] Meanwhile, the influence of the European Union, though positive, has been patchy. In the past several decades, the 'EU's good intentions have been met by Irish administrative mismanagement and politicking, especially in the RoI'.[18] This was clearly noticeable in the case of the Bird and Habitat Directive and the Nitrate Directive. The implementation of the Nitrate Directive, for instance, was delayed in the Republic until the summer of 2006, almost eleven years after its initial inscription in the EU environmental laws in 1995.

Another principal cause behind the poor implementation of EU environmental policies results from a lack of response from local institutions. The conflict between farmers and governmental groups around the implementation of EU directives 'is not simply about specific issues, such as the Nitrate Directive or cross-compliance, but above all is about the meaning and understanding of the "land", "countryside" and "rurality"'.[19] In other words, what is at stake is the term 'rural' itself, which consequently raises the questions of 'who should manage it, how and in what manner and for what purpose.'[20] This draws attention to the motto of 'Think globally, act locally'. Without a proper understanding of local communities and organizations and their role in implementing environmental laws, sustainable development remains a high ambition among the major policymakers in international spheres who have not succeeded in bridging the gap between

---

16   John Barry and Pat Doran, 'Environmental Movements in Ireland: North and South', in John McDonagh et al., eds, *A Living Countryside? The Politics of Sustainable Development in Rural Ireland*, 332.

17   Barry and Doran, 'Environmental Movements in Ireland', 332.

18   Brendan Flynn, 'Environmental Lessons for Rural Ireland from the European Union: How Great Expectations in Brussels get Dashed in Bangor and Belmullet', in John McDonagh et al., eds, *A Living Countryside? The Politics of Sustainable Development in Rural Ireland*, 53.

19   Barry and Doran, 'Environmental Movements in Ireland', 330.

20   Barry and Doran, 'Environmental Movements in Ireland', 330.

the local and the global. Likewise, national organizations that fail to acknowledge the accountability of local institutions end up with a lack of response from both local groups and international organizations.

When it comes to local institutions, regional communities become the major addresser and addressee of environmental issues in their locality. As Tim Forsyth has observed, '[m]any explanations of environmental degradation [...] have been constructed without the participation of the affected peoples, and without acknowledging how explanations may reflect social framings.'[21] In the case of rural Ireland, inappropriate policies have often led to various socio-economic problems for people including farmers, anglers and residents. The ongoing Shell to Sea campaign, which initially began as an opposition against the construction of the natural gas pipeline in the parish of Kilcommon in County Mayo, is a clear example of how local communities are constantly ignored by large commercial and governmental actors.

The overall failure to comprehend the significance and functionality of local communities in rural areas can be summarized in the flawed yet current assumption, especially in the Republic, that 'the term "rural" is still simply equated with farming interests'.[22] Such an equation is highly dismissive of the entire process of modernization in Ireland and the drastic de-agriculturalization of the countryside in the last century. In other words, despite the changes that have completely transformed rural Ireland into a modernized, industrialized environment, the countryside is still misunderstood as an atemporal, pastoral landscape. An atemporal landscape is a dead entity, susceptible to environmental degradation and cultural manipulation at the mercy of globalized, urban economies. Hilary Tovey refers to the change of land use for 'forestry, biomass production, golf courses and other recreational and tourist uses' besides the dereliction of less favourable sites as 'new types of exploitation' in the countryside:

---

21   Tim Forsyth 2003, 10; cited in Hilary Tovey, 'Managing Rural Nature: Regulation, Translation and Governance in the Republic of Ireland and Northern Ireland', in John McDonagh et al., eds, *A Living Countryside? The Politics of Sustainable Development in Rural Ireland*, 107.

22   Flynn, 'Environmental Lessons for Rural Ireland from the European Union', 54.

> The largely 'post-productivist' orientation of both state and population towards the rural encourages treating it as a place to be moulded increasingly to urban needs and demands, whether for recreation or for disposal of unwanted urban problems. Official actors see it as a space for prisons, landfill sites or incinerators, unofficial actors as a place to dump unwanted consumer goods and their by-products.[23]

Tovey's observation of the controversial uses of the rural landscape brings to mind the mid-nineteenth-century growth of capitalism and the gradual subjection of the countryside to what Karl Marx called 'the rule of the towns'.[24] In Ireland, not only did the Celtic Tiger transform the economic situation but also renegotiated the perception of the city and the country among citizens and policymakers to the point that sustainability in the rural environment was perceived as a threat to the economic security and social welfare of the cities. The notorious claim made by the Progressive Democrats in May 2007 regarding the policies of the Green Party destroying the Celtic Tiger economy is one example among many other misguided political claims that have affected sustainable development in Ireland. Misunderstanding sustainability often puts environmental preservation policies in opposition to 'development' and 'progress'. Lax environmental control and the pursuit of 'export-led strategies' without considering the ecological and, in the long term, social consequences of such decisions go back to 'the "developing world" character of Ireland's political economy'.[25] Economic security equally concerns members of the public who, according to the attitude surveys since the 1980s, have consistently placed environmental issues below other concerns such as 'orthodox economic growth, security and employment'.[26]

The main reasons behind the lack of public interest in environmental issues can be traced back to the scientific-oriented nature of environmental discourse in general and the exclusion of the public zone in decision-making

---

23 Tovey, 'Managing Rural Nature', 107.
24 Karl Marx and Fredrich Engels, *The Communist Manifesto* (Oxford: Oxford University Press, 1997), 7.
25 Susan Baker, 'The Evolution of the Irish Ecology Movement', in Wolfgan Rudig, ed., *Green Politics One* (Edinburgh: Edinburgh University Press, 1990), 47.
26 Whiteman1990; Devine and Lloyd 2000; cited in Barry and Doran, 'Environmental Movements in Ireland', 322.

processes in Northern Ireland and the Republic, in particular. In both jurisdictions, 'the governance and political structures for sustainable development are marked by weak or absent accountability processes. Unlike market actors, interests and imperatives, citizens have often been discouraged from participating in policy decision-making processes.'[27] The lack of acknowledgement extends to the Green Movement itself, which has similarly excluded the 'lay' knowledge through an overemphasis on scientific-led approaches. Despite the growing number of environmental organizations in both regions, Barry and Doran refer to the Green Movement in Ireland as 'one of the weakest in Europe.'[28] Each organization operates according to their own interpretation of 'rurality', 'sustainability' and 'economic growth' yet despite the slightly different route that each one takes, 'scientific management' seems to be the finish line of major environmental policies in Ireland.[29]

The issue of knowledge and sustainability is further complicated by the links among knowledge, power and justice. When it comes to the question of who owns the knowledge and how it is distributed, environmental issues lead to politically oriented concerns regarding power and justice. Tovey posits that 'scientific knowledge is owned and guarded by an "epistemic community" of experts for whom the public is insufficiently educated to participate in decision-making', which can be interpreted as an indication of the 'profoundly undemocratic' nature of the environmental management regime in the Republic.[30] As such, sustainable development exceeds the concern over the relative priority of 'development' versus 'sustainability' and turns into 'a site of contestation over the issue of *environmental knowledge* and its use in environmental management.'[31]

Over the past decades, there has been a gradual increase in pro-environmental attitudes and concerns among European citizens, which is congruent with the rise of the 'new' middle class, consisting of 'knowledge-based workers' employed in the welfare and education sectors. This emerging

27   Barry and Doran, 'Environmental Movements in Ireland', 323.
28   Barry and Doran, 'Environmental Movements in Ireland', 322.
29   Tovey, 'Managing Rural Nature', 110.
30   Tovey, 'Managing Rural Nature', 113.
31   Tovey, 'Managing Rural Nature', 117; *original emphasis.*

Countryside Narratives 93

class, which according to Inglehart's thesis, shares 'post-materialist' perspectives, is now concerned with 'personal autonomy, environmental amenity, identity and quality of life'.[32] In Ireland, however, until recently 'only a small percentage of people can be said to hold post-materialist values'.[33] Accordingly, there has been a significant difference in terms of public participation and environmental awareness in Ireland and the rest of Europe. Interestingly, however, the counterpart to this new middle class – people from labour backgrounds in Ireland – have implicit yet pro-environmental attitudes towards the environment. As Tovey has observed, 'the values espoused in a lot of Irish anti-pollution campaigns are those of family, community, locality and tradition rather than those of the international green movement'.[34] This draws the focus back on the issue of locality and community in the countryside. Perhaps, in Ireland as in the USA, 'environmental justice' would be a more suitable category whereby environmental campaigns can be associated with local interests and citizens' requirements from less privileged backgrounds.

A key initiative of the environmental justice movement, according to Schlosberg, 'is for "voice" and recognition which cannot, either in theory or practice, be separated from "community empowerments"'.[35] The denial of voice to local interests and campaigns regarding land and resource use and infrastructures 'is a main cause for local community mobilization on environmental and often public health and safety grounds'.[36] An environmental management agenda which does not 'recognize and incorporate a diverse range of knowledge of nature is likely today to be judged both ineffective

32   Barry and Doran, 'Environmental Movements in Ireland', 326.
33   Mary Kelly et al., *Cultural Sources of Support Upon Which Environmental Attitudes Draw: Second Report of National Survey Data*, 52, <www.ucd.ie/environ/reports/envirattitudessecondrept.pdf#search='environmental%20attitudes%20in%20Ireland>, accessed 6 April 2013.
34   Hilary Tovey, 'Environmentalism in Ireland: Modernisation and Identity', in Patrick Clancy et al., eds, *Ireland and Poland: Comparative Perspectives* (Dublin: University College Dublin, 1992), 285.
35   Schlosberg 2002; cited in Liam Leonard, Green Nation: The Irish Environmental Movement from Carnsore Point to the Rossport Five (Dundalk: Choice Publishing, 2006), 196.
36   Barry and Doran, 'Environmental Movements in Ireland', 327.

94   CHAPTER 3

and undemocratic, and hence itself "unsustainable".[37] Tovey's critique of
the environmental movement in Ireland, alongside that of Flynn, Barry,
Doran and others, calls for the recognition, integration and prioritization
of environmental laws within the main body of Irish constitutional laws.
Furthermore, the interconnectedness of environmental issues with social,
political and economic factors necessitates a higher degree of environmental
justice by acknowledging local communities and institutions, as well as an
integration of lay and expert knowledge and a higher degree of 'critiquing,
challenging and proposing alternatives to the underlying political economy
of the island as part of the transition to a more sustainable Ireland'.[38]

        Given the interconnectivity of environmental issues with wider cultural
considerations and the importance of the countryside in Irish literature, it is
no surprise that the same lack of knowledge regarding land and local communities also features representations of rural Ireland during the extended
Revival period. The flawed perception of 'rural' Ireland as 'real' Ireland in
revivalist narratives shows how literary portrayals of the countryside were
often subject to manipulation, misunderstanding and misrepresentation.
While certain features were romanticized, others were manipulated or
downsized in order to render an image of Ireland that fitted well with the
metanarrative of Irishness. The premise of 'real' Ireland as a rural, bucolic
landscape further marginalized the actual landscape and the rural community, once again hinting at the lack of an environmental sensibility in the
Irish sense of place promoted during the period.

Myth makers and rural dwellers – Rural Ireland in Irish Literary Revival

The Irish countryside, long portrayed as the embodiment of nationalist sentiments and a repository of Irish folklore and heritage, served
as a model for Ireland in the majority of the Revival and post-Revival

---

37   Tovey, 'Managing Rural Nature', 117.
38   Barry and Doran, 'Environmental Movements in Ireland', 337.

Countryside Narratives 95

narratives. Signifying both the countryside and a nation state, the English term 'country' exemplifies the interwoven notions of rurality and nationality. In nations with a colonial past, the countryside represents a place of authenticity and tradition as opposed to the foreign influence of the colonizing culture, crystallized in cities. In Ireland, the idea particularly gained currency from the nineteenth century onwards. The ongoing political conflict and major socio-political movements, such as the dissolution of the Irish Parliament by the Act of Union (1800), the Catholic Emancipation (1829) and the rise of the nationalist movements turned the Irish countryside into an ultimate source of interest for Irish writers, scholars and politicians who found in rural Ireland a model for unity and independence.

The countryside was well suited to meet the demands of the Irish Literary Renaissance, which on the one hand appealed to the foreign market through the revival of a literary version of Romanticism that had already faded in mainland Europe, and on the other, met the expectations of a nation at the verge of independence. Jean-Jacques Rousseau's 'noble savage' was to rise in the figure of the Irish peasant, who was considered good at heart, close to the land and uncorrupted by civilization. Furthermore, this 'authentic' specimen of Irish man/woman was in possession of the country's ancient folkloric tradition and conversed in the Gaelic vernacular, which had turned into a forgotten language by the second half of the century.

The landscape was valued for its scenic and picturesque qualities as well as its numberless historic landmarks that connected Ireland to the past. The pagan commemoration sites, early Christian monasteries and thousands of ringforts recorded the history of a civilization that was deemed by the Irish people to be richer and more heroic than that of their rivals, the English. These factors were enough to turn rural Ireland into a place of myth and romanticism regardless of the actual situation of many of the so-called heroic peasants who lived there. Cut off from the edge of the cities, malnourished and uneducated, plagued by famine, death and emigration, the rural dwellers of nineteenth- and early twentieth-century Ireland, whose number was diminishing rapidly, were a misrepresented, marginalized class in reality.

96   CHAPTER 3

The countryside appeared as the main setting in Irish narratives throughout the Revival period, from the novels of Maria Edgeworth, Sidney Owenson and William Carleton before the Great Famine to the heroic depictions of the peasantry by the iconic trio of W. B. Yeats, John Millington Synge and Lady Gregory. These narratives often failed to reflect a faithful picture of the country. Rural Ireland was usually reduced to a small geographical area, west of the Shannon. Villages in the north or non-Gaelic-speaking areas were almost a non-existent region on this literary map. In the words of Conor Cruise O'Brien, the Ireland commemorated by Yeats and his school consisted of 'an enormous West Coast and no North-East corner'.[39] At the same time, rural West – the locus of 'real' Ireland – was also marginalized, both economically and culturally. Less populated and poor, it was susceptible to losing its communities through emigration. The efforts of the Irish nationalist propaganda to 'make the whole country as like the West as possible'[40] was no less than to reduce the entire country to an image based on illusion and compensation, hence a *heterotopia*.[41] As the physical landscape was replaced by a cultural mindscape representing national identity, both the landscape and its conjoined cultures were pushed to the periphery. Charles Gavan Duffy's diary entry of his second visit to the West in the company of Thomas Carlyle in 1849 depicts a horrid picture of a dying countryside:

> We [Duffy and Carlyle] travelled slowly from Limerick to Sligo, and we found everywhere the features of a recently conquered country. Clare was almost a wilderness from Kilrush to Corofin.

> The desolate shores of Lough Corrib would have resembled a desert but that the stumps of ruined houses showed that not nature, but man, had been the desolator.

39   Conor Cruise O'Brien, ed., *The Shaping of Modern Ireland* (Toronto: University of Toronto Press, 1960), 21.
40   Fintan O'Toole, *The Lie of the Land: Irish Identities* (London: Verso, 1997), 14.
41   Michel Foucault in 'Of Other Spaces: Utopias and Heterotopias' refers to illusion and compensation as characteristics of the sixth principal of *heterotopias*. Foucault, Michel, 'Of Other Spaces: Utopias and Heterotopias', in *Architecture/Mouvement/Continuité*, 1984, <https://web.mit.edu/allanmc/www/foucault1.pdf>, accessed 1 April 2023.

Countryside Narratives 97

> Between Killala Bay and Sligo, during an entire day's travel, we estimated that every second dwelling was pulled down; and not cabins alone, but stone houses fit for the residence of a substantial yeomanry.[42]

Duffy's note on the condition of western Ireland during the Great Famine sets a striking contrast with popular images of the countryside before and after the Famine. The 'conquered country' of the Sligo region did not bear the slightest resemblance to the mystical and picturesque landscape of Yeats's Sligo. Neither did it appear as the site of the grand architecture and cultivated gardens of the Anglo-Irish 'Big House' novels. The 'heroic' peasantry in whose character and lifestyle Yeats had sought a 'Unity of Culture' turned into a nation of dirty, beast-like beggars, swarming the streets of Galway in Duffy's account:

> We saw on the streets of Galway crowds of creatures more debased than the yahoos of Swift – creatures having only a distant and hideous resemblance to human beings. Grey-headed old men, whose idiot faces had hardened into a settled leer of mendicancy, simious and semi-human, and women filthier and more frightful than the harpies, who at the jingle of a coin on the pavement, swarmed in myriads from unseen places, struggling, screaming, shrieking for their prey like some monstrous and unclean animal. In Westport the sight of the priest on the street gathered an entire pauper population, thick as a village market, swarming round him for relief. Beggar children, beggar adults, beggars in white hair, girls with faces grey and shrivelled; women with the more touching and tragic aspect of lingering shame and self-respect not yet effaced; and among these terrible realities, imposture shaking in pretended fits to add the last touch of horrible grotesqueness to the picture![43]

In its use of language and imagery, Duffy's diary re-narrates a colonial account of Irish people as poor, dirty, undignified and uncivilized. Despite reflecting certain aspects of the widespread famine in the countryside, Duffy's traveller perspective lacks an insight into the rather complex social class that was the peasantry, a social class obscured under the load of stereotypes from inside and outside Ireland. Similar accounts of

---

42 Charles Gavan Duffy, *Conversations with Carlyle* (London: Forgotten Books, 2013), 120.

43 Duffy, *Conversations with Carlyle*, 121.

98   CHAPTER 3

the countryside, which either romanticized the peasantry or incited pity (if not contempt) towards them, were popular in literary works.

For the likes of Maria Edgeworth and Lady Morgan, two of the earliest chroniclers of Irish life, the countryside served as a platform to argue for a reformation of the existing social system which had led to widespread inequality, poverty and misery in rural Ireland. In her novels *Castle Rackrent* (1800), *The Absentee* (1812) and *Ormond* (1817), Edgeworth criticizes the inefficiency of the absentee landlordism while portraying a varied cast of characters from tenants, stewards and agents to landlords and nobles. The general depiction of the peasant, though aimed at educating the public and making a plea for reform, still fell short of producing a different picture from the British stereotypes. Images of poverty, misery, drunkenness and indolence dominate the works of Edgeworth and her contemporaries, the majority of whom had unionist sympathies. The early conservatism and unionism gave way to a more robust plea for socio-political reform under the nationalist agenda at work in the narratives of the upcoming generation. Nevertheless, the representation of the Irish peasantry as 'naïve, close to animals, integrated to the landscape, out of history' continued throughout the period, which, in the words of Jacqueline Genet, 'nationalized the colonial attitudes'.[44]

In her 1782 letter to Fanny Robinson, Maria Edgeworth referred to the Irish people as 'perhaps the laziest civilized nation on the face of the Earth'.[45] However, she assigned this laziness – the most characteristic of Irish stereotypes – to the failure of the economic system and corrupt English management. In *Castle Rackrent*, the peasants are introduced as 'a set' or 'parcel of poor wretches'.[46] Yet, what makes Edgeworth's depiction of rural poverty, indolence and drinking different lies in her sympathy with peasants and in finding faults with the economic system, high tax rates, the indifference of the absentee landlords and the wickedness of the agents. In general, there is a prevailing ambiguity and distance in descriptions of country life in Edgeworth's Irish novels, which as Claude Fierobe comments, is a sign

44   Jacqueline Genet, 'Yeats and the Myth of Rural Ireland', in Jacqueline Genet, ed., *Rural Ireland, Real Ireland?* (Buckinghamshire: Colin Smythe, 1996), 141.
45   Maria Edgeworth, *Castle Rackrent* (Auckland: The Floating Press, 2010), 50.
46   Edgeworth, *Castle Rackrent*, 56.

Countryside Narratives 99

of Ireland being 'observed at a distance, examined with the critical and rather cold eye of an ethnologist avid for the truth'.[47] Like many of her characters – Glenthorpe, Ormond or Lord Colambre whose views of Ireland were based on their trips to the countryside – Edgeworth's knowledge of Ireland also stemmed from a traveller's perspective, distant, restricted and at times prejudiced.

Many of the early nineteenth-century narratives were predominantly concerned with Catholic Emancipation and experimental unionism. Lady Morgan, for instance, commented on her early romances as being 'written *for* and *in* the great cause of Catholic Emancipation'.[48] In fact, Morgan's *The Wild Irish Girl: A National Tale,* representing romantic Ireland, helped to create positive sympathies towards the Irish people among her English readership. Engaging with important political questions, she 'infused a new passion into a reviving Irish nationalism that carried through subsequent writers like the poet Anna Liddiard and on into the Young Ireland writers of the 1840s and the Rebellion of 1848'.[49]

However, it should be noted that the national and historical tales of the early nineteenth century were not necessarily in the service of nationalism, which was a complicated issue in Ireland compared to the situation in Scotland. What was accepted as 'loyalty and patriotism' in Scotland was viewed as 'rebellion' in Ireland.[50] In the words of Thomas Moore, nationalism was equal to 'treason' in the Anglo-Irish dictionary. Lady Morgan's portrayal of the peasantry was often more informed and informing than that of Maria Edgeworth. In a letter to Lady Morgan, Richard Philips, her publisher, claims that the novelist's accounts of Ireland are going to enlighten the world about the country: 'The world is not informed about Ireland, and I am in the situation to command the light to shine!'[51] Whether or

47   Claude Fierobe, 'The Peasantry in the Irish Novels of Maria Edgeworth', in Jacqueline Genet, ed., *Rural Ireland, Real Ireland?*, 62.

48   Cited in Robert Fitzroy Foster, *Words Alone: Yeats and His Inheritances* (Oxford: Oxford University Press, 2011), 11; *original emphasis.*

49   Stephen C. Behrendt, *British Women Poets and the Romantic Writing Community* (Johns Hopkins University Press, 2009), 245.

50   Foster, *Words Alone,* 24.

51   Sydney Owenson, *Lady Morgan's Memoirs: Autobiography, Diaries and Correspondence*, ed. William Hepworth Dixon (London: William H. Allen, 1862), 254.

not Lady Morgan succeeded in depicting a more realistic or sympathetic picture of country people, her novels still contained elements of stage Irishry. According to Jean Brihault, the idealized portraiture of the peasantry gives way to a more realistic grasp in Lady Morgan; yet, her characters are affected by the 'stage Irishman'.[52] Once again, we come across an indolent, drunk and poverty-stricken population; this time, however, we are also made aware of their virtues. In *The Wild Irish Girl*, Lady Morgan insists that the Irish are not instinctually indolent; the peasants wake up at dawn to go to the fields. She also reminds the reader that English agriculture is run by the Irish workforce. In *O'Donnel: A National Tale* (1814), the narrator states that 'a people who under circumstances of the greatest hardship, migrate annually to procure that labour which is denied them at home, cannot naturally be an idle people, however the means of industry may be denied them.'[53]

Like Maria Edgeworth, Lady Morgan was highly critical of the absentee landlordism, the corrupt economic system and negative stereotyping of Ireland by the English. Nevertheless, her narratives predominantly echo, like those of her contemporaries, the voice of an outsider, exemplified in the narrator's constant intrusion in the storyline for a chance to plead for reform. According to Jean Brihault, she could not 'have the peasants utter these arguments when she describes them on the brink of starvation, steeped in alcohol and exhausted. Hence the author's intrusion into the fiction where she plays the part of a witness and an accuser.'[54] In a way, the omniscient narrator's social commentary, combined with the journalistic tone of the novel, does not give the peasantry much of a chance to be heard from their own perspective. Thus, treated as an object of commentary rather than subject of a narrative on rural life, the peasantry becomes as static, lifeless and manipulated as representations of the Irish landscape in colonial and revivalist narratives.

Meanwhile, William Carleton from County Tyrone, whom young Yeats admired as 'the greatest novelist of Ireland, by right of the most Celtic

---

52 Jean Brihault, 'Lady Morgan: Deep Furrows', in Jacqueline Genet, ed., *Rural Ireland, Real Ireland?*, 71.

53 Sydney Owenson, *O'Donnel: A National Tale* (London: H. Colburn, 1814), 99.

54 Brihault, 'Lady Morgan: Deep Furrows', 78–9.

Countryside Narratives

eyes that ever gazed from under the brows of story-teller',[55] provided a more realistic picture of rural life due to his upbringing in the rural north. Carleton was the first novelist of his age to consider the Ulster peasantry in his writings. In the 1830 preface to *Traits and Stories of the Irish Peasantry*, he draws attention to the different state of affairs in the north and the sectarian conflicts which often marginalized the northern peasants from the peasantry in other parts of Ireland:

> These last – the Ulster Creachts, as they were formerly called – characteristically distinct from the Southern or Western Milesians as the people of Yorkshire are from the natives of Somerset; yet they are still as Irish, and as strongly imbued with the character of their country […]. Among these races, surrounded by Scotch and English settlers, and hid amongst the mists of their highland retreats, education, until recently, had made little progress; superstition, and prejudice, and ancient animosity held their strongest sway; and their priests, the poor pastors of a poorer people, were devoid of the wealth, the self-respect, and the learning which prevailed amongst their better endowed brethren of the south.[56]

Carleton documented the conditions of the peasantry based on personal experience and through his sharp eye for detail. *The Black Prophet: A Tale of the Irish Famine* (1847), based on the minor famine periods before *an Gorta Mór*, anticipated the catastrophic outcome of depending on the single crop system. Following the eruption of Mount Tambora in the East Indies, the climatic global calamity of lowered temperatures and flooding is vividly described in the early scenes of the novel:

> The whole summer had been sunless and wet – one, in fact, of ceaseless rain, which fell day after day, week after week, and month after month, until the sorrowful consciousness had arrived that any change for the better must now come too late, and that nothing was certain but the terrible union of famine, disease, and death which was to follow [….] A brooding stillness, too, lay over all nature; cheerfulness had disappeared, even the groves and hedges were silent, for the very birds had ceased

---

55   William Butler Yeats, 'Introduction', in William Carleton, *Stories from Carleton with an Introduction from W. B. Yeats* (London: Walter Scott; New York: W. J. Gage and Co., 1889), xiv–xvi.

56   William Carleton; cited in Colin Meir, *The Ballads and Songs of W. B. Yeats: The Anglo-Irish Heritage in Subject and Style* (London: Macmillan, 1979), 47.

to sing, and the earth seemed as if it mourned for the approaching calamity, as well as for that which had been already felt.[57]

Carleton's prophecy in *The Black Prophet* was no more than common sense. The increasing dependence of the Irish farmer on the potato crop led to a gradual distancing from the land and the laws of nature. In both *The Black Prophet* and Carleton's moral tale *Parra Sastha* (1845), it is the lack of knowledge and separation from the natural order that brings disaster.[58] The black prophet's common sense is a result of his close knowledge of the land through direct engagement and observation of the natural cycles and their impact on the environment. The prophecy, in other words, corresponds to Tim Ingold's insistence on the priority of intuition over reason in developing an ecological approach. Challenging the dichotomies of mind/feeling, reason/intuition and culture/nature, Ingold introduces a perspective whereby the perception of the environment is deduced from action and involvement in an actual place rather than from abstract reasoning. If intuition consists of the knowledge we apply on a day-to-day basis in a certain environment, then, it is 'based in feeling, consisting in the skills, sensitivities and orientations that have developed through long experience of conducting one's life in a particular environment.'[59]

Carleton's intuitive approach through first-hand familiarity with Irish country life and Gaelic language led to a portrayal of a more realistic 'picture of the social and educational deprivation' in rural Ireland.[60] In a way, Carleton's portrayal of the peasantry 'by-passes the Revival's idealistic view of the Irish peasant to make a direct link with Patrick Kavanagh's *The Great Hunger*.'[61] Although, in comparison with Kavanagh, Carleton came from a

---

57 William Carleton, *The Black Prophet* (Shannon: Irish University Press, 1972), 16–17.
58 Timothy Wenzell, *Emerald Green: An Ecocritical Study of Irish Literature* (Newcastle upon Tyne: Cambridge Scholars, 2009), 33–4.
59 Tim Ingold, *The Perception of the Environment: Essays on Livelihood, Dwelling and Skill* (London: Routledge, 2010), 25.
60 Daniel A. Harris, *Yeats: Coole Park and Ballylee* (Baltimore: John Hopkins University Press, 1974), 86.
61 Harris, *Yeats: Coole Park and Ballylee*, 86.

Countryside Narratives   103

considerably more advantageous background. In his 1843 introduction to *Traits and Stories,* Carleton wrote of his upbringing in a literate household:

> My father possessed a memory not merely great or surprising, but absolutely astonishing. He could repeat the whole of the Old and New Testament by heart, and was, besides, a living index to almost every chapter and verse you might wish to find in it [...]. As a teller of old tales, legends, and historical anecdotes, he was unrivalled, and his stock of them was inexhaustible. He spoke Irish and English language with nearly equal fluency.[62]

Carleton's childhood in the country and his knowledge of the linguistic gap between the Gaelic-speaking peasantry and the majority of the English-speaking writers gave him a point of view different from that of Maria Edgeworth and Lady Morgan, who were stylistically superior to him. He openly challenged the stereotypes and stage Irishry by referring to the language issue and was among the first writers to lament the publication of Irish literary works in foreign markets. Moreover, he urged for a national literature almost two generations ahead of W. B. Yeats. In *The Ned M'Keown Stories* (1881), Carleton compared the Irish writers to the absentee landlords:

> In truth until within the last ten or twelve years an Irish author never thought of publishing in his own country, and the consequence was that our literary men followed the example of our great landlords; they became absentees, and drained the country of its intellectual wealth precisely as the others exhausted it of its rents.[63]

Carleton's concern goes back to the sensitive issue of writing about Ireland at the time. The anxiety of representation put the Revival writers, the majority of whom were from the Protestant Ascendency, in a precarious situation regarding the authenticity of their accounts and the reception of their works inside and outside Ireland. Commenting on representations of Irish life in the nineteenth-century novels, Stephen Gwynn mentioned the sensitivity of writing about Ireland in an era where 'every book on an

62   William Carleton, *Traits and Stories of the Irish Peasantry,* 3rd edn (Dublin: William Fredrick Walkman, 1843), viii.
63   William Carleton, *The Ned M'Keown Stories* (Frankfurt am Main: Outlook Verlag GmbH, 2018), 9.

104   CHAPTER 3

Irish subject was judged by the effect it was likely to have upon English opinion':

> Ireland, though she ought to count herself amply justified of her children, is still complaining that she is misunderstood among the nations; she is forever crying out for someone to give her keener sympathy, fuller appreciation, and exhibit herself and her grievances to the world in a true light. The result is that kind of insincerity and special pleading which has been the curse of Irish or Anglo-Irish literature. I write of a literature which has its natural centre in Dublin, not Connemara; which looks eastward, not westward.[64]

Gywnn's perspective is indicative of a frustration among the literary class who, on the one hand, faced the challenge of resisting British stereotyping and representing Ireland in the foreign market, and on the other, had to bear the burden of proving their Irishness for the audience at home. The majority of these writers were Dubliners whose point of view was often marred by the physical and social distance that existed between them and their subject, the peasantry. Gwynn's contemporary and the most influential figure of the Revival, W. B. Yeats played an important role in popularizing the metanarrative of Irishness based on nationalist treatment of the Irish countryside. A generation later, Patrick Kavanagh challenged Yeats's depiction of the countryside by offering a counter-narrative to what he believed to be a 'myth' created in Dublin for Dubliners.[65]

W. B. Yeats and the persona of the 'peasant bard'

Yeats's rural Ireland accommodated an absentee population. By the time he was collecting stories about the country and fantasizing the rural dweller, the so-called 'heroic' peasantry had already joined the past. Even at the time of William Carleton and Maria Edgeworth, the peasantry they portrayed had already ceased to exist, and they were aware of

64   Stephen Gwynn, *Irish Books and Irish People* (Dublin: Talbot Press, 1919), 8–9.
65   Genet, 'Yeats and the Myth of Rural Ireland', 148.

Countryside Narratives 105

it. In his preface to *Tales and Sketches Illustrating the Character of the Irish Peasantry* (1845), Carleton wrote: 'Many of the characters contained in the following volume have already ceased to exist, and are consequently the property of history. Others are still in being, but ere long they too will have disappeared.'[66] In her preface to *Castle Rackrent*, Maria Edgeworth also reminded the reader that the characters in the book were no longer part of the existing social life of the country:

> The editor hopes his readers will observe, that these are 'tales of other times'; that the manners depicted in the following pages are not those of the present age; the race of the Rackrents has long since been extinct in Ireland, and the drunken Sir Patrick, the litigious Sir Murtagh, the fighting Sir Kit, and the slovenly Sir Condy, are characters which could no more be met with at present in Ireland, than Squire Western or Parson Trulliber in England.[67]

The backward view of the countryside was part of the Revival's zeitgeist. The literary journals and magazines of the time, including the *Nation* and *Dublin University Magazine*, were active in promoting Schlegel and Carlyle's belief that 'the historian was a prophet facing backwards'.[68] This reliance on the past, as explained in the previous chapter, was part of the nostalgic characteristic of a postcolonial literature with the aim of reconstructing an ideal nation modelled after the pre-Conquest culture. The further the countryside moved towards modernization, the more valuable the past and its idylls became; consequently, the Irish writers looked further backward in search of an 'authentic' cultural heritage.

The Ireland of Yeats's youth had already undergone major socio-economic and demographic transformations. What was once a predominantly rural country in the nineteenth century was on its way to becoming one of the most urbanized states in twentieth-century Europe. In less than three decades after the Famine, Ireland entered an era of dramatic demographic changes; '[m]entalities, social relationships, people's behaviour in general considerably evolved and the rural society looked to the future

---

66 Carleton, *Tales and Sketches Illustrating the Character of the Irish Peasantry*, ix.
67 Edgeworth, *Castle Rackrent*, 42–3.
68 Foster, *Words Alone*, 59.

with new eyes and the past acquired a new value.'[69] The rapid demographic growth – as a result of economic transformation – drastically altered rural Ireland. A great number of small farmers and villagers emigrated, and those that stayed behind chose celibacy. The modernization and urbanization of Ireland as a non-industrial country brought about an existential gap that Yeats and his contemporaries tried to fill in by returning to 'their origins' or, as Foucault observed, 'in the analysis of their very historicity.'[70]

For Yeats, the peasantry's way of life strengthened his 'hope of creating a Unity of Culture',[71] uncorrupted by modernity. Moving towards an independent future, modern Ireland had lost its connection to the countryside and as such, lost sight of its collective past. Thereby, by replacing history with myth and reducing the countryside into a purely geographical entity, the Irish Literary Revival managed to free the landscape of the socio-political complexities that dominated the modern countryside. This cultural mutation had the greatest impact on rural Ireland. As Maignant points out, rural dwellers, 'dehistoricized by the conquest', made up of lower classes of society and less educated than their urban counterparts, were 'by definition, denied access to historical consciousness'.[72] The rural community's only access to the past was restricted to their 'habitus'; that is, what they had inherited from their previous generations and adapted to their own situation.[73] As such, the rural society lacked a history, which made it susceptible to manipulation from outside.

The revivalists were intent on retrieving a collective consciousness based on the character of the peasant, who became the 'everyman' of this cultural stage. The peasants' close-to-nature and down-to-earth way of life as well as their connection to the oral literary tradition of Ireland through stories, ballads and songs renewed hopes of restoring Ireland into what Genet termed 'a "holy land" of the imagination'.[74] The Irish Literary

---

69 Catherine Maignant, 'Rural Ireland in the Nineteenth Century and the Advent of the Modern World', in Jacqueline Genet, ed., *Rural Ireland, Real Ireland?*, 26–7.

70 Cited in Maignant, 'Rural Ireland in the Nineteenth Century', 27.

71 Genet, 'Yeats and the Myth of Rural Ireland', 145.

72 Maignant, 'Rural Ireland in the Nineteenth Century', 27.

73 Maignant, 'Rural Ireland in the Nineteenth Century', 27.

74 Genet, 'Yeats and the Myth of Rural Ireland', 142.

Countryside Narratives 107

Renaissance assimilated the peasant as a prototype of Irishness, based on similarities to ingredients of a past culture which in most cases were forged or at least exaggerated. They were deemed close to the Celtic race of heroes and warriors who dwelt in Ireland before the Conquest. Their proximity to a more natural environment and their connection to the soil was a reminder of Finn and his warriors' residence in 'nature'. Their belief in the existence of the *Sidhe* was compared to the pre-Christian belief in the ancient gods and goddesses of Ireland. The storytelling tradition and love of rhyme were also reminders of the Celtic bardic order.

The significance of the peasantry for Yeats extended beyond the characterization of rural life towards a representation of the entire Irish culture. The Irish peasant was not a mere stock character in Yeats's tales of heroic Ireland; she or he served as an esoteric symbol, a persona hiding the 'true' artist. In *A Vision* (1925), Yeats 'systematizes the perception of the relationship between the artist and the peasant. The man of phase 17 (Yeats himself, Shelley, Dante and other artists) derives his mask from phase 3, the peasant.'[75] Carleton, for instance, was not only a rural poet from County Tyrone; for Yeats, he embodied the 'true' peasant who was 'at last speaking, stammering, illogically, bitterly, but nonetheless with the deep and mournful accent of the people'.[76] According to Genet, Yeats's 'interest in the character of the countryman merges with his effort to transform Irish culture, spiritualize the native soil, revive traditions and awaken the national imagination'.[77] It was above all the proximity of the peasant to the land or symbolically, his marriage to 'rock and hill'[78] that made him a suitable model for representing Irishness.

Yet as mentioned earlier, the recurrent identification of the peasant with the land created a character free of socio-political complexities. The land, or rather the aesthetic appreciation of it in the form of the landscape, turned into a background for connecting the dehistoricized peasant to the context of Yeats's stories. Once again, the land turned into a dead entity,

75   Genet, 'Yeats and the Myth of Rural Ireland', 152.
76   William Butler Yeats, *Representative Irish Tales* (G.P. Putnam's Sons, 1891), 28.
77   Genet, 'Yeats and the Myth of Rural Ireland', 139.
78   The phrase appears in William Butler Yeats, *Autobiographies* (London: MacMillan Press, 1973), 193–4.

pushing the imaginary peasants who populated Yeats's countryside further towards abstraction. In other words, Yeats's lack of interest in the socio-political or socio-environmental reality of the countryside undermined the peasantry 'as a social group'.[79] When Yeats suggested Aran Islands to J. M. Synge as a place where Irish culture existed in its purest form, he was aware that the relevant distance of the islanders from the socio-political disturbances of the age would have made them a 'pure' specimen for his study. What he was looking for was an isolated sample, with 'the least developed' economic situation.[80]

Among Yeats's own array of rural characters – the shepherd, goatherd, gleeman, storyteller, blind poet, hermit, fool and the like – the 'peasant bard' was perhaps the most prototypic representative of rural Irish culture. Yeats revisited this popular character throughout his canon: He is the Cumhal McCormac of *The Secret Rose* (1896) collection; we come across him in the reincarnation of the eighteenth-century Gaelic poet Eoghan Rua Ó Súilleabháin (Owen Roe O'Sullivan) in *The Stories of Red Hanrahan* (1892–1903); later on, he is the blind Raftery of nineteenth-century Ireland whose shadow dwells in Yeats's tower. In short, the peasant bard of the Yeatsian fiction is a wandering outcast who has a curious relationship with the supernatural; his bitter tongue and cursing habit have alienated him from the people, and his love/hate relationship with the environment separates him from the rest of the peasantry. Cumhal McCormac in *The Secret Rose* and Hanrahan in *The Stories of Red Hanrahan* are both wandering bards based on the Gaelic theme of '*consuetude peregrinandi*' or 'White Martyrdom',[81] where the outcast poet, king or hermit left his birthplace and companions and turned into a wandering character in the wild. While Yeats's characters are inspired by the Gaelic past of Ireland, they express 'attitudes totally foreign to the eighteenth-century Gaelic tradition',[82] and represent instead the poet's construction of a certain identity type.

Nevertheless, Yeats's depiction of the peasantry evolved throughout his prolific career. He was, in Genet's conviction, 'too great a poet to be

79   Genet, 'Yeats and the Myth of Rural Ireland', 148.
80   Genet, 'Yeats and the Myth of Rural Ireland', 149.
81   Robin Flower, *The Irish Tradition* (Oxford: Clarendon Press, 1966), 19.
82   Meir, *The Ballads and Songs of W. B. Yeats*, 44.

Countryside Narratives   109

satisfied with an artificial poetic myth'.[83] He showed a great degree of concern with representing the spirit of the peasantry through his attempts
at grasping their language, habits, customs and beliefs. In his preface to
Cathleen Ni Houlihan (1902), dedicated to Lady Gregory, he mentioned
his childhood memories of Rosses Point and Ballisodare, where he was first
acquainted with the songs and stories that appear in the first edition of
The Celtic Twilight (1893). He further referred to his residence in London
as the period that distanced him from 'the Irish way' despite his attempts
at keeping the memory of the countryside alive by reading every book or
old newspaper:

> I began to forget the true countenance of country life [...]. Then you brought me
> with you to see your friends in the cottages, and to talk to old wise men on Slieve
> Echtge, and we gathered together, or you gathered for me, a great number of stories
> and traditional beliefs. You taught me to understand again, and much more perfectly
> than before, the true countenance of country life.[84]

In the second edition of *The Celtic Twilight* (1902), Yeats was concerned
with reflecting the voice of the country people, echoing their accents and
incorporating their energetic and earthly cadence to his stories. For him,
the peasantry's speech was free from the abstractions that had characterized the Victorian prose; it was a 'living speech, flowing out of the habits
of their lives'.[85] In a letter to John Quinn on September 16, 1905, he insisted that 'the element of strength in poetic language is common idiom,
just as the element of strength in poetic construction is common passion'.[86] When the myth exploded, as it did in his later poetry, the vice and
virtues of rural life were depicted in greater depth. The peasant character
in Yeats's late poems turns out to be more complex, sometimes fearful and
cowardly and sometimes bold and heroic. He could be banal, wise or spiritual. In the end, Yeats created an anti-hero in the same familiar persona
of Moll Magee, Red Hanrahan and Crazy Jane, all solitary characters,

83   Genet, 'Yeats and the Myth of Rural Ireland', 149.
84   William Butler Yeats, *The Variorum Edition of the Poems of W. B. Yeats*, ed. Peter
      Allt and Russell C. Alspach (New York: Macmillan, 1966), 232.
85   Allan Wade, ed., *The Letters of W. B. Yeats* (London: Rupert Hart-Davis, 1954), 462.
86   Wade, *The Letters of W. B. Yeats*, 462.

alienated and cast away from society. Their suffering stemmed from a social system to which they did not belong; their condition was a critique of the materiality of their community, of the misunderstandings that stigmatized the peasantry and pushed them further towards the periphery.

In portraying a character such as Crazy Jane, for whom the dichotomies of body/soul and fair/foul were non-existent, Yeats succeeded in deidealizing the previous masks. The new mask, in Genet's view, possessed a 'concrete vigour' which saved him from 'the idealization which tended to devitalize him in the eighties'.[87] Corrupted by modernism and materialism, the new persona was perhaps closer to the city dweller. The characters of *The Secret Rose* collection seem to have more affinity with the Irish middle class: 'They are closer to Dublin Shopkeepers [...] than to Biddy Hart, Paddy Flynn or Mary Battle in *The Celtic Twilight*.'[88] The new persona also reflected the new rural class, as the boundaries which had previously separated the country and the city merged in the new century. Overall, Yeats's primary interest in rural Ireland, as he explained in *Autobiographies*, continued to be a preoccupation with examining his own personality: 'I did not examine [...] the true thoughts of those I met, not the general tradition of the country, but I examined myself a great deal.'[89] Yeats's obsession with masks and preoccupation with exploring his own true self were perhaps what deterred him from catching – in his own words – 'the true spirit of Irish life in the country', a countenance that shows a truer colour in Kavanagh's portrayal of the countryside.

87   Genet, 'Yeats and the Myth of Rural Ireland', 152.
88   Genet, 'Yeats and the Myth of Rural Ireland', 150.
89   Yeats, *Autobiographies*, 201.

CHAPTER 4

Towards a Poetics of Dwelling: Patrick Kavanagh and the Countryside

Patrick Kavanagh: The ploughman poet and early influences

Patrick Kavanagh was a minor but promising young poet prior to his arrival in Dublin in 1931. His early poems appeared from 1929 in literary journals and magazines including the *Irish Statesman, Dublin Magazine, Irish Times,* and *Irish Independent.* His first volume of poetry *Ploughman and Other Poems* and his first novel *The Green Fool* were published before his settlement in Dublin in 1939. A study of Kavanagh's early work highlights major influences in his poetic career, among which the influence of the Irish Literary Renaissance and the so-called 'myth of Irishness' was not only seen in his writing but also in his conduct. His sixty-mile walk from Monaghan to Dublin in December of 1931 to meet his mentor George Russell (AE) and his 'exaggeratedly "countrified"'[1] appearance were signs of the younger poet's awareness of what the literary society in Dublin was looking for and his readiness to enact it. The 'peasant bard' of the Irish Literary Revival had finally arrived in Dublin to sing of the peasantry. His humble background and lack of formal education were advantageous in assigning him a role W. B. Yeats and his contemporaries had forged as an image of 'authentic' Irish identity, a concept that older Kavanagh repudiated in his poetry and prose.

---

1   Antoinette Quinn, *Patrick Kavanagh: A Biography* (Dublin: Gill and Macmillan, 2001), 70.

112   CHAPTER 4

Despite being 'a late starter in literature'[2] and leaving school at the age of thirteen, reading became Kavanagh's major hobby, especially after the ownership of Reynold's farm at the age of twenty-one. Paddy in *The Green Fool* and Tarry in *Tarry Flynn* are both daydreamers who often carry a torn copy of a book with them on the farm. Paddy's account of his library among the briars in the field is an autobiographical account of Kavanagh's early love of poetry and the unusual circumstances of his self-education which consisted of schoolbook rhymes, street ballads, popular writers in *Old Moore's Almanac* and *Palgrave's Golden Treasury* as well as canonical Romantic and Victorian poets. He also read the popular and religious magazines which circulated in his native townland of Mucker in Inniskeen, including *Sunlight Soap Almanac*, *The Messengers of the Sacred Hearth* and *Ireland's Own*.

Early poems such as 'Ploughman' and sections from *The Green Fool*, which he later regretted having written, register the Revival's diction and Georgian pastoral imagery. At times his poetry censures the reality of farm life. Quinn calls Kavanagh's early poetry 'a prettified version of reality' built on 'deception'.[3] Phrases such as 'Tranquillity walks with me / And no care', 'Joy that is timeless' and 'a star-lovely art / In a dark sod'[4] echo a Yeatsian west-of-Shannon narrative of bliss and beauty. His poetry at this stage is archaic in imagery and outmoded in diction, which in Holliday's opinion is a 'pale attempt at employing AE's mystical Aestheticism'.[5] On the other hand, this early sentimentality captured at its best what Oona Frawley has called 'the mood of a generation that was shifting the population centres of Ireland'.[6] High unemployment rates, emigration, and celibacy continued

2   Quinn, *Patrick Kavanagh: A Biography*, 15.
3   Quinn, *Patrick Kavanagh: A Biography*, 78.
4   Patrick Kavanagh, 'Ploughman', in *Collected Poems* (London: Penguin Books, 2005), 7.
5   Shawn Holliday, 'Patrick Kavanagh (1904–1967)', in Alexander G. Gonzalez, ed., *Modern Irish Writers: A Biocritical Source Book* (Westport: Greenwood Press, 1997), 140.
6   Oona Frawley, 'Kavanagh and the Irish Pastoral Tradition', in Stan Smith, ed., *Patrick Kavanagh* (Dublin: Irish Academic Press, 2009), 85–6.

Towards a Poetics of Dwelling 113

to drain the countryside in the first decades of the twentieth century and even after Kavanagh had left Monaghan for Dublin.

Kavanagh himself referred to his early meditative verse as 'mere juvenilia';[7] yet, what is rewarding about his early vision is the employment of a type of imagery derived from direct engagement with his immediate surroundings. He was a keen observer of what appeared to be a pastoral landscape populated with birds and trees. 'Four birds', one of his earliest poems, is a simple, descriptive verse about the familiar birds in the poet's environment, the kestrel, owl, lark and corn-crake. Compared to Yeats's bird imagery in *The Wanderings of Oisin*, the osprey, eagles, seagulls, etc., Kavanagh's birds carry no supernatural significance; at most, they imbue the marginalized landscape of rural Ulster with a tangible, romantic touch. In 'To a Blackbird', he apostrophizes the bird as 'O pagan poet' and refers to it as his 'kindred' in a style that echoes the early Irish pastoral tradition, celebrated by hermit poets in search of spirituality in nature. This pantheistic overture continues throughout the length of Kavanagh's poetry and crystallizes in his two novels, but the change of circumstances in his later poetry, most importantly his residence in Dublin, led to a gradual change in his poetics from rural pastoralism to the urban pastoral or post-pastoral, a notion that is examined in greater depth in Chapter six.

Oona Frawley distinguishes between the Irish pastoral before and after the Conquest based on the genre's engagement with nostalgia. Early pastoral is more or less a subcategory of the classical genre. Hermit and bardic poetry before the thirteenth century were predominantly dedicated to the beauties of nature and the landscape. From the Norman invasion onwards and the consolidation of power by the Catholic Church, nature became a site for nostalgia, 'a place from which to lament the passing or loss or changing of culture'.[8] In other words, medieval Irish poetry 'mourned the loss of a cultural world', hence moved 'towards a pastoral form that is at once realistic and acknowledging of beauty while containing a coded reading of cultural change'.[9]

---

7   Patrick Kavanagh, *A Poet's Country, Selected Prose*, ed. Antoinette Quinn (London: Penguin Books, 2003).
8   Frawley, 'Kavanagh and the Irish Pastoral Tradition', 76.
9   Frawley, 'Kavanagh and the Irish Pastoral Tradition', 76.

Kavanagh's pastoralism is not classical or Irish in any restrictive sense. Unlike revivalist narratives that saw in post-Conquest Irish pastoral a model for reviving a lost culture, Kavanagh's rural-pastoral dismisses such nostalgic references to the past and instead focuses on the here and now. His is a depiction of the country's merits and beauties as well as its banalities and hardships. Old wooden gates, blackbirds, trees and flowers are celebrated. Farming details along with the poet's mention of the cycle of seasons also give his verse the tension that is characteristic of the georgic mode. Sometimes, spraying the potatoes becomes the most pleasing and heroic of tasks in *Tarry Flynn*; other times, it turns into a denigrating activity on Reilly's farm, with Tarry clad in his patched trousers and his back soaked from the leaking spray can.

The spiritual hunger of the country people, the stasis of rural life and its attachment to tradition as well as the pettiness of family feuds and problems make up a rather bleak countryside in Kavanagh's later poems including *The Great Hunger* (1942), which is an example of antipastoral. Yet, antipastoral 'for all its nay-saying' is still a version of the pastoral, as Declan Kiberd points out.[10] Kavanagh's antipastoral engages with the common elements of the pastoral, 'even if simply because of the politicized nature of earlier writing on these themes'.[11]

According to Seamus Heaney, Kavanagh's early poetry is written under the influence of a Blakean notion of consciousness in *Songs of Innocence and Experience*. Verses from *Tarry Flynn* and poems like 'Shancoduff', 'A Christmas Childhood' and 'Spraying the potatoes' reflect 'the growth of a poet's mind'.[12] In other words, Kavanagh's sense of place invokes a mixed feeling of attachment and alienation at the same time. The early poems construct the very dynamics of a landscape which, perhaps for the first time since the Revival, emerges as a living and temporal entity. Kavanagh achieves this through an act of disclosure, which is the result of a dwelling perspective. Dwelling is more than inhabiting the earth; it is a

---

10   Declan Kiberd, *Inventing Ireland: The Literature of the Modern Nation* (London: Vintage Books, 1996), 489.

11   Frawley, 'Kavanagh and the Irish Pastoral Tradition', 72.

12   Seamus Heaney, *Preoccupations: Selected Prose, 1968–1978* (New York: Farrar, Straus, and Giroux, 1989), 120.

Towards a Poetics of Dwelling

way of communicating with and perceiving the environment particular to human beings as the only living phenomena conscious of their existence. Dwelling is dynamic; it is a process that involves 'the long-term imbrication of humans in a landscape of memory, ancestry and death, of ritual, life and work'.[13] In Heideggerian etymology, dwelling is closely connected to *Dasein* (being-in-the-world) and characterized by 'sparing and preserving'[14] the land. Kavanagh's poetry manifests a complex relationship between the poet-farmer and his surrounding environment and offers a view of the landscape and peasantry beyond revivalist and colonial stereotypes.

Kavanagh's active engagement, intuitive knowledge of the countryside and attention to detail can also be interpreted in relation to Tim Ingold's 'poetics of dwelling',[15] which is a derivative of Martin Heidegger's later philosophy and influenced by the works of prominent anthropologists Gregory Bateson and Claude Lévi-Strauss. In *The Perception of the Environment*, Ingold questions the view of the environment as dead, unengaging and separate from humans and acknowledges instead its dynamism, relativity and temporality through the following principles: First, the environment is always a relative term; 'that is, to the being whose environment it is'. Second, the environment is a process rather than a complete entity in itself, which means as long as 'environments are forged through the activities of living beings [...] they are continually under construction'. Third, there is a fundamental difference between 'environment' and 'nature' which 'corresponds to the difference in perspective between seeing ourselves as beings *within* a world and as beings *without* it'.[16]

The former view of the environment leads to an 'ecological' approach towards the ecosphere, where each phenomenon, whether human or non-human, endowed with life or still, becomes an engaging part of the entire process that makes a 'lifeworld' – Ingold's parallel terminology for the term 'environment'. Thereby, Ingold's ecological approach depends on a

13   Greg Garrard, *Ecocriticism* (New York: Routledge, 2004), 108.
14   Martin Heidegger, *Poetry, Language, Thought* (New York: Harper & Row, 1975), 149; *original emphasis*.
15   Tim Ingold, *The Perception of the Environment: Essays on Livelihood, Dwelling and Skill* (London: Routledge, 2010), 11.
16   Ingold, *The Perception of the Environment*, 20; original emphasis.

proper understanding of the environment and organisms as well as their interconnectedness:

> A properly ecological approach [...] is one that would take, as its point of departure, the whole-organism-in-its-environment. In other words, 'organism plus environment' should denote not a compound of two things, but one indivisible totality. That totality is, in effect, a developmental system [...], and an ecology of life – in my term – is one that would deal with the dynamics of such systems.[17]

Borrowed from Bateson's phrase 'genuine ecology of mind', Ingold's 'genuine ecology of life' presents a more ecofriendly view of the environment by engaging man and environment in a mutually constructive relationship where the health and functionality of one depends on the other. Such an ecology is highly intuitive. Intuition consists of the knowledge each organism develops through interaction with its immediate environment throughout a life cycle and is prerequisite to the survival of each organism; as such, it is prioritized to reason in Ingold's subversion of the dichotomous understanding of the human-environment relationship.

Kavanagh's poetics of dwelling offers a portrayal of the countryside based on active engagement and constructs a narrative based on sensory perception and intuition. As a small farmer in Mucker and being a keen observer of his environment, he was able to present a close view of the parish community in rural Monaghan and captured details which often went unnoticed by the city poets and the novelists of his and previous generations. Details such as the quality of clay, the cycle of seasons, the soundscape of the countryside and other banal as well as spiritual dimensions of living in the rural north came to life in Kavanagh's poetry and novels and became a point of reference for the future generation of Irish poets, north and south of the border.

---

17   Ingold, *The Perception of the Environment*, 19.

The education of attention: Kavanagh's eye for detail

Kavanagh was a keen observer of the living and non-living entities in the landscape. Details which at first might seem cumbersome become indispensable to the perception of the poet's environment. They are not employed as decorative devices which simply add to the ambience of rural life, nor serve the purpose of poetic description per se; rather, the poet's watchful eye in Monaghan and later in Dublin creates the tangible experience of being part of a certain environment – rural or urban – built upon personal experience. The landscape is enlivened with trees, birds, crops, hills and rivers; the cityscape is characterized by street names, canal banks and bridges, and both are peopled with true-to-life characters such as Tarry Flynn, Paddy, Patrick Maguire, lovers, and passers-by.

Seamus Heaney compared Kavanaghs' attention to detail in 'A Christmas Childhood' to 'the child's open-eyed attention to the small and the familiar'. His sensibility 'is acutely of its own time and place, and his region is as deep not as its history but as his own life in it'.[18] This is while the majority of the Revival and post-Revival narratives relied on the notion of land as a stable entity out of a 'desperate hope'[19] to bypass the country's turbulent history and to restore stability and continuity to a nation of diverse social, religious and political convictions. Kavanagh's poetic imagination, however, was rooted in his personal environment, and his narratives, for the most part, remained free of the cultural anxiety that characterized the previous generation's engagement with questions of land and identity. His relationship with place oscillates between love and hate, a sense of attachment accompanied by frustration. His poetic personae, the embodiment of this complicated relationship, are often trapped in what seems like a stagnant, rural landscape. However, the stasis is a result of the oppressive social mechanisms that govern the countryside;

---

18   Heaney, *Preoccupations*, 142.
19   Patrick Sheeran, 'The Narrative Creation of Place: Yeats and West of Ireland Landscapes', in Anne Buttimer and Luke Wallin, eds, *Nature and Identity in Cross-Cultural Perspective* (The Netherlands: Kluwer Academic Publishers, 1999), 287.

furthermore, the sense of entrapment is reinforced by the harsh realities of farming. The actual landscape, on the other hand, remains in constant change, and Kavanagh's attention to detail offers an understanding of the human-environment relationship from the perspective of a participant in the socio-environmental matrix of rural life.

Instead of imposing his view of the countryside as a fixed construction, Kavanagh teaches the reader where to look and by drawing attention to colours, sounds, scents and textures helps to transform the passive reader into an active observer who participates in the discovery of meaning embedded in the environment. An example is Tarry's watchful eyes in *Tarry Flynn*; through Tarry's moving vision, Kavanagh discloses a panoramic – rather than a flat – view of the landscape. One learns about the hills in the distance, the potato pit, the briars at the corner of the field as well as the local community who are engaged in some activities. He instructs the reader to look 'around' rather than to look 'at'. This is what Ingold calls 'the education of attention',[20] a phrase he had borrowed from Gibson in order to explain how the environment is understood through sensory perception, and how knowledge is transferred in an ongoing engagement within the environment. Referring to the transmission of knowledge from one generation to another in tribal cultures, Ingold emphasizes the importance of *showing* as a way of instructing the inexperienced observer about the knowledge inherent in the environment:

> To show something to somebody is to cause it to be seen or otherwise experienced – whether by touch, taste, smell or hearing – by that other person. It is, as it were, to lift a veil off some aspect or component of the environment so that it can be apprehended directly. In that way, truths that are inherent in the world are, bit by bit, revealed or disclosed to the novice. What each generation contributes to the next, in this process, is an *education of attention* (Gibson 1979: 254). Placed in specific situations, novices are instructed to feel this, taste that, or watch out for the other thing. Through this fine-tuning of perceptual skills, meanings immanent in the environment – that is in the relational contexts of the perceiver's involvement in the world – are not so much constructed as discovered.[21]

20 Gibson 1979, 254; cited in Ingold, *The Perception of the Environment*, 21.
21 Ingold, *The Perception of the Environment*, 21; my emphasis.

Towards a Poetics of Dwelling 119

The education of attention implies a type of learning that brings about knowledge. One does not become simply 'more knowledgeable' through the accumulation of information. Rather, knowledgeability consists 'in the capacity to situate such information and understand its meaning, within the context of a direct perceptual engagement with our environments. And we develop this capacity [...] by having things shown to us.'[22] For Kavanagh, the knowledge of the countryside comes from the inside. Whether viewing it from within the parish, for example, on the field while spraying the potatoes or reminiscing about the harvest season while in Dublin – hence reliving the moments through memory and association – Kavanagh remains a participant in his own narrative. He is able to present a vista the understanding of which is inseparable from an understanding of the seasons, crops, quality of soil, harvest time, trees, birds and cattle. Take for instance the poet's sensitivity to the seasonal changes and the time of the year when a specific activity is taking place. The poems 'After May', 'April', 'March', 'April Dusk' and 'October 1943', as obvious from their titles, are seasonal poems in which the mention of the month binds the activity to a living environment. The time of the year informs the reader – the novice – whether it is the calving season or harvest time, or if it is time for planting a tree or harrowing the field; in other words, the environment is built around these time-specific activities.

Regardless of whether the changes are cyclical like that of the seasons or embody more permanent and serious alterations such as the advance of farming life in the parish, Kavanagh's countryside remains dynamic. This element is present in most of his early poetry which often reflects the growth of an entity interconnected with that of another. Examples include 'To a Late Poplar', 'Beech Tree' and 'Poplar Memory', poems that deal with Kavanagh's passion in real life, i.e. trees. In 'Beech Tree', for instance, he writes of planting a beech in February, protecting it from 'goats with wires'[23] and waiting for it to come with leaves during spring. In 'The Poplar Memory', the planter is the poet's father, and the tree becomes a point of reference to indicate the passage of time.

22   Ingold, *The Perception of the Environment*, 21; original emphasis.
23   Kavanagh, 'Beech Tree', *Collected Poems* 9.

Temporality is one of the primary characteristics of the landscape. Ingold uses the term 'taskscape', which implies 'a pattern of dwelling activities',[24] in order to describe the temporality of the landscape through the activities that take place therein. To make his point clear, he offers an interpretation of Pieter Bruegel's *The Harvesters* (1565). The painting depicts the month of August where a group of peasants are working in the field while others rest by the shadow of a pear tree. The colour composition and the portrayal of certain agricultural tasks make the painting a miniature example of the real landscape. Observing the human activity in the painting as well as the natural and artificial phenomena, such as the nearby tree and the church in the distance, Ingold points to Bruegel's landscape being under formation as time passes and how people 'shape the landscape' as they dwell on it.[25] In specific, the pear tree becomes a point of reference which 'draws the entire landscape around it into a unique focus' by bridging 'the gap between the apparently fixed and invariant forms of landscape and the mobile and transient forms of animal life', which is 'visible proof that all these forms, from the most permanent to the most ephemeral, are dynamically linked under transformation within the movement of becoming of the world as whole'.[26]

Similar to the taskscape in Bruegel's painting, Kavanagh's taskscapes indicate the temporality of the environment. As Bruegel's pear tree embodies a history of development from its own growth to the passage of time in the village, Kavanagh's landscapes are populated with living and non-living entities whose existence is bound with that of one another. Nevertheless, Kavanagh's countryside is austere and free from the idealizations that characterize Bruegel's genre paintings, which aimed at capturing a pastoral environment modelled on a period of prosperity in the Netherlands. While Kavanagh's view of the field and peasants emanate from an insider's vantage point, Bruegel, as Gibson notes, was inclined to 'depict peasants very much as a wealthy landowner would have viewed them, as the anonymous tenders of his fields and flocks'.[27] Kavanagh's personae, on the other hand,

24 Ingold, *The Perception of the Environment*, 157.
25 Ingold, *The Perception of the Environment*, 157.
26 Ingold, *The Perception of the Environment*, 205.
27 Walter S. Gibson, *Bruegel* (London: Thames and Hudson, 1977), 157–8.

Towards a Poetics of Dwelling 121

often have a name with whom we can identify, and it is through *their* vista that the reader is offered a glimpse of the farming community through the activities that take place in the landscape.

The farming community: Acting, perceiving, dwelling

Many of Kavanagh's characters are members of a farming community. Before harbouring dreams about becoming poets, both Paddy and Tarry are minor farmers who participate in the social and agricultural activities of their community. The majority of Kavanagh's poems from 1929 to 1946, including 'The Hired Boy', 'Spraying the Potatoes', 'To the Man after the Harrow', 'Plough Horses', 'Temptation in Harvest' and 'In Memory of My Mother' refer to an aspect of farming and agriculture. If as Ingold insists, 'ways of acting in the environment are also ways of perceiving it',[28] then the perception of Kavanagh's environment is dependent upon the perception of the farming community in rural Monaghan and the activities therein; that is, harrowing, seeding, spraying, tilling and harvesting the crops as well as selling and bargaining in local fairs and markets, taking care of poultry and cattle, going on pilgrimage, storytelling, dancing and other local events. These details alongside the gossips and rumours circulating in the parish and nearby towns take such importance in Kavanagh's narratives that they no longer serve as a simple backdrop to an unfolding story; rather, they become the story – an account of humble origins made spectacular in the poet's treatment of the banal and mundane. Tarry's most romantic and poetic revelations come to him while he is busy pulling out turnips or draining the land. The origins of the 'lea green poem' ('The Ploughman') comes from 'A kicking mare in a rusty old plough tilling a rood of land for turnips'.[29]

In chapter 'Life and Death' of *The Green Fool*, Paddy describes the ins and outs of slaying a pig and selling it at the local market.[30] This information

28 Ingold, *The Perception of the Environment*, 9.
29 Patrick Kavanagh, *The Green Fool* (London: Penguin Books, 2001), 219.
30 Kavanagh, *The Green Fool*, 181–3.

is described with such precision and force that one is bound to ask why Kavanagh inscribes such rural details in a novel addressed to an urban readership in London and Dublin. This is important information; far from constructing a rural setting per se or idealizing the country tasks, Kavanagh informs the reader of the reality of the Irish countryside in the first decades of the twentieth century. The novel offers a critique of the restrictive rural communities in a country soaring towards modernism and the marginalization of small Catholic villages and townlands in Ulster.

It is noteworthy that the gradual modernization of farming methods in Ireland did not take place until the 'widespread diffusion of the tractor' after the Second World War.[31] What was available at the time were a few simple yet highly valued old farm tools: 'a spade, a rake and a shovel'. The bigger farms also required the use of a 'plough, harrow and roller'.[32] The introduction of the improved equipment was not welcomed at first since the alterations did not necessarily mean a more feasible farming method but one that broke with tradition. Of this equipment, the plough has been the single oldest farming tool in Ireland, and 'modifications made to it mirror the development of Irish agriculture'.[33] When the improved plough was introduced, it often steered some unwelcome reactions. In *The Green Fool* Paddy reminds the reader of the deep respect the country people had for the plough: 'In a quiet way it was an idol. To tamper with a plough was a dark sin: "The unluckiest thing ye ever done", I was told.'[34]

Borrowing farm equipment and animals for ploughing was a common practice in the countryside. Kavanagh continuously refers to borrowing an ass from one of the neighbours: Kerr's ass in a poem of the same name and Cassidy's ass in *The Green Fool* are two examples. After buying an old mare called Brown Bess, Paddy narrates the account of a humorous yet 'painful' joined ploughing with his neighbour, painful since the old mare happens to be a kicking mare. This ploughing partnership was called

31   Anne O'Dowd, 'Folklife and Folk Traditions', in Desmond Gillmor, ed., *The Irish Countryside: Landscape, Wildlife, History, People* (New York: Barnes and Noble Books, 1989), 121.
32   O'Dowd, 'Folklife and Folk Traditions', 121.
33   O'Dowd, 'Folklife and Folk Traditions', 122.
34   Kavanagh, *The Green Fool*, 96.

Towards a Poetics of Dwelling 123

'comhar' and was customary until recently in most parts of the countryside, especially among small farmers. In *The Green Fool*, we read about *comhar* from Paddy's perspective:

> You could tell a plough which was being drawn by a joined team: there would always be two men following the plough. A man whose stock of farming implements didn't include, say, a harrow tried to form a join with a man who had a harrow.[35]

Other than farming, participation in fairs and local markets were the major source of business and livelihood in the countryside. According to O'Dowd, '[f]airs were the most important event through rural Ireland until the 1950s, since which they have been largely replaced by livestock auction marts.'[36] There is a recurrent reference to fairs and markets among other socio-economic activities in Kavanagh's parish. In the highly evocative poem 'In Memory of My Mother', Kavanagh remembers his late mother as not 'lying in the wet clay' but walking 'among the poplars' on her 'way to the station' or 'Going to second mass' and meeting the poet 'On a fair day by accident, after / The bargains are all made'.[37] The memories are kinaesthetic and the dynamic environment in which the poet commemorates his mother gives her an air of life and mobility rather than death.

The introduction of the radio and television since the 1960s replaced many of the old methods of entertainment in the country, including storytelling, singing tunes and dancing, which were also part of Kavanagh's countryside. Another important component of rural life was and to some extent continues to be visiting holy wells and going on patterns, a pre-Christian ritual which was later adapted to the Christian practice of devotion to the patron saint of a parish on a feast day or the nearest Sunday called a Pattern Sunday. Among them, going to Lough Derg, Saint Patrick's purgatory in county Donegal, has been a popular subject among northern poets and writers from the time of William Carleton to Seamus Heaney. *Lough Derg*, one of Kavanagh's longer poems, provides an insight into the marginalized

---

35 Kavanagh, *The Green Fool*, 213.
36 O'Dowd, 'Folklife and Folk Traditions', 132.
37 Kavanagh, 'In Memory of My Mother', *Collected Poems* 129.

124   CHAPTER 4

Catholic community of the north, suffering from unemployment, high
celibacy rates and poverty.

'Homeric utterances' in the 'banal beggary' of the countryside: *Lough Derg*

Written in June 1942, *Lough Derg* is the account of a three-day pilgrimage
to Lough Derg in County Donegal. Kavanagh had formerly written about
the pilgrim site in *The Green Fool*, as young Paddy goes on pilgrimage
with a couple of neighbours and comes across a mixture of superstition,
humble piety, misery and hope in religious salvation. In the poem, the
'banal beggary'[38] of the people who have travelled from Cavan, Leitrim
and Mayo and 'From all the thin-faced parishes where hills / Are perished noses running peaty water' is described in detail to provoke and vex.
There is an underlying critique of a social system which has caused widespread unemployment, hunger, celibacy and poverty, mentioned through
the pilgrims' prayers. *Lough Derg* is also among the few references to the
Second World War in the body of Kavanagh's work.

> Then there was war, the slang, the contemporary touch,
>
> The ideologies of the daily papers.
>
> They must seem realer, Churchill, Stalin, Hitler,
>
> Than ideas in the contemplative cloister.[39]

Yet, it is the very 'ideas in the contemplative cloister' of Lough Derg
that concerns him. Against the backdrop of the Second World War in
Europe, Kavanagh chooses to give importance to the 'mean' and banal
longings of men and women who have travelled far for redemption; some
barefooted, some with gravels in their boots. Redemption for a hungry

---

38   Kavanagh, 'Lough Derg', *Collected Poems* 107.
39   Kavanagh, 'Lough Derg', 101.

Towards a Poetics of Dwelling 125

people, however, implies more than an abstract religious notion, in the same way that their hunger speaks of a deeper deprivation beyond corporeal limits. For them, redemption comes only when they are freed from the knot tied to their feet of the wet, cold clay of their parish, as Kavanagh remarks in his other long poem *The Great Hunger* (1942).

Among the pilgrims, a woman is praying for her husband's health and for her son to 'pass the Intermediate' and for her daughter to 'do well in music'. She asks that her aunt may remember them in her will. She prays for good weather and for her indigestion.[40] A young girl is asking to be liberated from living in a household 'With arguments going on and such as bother / About the half-boiled pots and unmilked cows'.[41] 'How Longer/ Must a fifty-shilling-a-week job be day-dreaming?' wonders another pilgrim, who needs a job to be able to 'settle down and marry'.[42] The poet continues:

This was the banal

Beggary that God heard. Was he bored

As men are with the poor? Christ Lord

Hears in the voices of the meanly poor

Homeric utterances, poetry sweeping through.[43]

In these small prayers and litanies, Kavanagh gives us a glimpse to the depth of a people's common miseries, needs, hopes and fears; yet in doing so, he adds an epic dimension to them, one that supersedes the seriousness of the war in Europe:

The battles where ten thousand men die

Are more significant than a peasant's emotional problem.

But wars will be merely dry bones in histories

And these common people real living creatures in it [...].[44]

40   Kavanagh, 'Lough Derg', 105.
41   Kavanagh, 'Lough Derg', 106.
42   Kavanagh, 'Lough Derg', 106.
43   Kavanagh, 'Lough Derg', 107.
44   Kavanagh, 'Lough Derg', 101.

126   CHAPTER 4

The reality of the people's miseries and the force with which Kavanagh narrates their prayers is a reminder of a later poem 'The Epic'. Having realized the importance and relevance of the small affairs in his parish, the poet chooses to write of Ballyrush and Gortin, leaving the war behind in the understated phrase 'Munich's bother'.[45] Lough Derg is not merely a site of pilgrimage or religious devotion. First and foremost, it is a 'physical' place with interwoven layers of myth, history and memory that manifest themselves in the very structure of the well. In other words, Kavanagh builds an environment around its participants, from trees in the landscape to the people who have left the place and from the memory of the Famine and the saints to the people who still live nearby:

> The middle of the island looked like the memory
>
> Of some village evicted by the Famine,
>
> Some corner of a field beside a well,
>
> Old stumps of walls where a stunted boortree is growing.
>
> These were the holly cells of saintly men –
>
> O that was the place where Mickey Fehan lived
>
> And the Reillys before they went to America in the Fifties.
>
> No, this is Lough Derg in County Donegal –
>
> So much alike is our historical
>
> And spiritual pattern, a heap
>
> Of stones anywhere is consecrated
>
> By love's terrible need.[46]

Building is dwelling, and as a dweller, Kavanagh is aware of how the historical cycle of the community is intertwined with that of the spiritual history of the place. By mixing the banal and the spiritual, something at which Kavanagh shows great mastery, rural life becomes tangible. It is

45   Kavanagh, 'Epic', 184.
46   Kavanagh, 'Lough Derg', 93–4.

no longer a so-called 'pristine' environment where the peasantry is presented as simple and heroic, nor a famine-ridden landscape with dirty, beast-like inhabitants. Rather, in the middle of their seemingly small and common demands, Kavanagh brings to focus the complexity of their hard rural life and dignifies their struggles as proper subject matter for poetry. While manifesting the beauties of the landscape, Kavanagh also allows the reader to touch the hard clay and feel the burden that lays upon the shoulders of the villagers.

'The Apocalypse of Clay': *The Great Hunger*

If Kavanagh's rural poetics has a single keyword that embodies the Irish countryside as a lived-in and living environment, the word is 'clay'. When Yeats in 'Municipal Gallery Revisited' wrote that 'All that we did, all that we said or sang / Must come from contact with the soil',[47] the soil was for him more of a symbol than a tangible reality. In contrast, Kavanagh wrote of the 'real' thing, of the touch of clay. His descriptions of the countryside, both the landscape and its social reality, are often enhanced by the use of 'clay' or a similar term in an adjective or phrase that embeds the social experience in the actual environment. It is noteworthy that soil denotes fertile ground whereas nothing grows in clay, which might refer to Kavanagh's use of the term as a reference to the arid social atmosphere of small rural communities in the north. This being said, he often used both terms interchangeably, and the connotations of the terms vary in different lyrics and prose pieces. Nevertheless, the connection between the persona and his/her environment remains solid. In 'A Christmas Childhood', Kavanagh writes about eating 'the knowledge that grew in clay'.[48] In 'Temptation in Harvest', the clay has the capacity 'to seduce' the

---

47 William Butler Yeats, 'Municipal Gallery Revisited', in Peter Allt and Russell K. Alspach, eds, *The Variorum Edition of the poems of W. B. Yeats* (New York: Macmillan, 1966), 603.

48 Kavanagh, 'A Christmas Childhood', *Collected Poems* 39.

128 CHAPTER 4

poet's heart. The 'Stony Grey Soil' of Monaghan is the object of love and hate. *The Great Hunger* ends with 'the apocalypse of clay',[49] and so on and so forth.

Adjectives are of utmost importance. The sod is described in various places as 'dark', 'sticky', 'stony', 'hard', 'good', 'fertile', 'wet' and the like. In *The Green Fool*, Paddy makes frequent references to how the soil feels in his hands: 'The soil was heavy, sticky, and lumpy.' His own mind is described as 'clay-heavy'.[50] Similar analogies such as 'mud-gloved fingers', 'Clay-wattled moustache', 'twisting sod' and 'Clayly hours'[51] set the tone for Kavanagh's critique of the restrictive rural community in *The Great Hunger*. Written and published in 1942, *The Great Hunger* is an epic manifesto of an anti-revivalist view of Irishness. In the words of Kavanagh's biographer Antoinette Quinn, the poem is 'a prophetic condemnation of rural Ireland'.[52] John McDonagh believes the poem played a crucial role in 'the gradual destruction of de Valera's idealised peasant who had, for centuries, epitomised the rural, Catholic, heterosexual, farming heart of Ireland'.[53] Terence Brown has referred to *The Great Hunger*, along with *Lough Derg* and *Tarry Flynn* as being 'among the most authentic reports from an indigenous Irish world which, since William Carleton opened its realities to inspection in the nineteenth century, had endured various forms of literary misrepresentation, exploitation and creative re-invention'.[54]

The poem is dominated by Kavanagh's use of the word 'clay', which from the very beginning helps register an authoritative and biblical tone: 'Clay is the word and clay is the flesh',[55] and after a series of apocalyptic observations,

49   Kavanagh, 'Temptation in Harvest', *Collected Poems* 121; 'Stony Grey Soil', *Collected Poems* 38; 'The Great Hunger', *Collected Poems* 89.
50   Kavanagh, *The Green Fool*, 103, 244.
51   Kavanagh, 'The Great Hunger', *Collected Poems* 64–9.
52   Antoinette Quinn, *Patrick Kavanagh: Born-Again Romantic* (Dublin: Gill and Macmillan, 1991), 389.
53   John MacDonagh, 'The Great Pyramids of Carlingford Lough: John Hinde and the De Valerian Utopia', in Alison O'Malley-Younger and Frank Beardow, eds, *Representing Ireland: Past, Present and Future* (Sunderland: University of Sunderland Press, 2005), 41.
54   Terence Brown, *The Literature of Ireland: Criticism and Culture* (Cambridge: Cambridge University Press, 2010), 22.
55   Kavanagh, 'The Great Hunger', 63.

Towards a Poetics of Dwelling

it ends with 'the hungry fiend' who 'sings the apocalypse of clay / In every corner of this land'.[56] The landscape is stripped bare of its former romantic associations that depicted the soil and the peasants' adherence to it as a sign of authenticity in Irish culture. So is the peasant liberated 'from the cosy imagination of the nation into the painful reality of contemporary existence'.[57] The image of the heroic countryman, the peasant bard or the gleeman of the Yeatsian canon is now reduced to a bunch of 'potato-gatherers' moving like 'mechanized scare-crows' in the field, where the poet struggles to find 'some light of imagination' in the 'wet clods'.[58]

Although Kavanagh later denounced *The Great Hunger* for its tragic qualities and lack of humour, the poem remains a turning point in the mainstream literary perception and representation of the Irish countryside. According to Seamus Heaney:

> [I]f *The Great Hunger* did not exist, a greater hunger would, the hunger of a culture for its own image and expression, it is a poem of its own place and time, transposing the grief of the past [...] into the distress of the present, as significant in the Irish context as Hardy's novels were in the English, socially committed but also committed to a larger, more numinous concept of love whose function he decreed was not to look back but 'to look on'.[59]

As in Kavanagh's other accounts of the country, there is no sign of a nostalgia for a so-called glorious past in *The Great Hunger*. What exists is the spiritual hunger of a community of peasants who live in the 'now' and 'here' of the poet's time and place. There is no anxiety in making direct reference to the Great Famine; neither is there a need for replacing history with myth. In contrast, Kavanagh rescues the countryside from the stagnant literary representations that continued to view rural Ireland in terms of its significance to some nationalist ends.

Kavanagh defamiliarized the familiar landscape of the nineteenth- and early twentieth-century narratives through a subversion of its most dominant actor – the peasant. It is only when the character is freed from

---

56 Kavanagh, 'The Great Hunger', 89.
57 McDonagh, 'The Great Pyramids of Carlingford Lough', 41.
58 Kavanagh, 'The Great Hunger', 63.
59 Heaney, *Preoccupations*, 126.

130   CHAPTER 4

the burden of myths and stereotypes that the reader is able to perceive the distance between the nationalist/romantic treatments of the peasant and Kavanagh's bleak, yet more in-depth portrayal. Throughout the poem, Kavanagh reminds the reader of the contrast between these two perspectives. Blind religious faith, hard work, misery and ignorance characterize Maguire, the peasant, and his countryside; yet, the 'passing world' which stares but does not stop to 'look closer'[60] deems the peasant as the source of 'all cultures' and 'all religions', and an inspiration without whom 'civilization must die':[61]

> The world looks on
>
> And talks of the peasant:
>
> The peasant has no worries;
>
> In his little lyrical fields
>
> He ploughs and sows.[62]

Kavanagh's whimsical irony is addressed at Yeats's idea of 'Unity of Culture' in the character of the peasant. As mentioned earlier, the 'Revival's conception of the peasant as a politico-cultural artifact'[63] had created an imaginary figure which was a reaction to British stereotyping, and Kavanagh's reaction to it is bitterly ironic. What he was fighting against was the very idea of the Yeatsian peasant, 'a myth, born in Dublin, for Dubliners'.[64] In 'Self-Portrait', which was originally delivered in a television programme in 1962, Kavanagh referred to the myth of Irishness as 'a form of anti-art', 'an undignified business – the trade of enemies and failures'.[65]

60 Kavanagh, 'The Great Hunger', 76.
61 Kavanagh, 'The Great Hunger', 85.
62 Kavanagh, 'The Great Hunger', 85.
63 Stan Smith, 'Introduction: Important Places, Times', in Stan Smith, ed., *Patrick Kavanagh* (Dublin: Irish Academic Press, 2009), 10.
64 Jacqueline Genet, *Rural Ireland, Real Ireland?* (Buckinghamshire: Colin Smythe, 1996), 148.
65 Kavanagh, *A Poet's Country, Selected Prose*, ed. Antoinette Quinn (London: Penguin Books, 2003), 309.

Towards a Poetics of Dwelling 131

For Kavanagh, the myth had degraded the peasant to 'half a vegetable'.[66] Phrases such as 'The peasant who is only one remove from the beast he drives' and 'An ignorant peasant deep in dung'[67] depict the poet's impatience with the matter of Ireland and the over-simplistic representations of rural life and characters. Kavanagh reacted to the very term 'peasant' that for him – as for the majority of the rural farming class – did not entail a proper representation of the people in the countryside. Neither was the term representative of Irish national identity. Instead, it was associated with ignorance, in Kavanagh's belief, who called the peasantry 'all that mass of mankind which lives below a certain level of consciousness'.[68]

Kavanagh juxtaposes the view of the countryside from outside and inside on various occasions, and at times, the juxtaposition leads to an absurd sense of humour and sarcasm. Earlier in the poem, Kavanagh comically refers to Maguire's 'happiest dream' as cleaning 'his arse / With perennial grass'.[69] Later, in part XIII, he writes of the travellers who 'touch the roots of the grass and feel renewed / When they grasp the steering wheels again' (85). What does Kavanagh imply in this sarcastically comical reference to the grass? Is the peasant unable to appreciate the beauty of his own surroundings? Does Maguire belong to the less sensitive class of peasants such as Eusebius and Tarry's mother in *Tarry Flynn*? Or, has spiritual hunger dried all poetic taste and replaced it with, instead, practicality and lack of affection?

Kavanagh's unromantic portrayal of the peasant and his contrast with the tourist's superficial perspective is an intended mockery of the way the likes of Yeats and his generation, who were tourists in the countryside, idealized the peasants and their suppressing rural environment. In 'A Poet's Country', an essay published in 1953, Kavanagh makes a comparison between the poet and the tourist based on the observation of beauty: 'No poet ever travelled in search of beauty', he wrote; beauty comes 'obliquely' when you are busy with common things. The tourist, however, 'is in a hurry; he demands quick returns of the picturesque and the obvious'.[70]

---

66 Kavanagh, 'The Great Hunger', 85.
67 Kavanagh, 'The Great Hunger', 85, 76.
68 Kavanagh, *Selected Prose*, 312.
69 Kavanagh, 'The Great Hunger', 67.
70 Kavanagh, *Selected Prose*, 28–9.

For the likes of Tarry Flynn, beauty is hidden in common things, things that he is ashamed of loving: 'Stones, clay, grass, the sunlight coming through privet hedge.'[71] The omniscient narrator asks: 'Why did he love such common things? He was ashamed of mentioning his love; these things were not supposed to be beautiful.'[72] Maguire, on the other hand, is not as sensitive or poetic as Tarry. His convictions might be simplified in his worries about whether or not 'to cross-plough' a turnip field in the middle of his prayers. However, Kavanagh does not stop here: In part III, Maguire's fourteen-hour daily routine, featuring common chores on the farm, ends with a sudden realization of the presence of some transcendent truth in the midst of everyday banalities:

No worry on Maguire's mind this day

Except that he forgot to bring his matches.

'Hop back there, Polly, hoy back, woa, wae.'

From every second hill a neighbour watches

With all the sharpened interest of rivalry.

Yet sometimes when the sun comes through a gap

These men know God the Father in a tree:

The Holy Spirit is the rising sap,

And Christ will be the green leaves that will come

At Easter from the sealed and guarded tomb.

[...]

Maguire learns

As the horses turn slowly round the which is which

Of love and fear and things half born to mind.

He stands between the plough-handles and he sees

71 Patrick Kavanagh, *Tarry Flynn* (London: Penguin Books, 1978), 172.
72 Kavanagh, *Tarry Flynn*, 172.

Towards a Poetics of Dwelling 133

> At the end of a long furrow his name signed
>
> Among the poets, prostitutes. With all miseries
>
> He is one.[73]

Through wry observation, Kavanagh constructs a complex character that is torn between the banal and the spiritual. The lines 'Yet sometimes when the sun comes through the gap / These men know God the Father in a tree' echo the pantheism of Tarry Flynn or Paddy in *The Green Fool*, in spite of their lack of Catholic piety. Similarly, the juxtaposition of poets and prostitutes in the last line, separated with a single comma, hints to the ambiguous and close relation between Maguire's labour on the farm and moments of transcendence or the complexities of the peasant's mind and his seemingly simplified convictions. After all, Maguire's life remains hidden and unapprehended for the most part: 'Nobody will ever know how much tortured poetry the pulled weeds on the ridge wrote / Before they withered in the July sun'.[74]

In depicting the complicated and, at times, adverse relationship between the peasant and the environment, Kavanagh states his early disillusionment with the simplistic assumption of the peasantry's idealized relationship with nature. In *Tarry Flynn*, nature turns against Tarry time and again. For example, just as he hopes that it rains in 'bucketfuls' for the local event to be dismissed, the day proves fair and sunny.[75] In *The Great Hunger*, Maguire's masturbation into the ashes – a subtle hint at his celibacy or impotence – is juxtaposed with the field's fertility and regeneration. The cruel grip of nature with which Kavanagh ends the story of Tarry Flynn also characterizes the doomed destiny of Maguire in *The Great Hunger*. Removed to the degree of beasts and vegetables, the peasant's bond with nature remains inseparable even in death:

> Maguire is not afraid of death, the Church will light him a candle
>
> To see his way through the vaults and he'll understand the

---

73 Kavanagh, 'The Great Hunger', 68.
74 Kavanagh, 'The Great Hunger', 76.
75 Kavanagh, *Tarry Flynn*, 150.

134   CHAPTER 4

Quality of the clay that dribbles over his coffin.

He'll know the names of the roots that climb down to tickle his feet.

And he will feel no different than when he walked through Donaghmoyne.

If he stretches out a hand – a wet clod,

If he opens his nostrils – a dungy smell;

If he opens his eyes once in a million years –

Through a crack in the crust of the earth he may see a face nodding in

Or a woman's legs. Shut them again for that sight is sin.[76]

Kavanagh's reference to the peasant's commitment and his symbolic marriage to the land through death is more vexing than Yeats's 'funereal' sense of place. While, in Yeats, there remains a post-mortem vision from the surface of the earth where the Yeatsian persona admonishes the next generation of Irish poets to 'learn their trade' and to sing of the peasantry,[77] Kavanagh's peasant, it seems, 'can neither be damned nor glorified'.[78] All that awaits him in death, as in life, is a religious obsession with guilt and the cruel grip of a nature that knows no 'unearthly laws':

The earth that says:

Patrick Maguire, the old peasant, can neither be damned nor glorified;

The graveyard in which he will lie will be just a deep-drilled potato-field

Where the seed gets no chance to come through

To the fun of the sun.

The tongue in his mouth is the root of a yew.

Silence, silence. The story is done.

[...]

The hungry fiend

76   Kavanagh, 'The Great Hunger', 88.
77   Yeats, 'Under Ben Bulben', 639–40.
78   Kavanagh, 'The Great Hunger', 89.

Towards a Poetics of Dwelling 135

Screams the apocalypse of clay

In every corner of this land.[79]

Maguire's clay-bound death brings to mind Tarry's clay-bound life. In the last chapter of *Tarry Flynn*, we read: 'The present tied him in its cruel knots and dragged him through bushes and briars, stones and weeds on his mouth and nose.'[80] In *The Green Fool*, Paddy talks about the difficulty of freeing oneself of the grip of the land and its jealousy towards literature: 'The land, when once it gets a grip on a man, will not easily let him go. The land is jealous of literature, and in its final effort to hold a poet offers him, like a despairing lover, everything, everything.'[81] While there seems to be no salvation for the old peasant at the end of *The Great Hunger*, the tight grip of nature is not always cruel. There is something comforting and homely amidst the vexing description of the peasant's clay-bound destiny in *Tarry Flynn* or poems where Kavanagh writes of a love/hate relationship towards his native soil.

'Stony Grey Soil', 'Inniskeen Road, July Evening' and 'Shancoduff' are among Kavanagh's most quoted parochial poems which deliver a strong sense of place. This sense of place, however, does not simply denote one's attachment to or love for a particular place. Sometimes the relationship is that of detachment or contempt. One's local environment could be a hindrance to his or her growth as a poet, as Kavanagh hints in the famous lines from 'Stony Grey Soil':

O stony grey soil of Monaghan

The laugh from my love you thieved;

You took the gay child of my passion

And gave me your clod-conceived.

[...]

79 Kavanagh, 'The Great Hunger', 89.
80 Kavanagh, *Tarry Flynn*, 174.
81 Kavanagh, *The Green Fool*, 245.

136 CHAPTER 4

You flung a ditch on my vision

Of beauty, love and truth.

O stony grey soil of Monaghan,

You burgled my bank of youth![82]

In the depths of Kavanagh's frustration with what detains him from growth, there is a 'clod-conceived' passion that makes him the poet he is. Later in life, Kavanagh regretted having left his farm and settled in Dublin to pursue his career as a poet. The nostalgic tone of 'Temptation in Harvest', for instance, represents the point of view of one who has reconciled with his early object of love/hate – the land. The cruel grip of nature, represented in the line 'the devilry of the fields'[83] is now transformed into the poet's passionate care for his farming life: 'The ricks are now my care.'[84]

A parochial sense of place: Kavanagh's sacerdotal care

In a lecture delivered at Ulster Museum in 1977, Seamus Heaney drew a line of difference between two senses of place in Irish poetry: 'One is lived, illiterate and unconscious, the other learned, literate and conscious.'[85] In comparison to Montague's learned etymology of placenames or Hewitt's rationalization of his northern roots, Kavanagh's placenames 'stake out a personal landscape, they declare one man's experience, they are denuded of tribal or etymological implications. Mucker, Dundalk, Inniskeen, provide no *frisson* beyond the starkness of their own dunting, consonantal noises.'[86]

---

82 Kavanagh, 'Stony Grey Soil', 38.
83 Kavanagh, 'Temptation in Harvest', 121.
84 Kavanagh, 'Temptation in Harvest', 122.
85 Heaney, *Preoccupations*, 131.
86 Heaney, *Preoccupations*, 140.

Towards a Poetics of Dwelling

What sets Kavanagh's view of the landscape apart is his invocation of a sense of place that is parochial. The 'parochial mentality', according to the poet himself, is based on 'the right type of sensitive humility' towards one's place and is not to be mistaken for provincialism.[87] 'The provincial has no mind of its own' and looks towards the metropolis; the parochial, on the other hand, 'is never in doubt about the social and artistic validity of his parish'.[88] Kavanagh does not offer a history of placenames; nor do his land/cityscapes carry nationalistic nuances. His ecology, according to Heaney, offers a 'felt knowledge of place',[89] a knowledge that is personal and based on the poet's momentary response to his surroundings. An example is Kavanagh's love for the hills around Reynolds farm, which is reflected in Paddy's passion for the hills surrounding Rocksavage far in *The Green Fool*:

> There were *good* names on these hills even though their soil was sticky and scarce of lime. Poets had surely put the names on them. Translated from the Gaelic they were: 'The Field of The Shop', 'The Field of The Well', 'The Yellow Meadow', 'The Field of The Musician'.[90]

At first glance, Kavanagh seems to be a namer in a Yeatsian fashion. His beloved hills remind one of the 'Seven Woods of Coole' and Yeats's enthusiasm in their mythology. The Monaghan placenames – Gortin and Ballyrush, Dundalk and Drumnei – might have a slight undertone of Yeats's Coolooney, Coole or Innisfree; yet, these places are not seen by the poet as more 'Irish' or 'authentic' than any other place. There is no learned invocation of landscape in Paddy's naming of the hills; the names of the hills are simply remarked as 'good' names. In other words, there is no insistence on praising or elevating the hills beyond the poet's personal affection towards them. In his famous essay 'Self Portrait', Kavanagh insisted that he had 'no belief in the virtue of a place'.[91] At this stage, Kavanagh's sense of place is not a conscious affirmation of his Irishness. These places are celebrated because they are part of the poet's intimate landscape. What

---

87 Kavanagh, *Selected Prose*, 237.
88 Kavanagh, *Selected Prose*, 10.
89 Heaney, *Preoccupations*, 132.
90 Kavanagh, *The Green Fool*, 204; *my emphasis*.
91 Kavanagh, *Selected Prose*, 309.

138   CHAPTER 4

is distinctive about his invocation of placenames, therefore, is a parochial perspective that gives 'the unremarkable countryside around Inniskeen a remarkable presence in the Irish literary landscape'.[92]

Kavanagh's perception of his local flora and fauna is free from the learned knowledge of the books. In 'On Reading a Book of Common Wild Flowers', the poet confesses his love for the fleabane, the burnet saxifrage and the autumn gentian long before knowing their names:

> O the greater fleabane that grew at the back of the potato-pit.
>
> I often trampled through it looking for rabbit burrows!
>
> The burnet saxifrage was there in profusion
>
> And the autumn gentian –
>
> I knew them all by eyesight long before I knew their names.
>
> We were in love before we were introduced.[93]

He is more of a 'knower' than a namer. His sense of place is 'emotional and definitive',[94] and the knowledge of his surroundings is practical and personal. According to Mc Elroy, '[w]hether Kavanagh recounts the significance of local plant life' in this poem 'or celebrates, as he does in the later "Canal Bank Walk" [...], his overriding concern is with the parish as a limited and liminal – but luminous – habitat space.'[95] The use of personal possessive adjectives in poems such as 'Stony Grey Soil' and 'Inniskeen Road, July Evening' shows a sense of intimacy between the poet and his surroundings, which in terms of Aldo Leopold's 'land ethics' is the first stage of an ecologically - evolved response to the environment. In 'Shancoduff', the same hills that have been forsaken by 'water-hen and snipe' are referred to as '*my* hills';[96] they are the poet's 'Alps' just as

---

92   Irene Gilsenan Nordin, 'The Place of Writing in the Poetry of W. B. Yeats and Patrick Kavanagh', *Nordic Journal of English Studies* 2 (2014), 49–50.

93   Kavanagh, 'On Reading a Book on Common Wild Flowers', *Collected Poems* 200.

94   Heaney, *Preoccupations*, 145.

95   James McElroy, 'Ecocriticism and Irish Poetry: A Preliminary Outline', *Estudios Irlandeses* 6 (2011), 59.

96   Kavanagh, 'Shancoduff', *Collected Poems* 21; *my emphasis*.

Towards a Poetics of Dwelling

the stretch of road in 'Inniskeen Road, July Evening' is his kingly possession: 'A road, a mile of kingdom, I am king / Of banks and stones and every blooming thing.'[97]

For Heaney the term 'blooming' in the above line is key to the ambiguous stance of the poet somewhere between attachment and detachment, of being 'at once marooned and in possession'.[98] In the northern dialect, blooming means bloody or annoying while the reference to banks and stones could also imply thriving and growing. There is a hidden note of detachment in the monotony, solitude and poverty of the hills in 'Shancoduff'; yet, it seems that Kavanagh is more in touch with his dwelling when he seeks detachment, a theme that he explored fully in both his novels. Paddy's love for Rocksavage farm and its surroundings is a result of his labour on the field as well as his intimate knowledge of the place: 'I worked in all the fields of Rocksavage and developed a homelover's sentiment for them. I knew every corner of those fields, and every well and stream.'[99] He later speaks of the importance of the farm in his life and particularly addresses the significance of the trees:

> Rocksavage filled a great place in our lives. Before the War there were thousands of beautiful trees on the farm. Close to our school these trees leaned over the wall and dropped us nuts – monkey-nuts for making toy-pipes, horse-chestnuts of which we made whistles and hazel-nuts which we ate.
>
> Then came the timber-hunger and the trees began to fall.
>
> 'O what will we do for timber?
>
> The last of the woods are down.'
>
> No wonder the old Gaelic poet, lamenting the destruction of the woods of Kilcash, sang so sadly.[100]

---

97 Kavanagh, 'Shancoduff', 21.
98 Heaney, *Preoccupations*, 118.
99 Kavanagh, *The Green Fool*, 62.
100 Kavanagh, *The Green Fool*, 63.

Paddy's view of the trees, from a schoolboy's perspective to the later lyrical appreciation of the beauty in nature, awakens a sense of care the lack of which is associated with barbarism:

> Rocksavage trees were sold by auction. The man who bought one cut down five as there was nobody to stop him. Father didn't buy any of the trees. There were no young, strong men in our house to help. There was no love for beauty. We were barbarians just emerged from the Penal days.[101]

Paddy's sentient ecology is not restricted to trees. After owning the farm, he talks about the wildness of the briars, of the place being 'a sanctuary for hares and rabbits', and how he does not 'disturb their briary haunts'.[102] During the Carrick fair, where Paddy and his friend are hired to work as farm hands, he is shattered by the cruelty of the owners towards their animals. At first, he does not understand what 'feeding' signifies when an owner complains about the donkeys. His innocence is immediately ridiculed:

> 'Oats and hay you give them, I suppose?'
>
> [...]
>
> 'Hay and oats be no good to asses,' he said 'The stick is what they get when they begin to get drowsy. Why, man, if ye saw an ass after his feed he's as lively as a red-bellied bee in a June meadow. If ye come with me I'll show ye the asses a-feedin'.'
>
> 'I don't want to see it,' I said.[103]

Paddy's sensitivity towards animals continues throughout the volume. In 'The Outlaws' chapter, he narrates the illegal attempt to catch salmon in the river through 'salmon-gaffing' and calls it 'cruel work'.[104] Similar passages run through Kavanagh's body of work where the poet's appreciation and sympathy for his environment present a sentient understanding of the country's hills and rivers as well as its domestic and wild animals. There is an environmental awareness in Kavanagh's poetry and prose that does not originate

---

101 Kavanagh, *The Green Fool*, 63.
102 Kavanagh, *The Green Fool*, 207.
103 Kavanagh, *The Green Fool*, 118.
104 Kavanagh, *The Green Fool*, 139.

Towards a Poetics of Dwelling

from adherence to any institution or movement; rather, it is influenced by a sense of place based on the poet's intuition and direct contact with the land. In contrast to the recent pro-environmental or environmentally-informed narratives, Kavanagh's sentient ecology does not carry any explicit ecological message. It is built on individual response and sensitivity to his environment. This is what Heaney refers to as Kavanagh's 'pastoral care' which in his view is as much sacerdotal as it is literary.[105]

Conclusion

While Kavanagh's departure from the influence of the Irish Literary Renaissance did not take place until later in his poetic career, his early works showcase a sense of place rich with nuances absent from revivalist narratives. His landscapes and characters were contemporaneous with his own time and place. The backward-look, part of the Irish *zeitgeist*, was missing from his poetry. When there is nostalgia, it is a personal sentiment which delivers homesickness. Kavanagh's countryside is a network of complex socio-environmental relations, where sense of place and Irishness are explored in new ways. Kavanagh's countryside also serves as an example of how one's perception of the environment changes according to one's distance or proximity to it as well as being dependent on one's level of engagement. The poet's ability to see beyond the picturesque and scenic features of the landscape and his insight into the social reality of the rural community of southern Ulster emancipated his poetry from the idealizations which had dominated the literary representations of rural Ireland since the nineteenth century. The countryside does not simply represent nature or authenticity in Kavanagh's work for, to repeat Ingold, 'the world can only exist as nature for a being that does not belong there'.[106] Kavanagh was a dweller and for him, the countryside remained first and foremost a dwelling, an environment in the making.

---

105 Heaney, *Preoccupations*, 121.
106 Ingold, *The Perception of the Environment*, 20.

CHAPTER 5

City Narratives: An Urban Sense of Place in Modern Irish Literature

Urban ecocriticism: An oxymoron?

Neil Evernden, in 'Beyond Ecology', points to the absence of a sense of place in cities. The 'environmental repertoire', according to him, is 'vastly diminished in urban life, perhaps to the point of making genuine attachment to place very difficult'.[1] Evernden's reference to the lack of an environmental repertoire in cities is a classic example of the overly pastoralized perception behind first-wave ecocriticism which demonized the city. According to Andrew Ross, '[i]n the dominant environmental literature, the city is sick, monstrous, blighted, ecocidal, life-denying, parasitical'; no wonder 'urban ecocriticism' is often 'considered an oxymoron'.[2]

The common interpretation of a sense of place in terms of topophilia and attachment is also problematic in terms of ignoring the wide range of interactions that develop between humankind and the environment as well as restricting the meaning of the term environment to wide open spaces. Given that more than half of the world population is classified as

[1]   Neil Everden, 'Beyond Ecology: Self, Place, and Pathetic Fallacy', in Cheryll Glotfelty and Harold Fromm, eds, *The Ecocriticism Reader: Landmarks in Literary Ecology* (Athens: University of Georgia Press, 1996), 100–1.

[2]   Andrew Ross, 'The Social Claim on Urban Ecology', in Michael Bennett and David W. Teague, eds, *The Nature of Cities: Ecocriticism and Urban Environments* (Arizona: The University of Arizona Press, 1999), 16.

144   CHAPTER 5

urban or suburban, rising to 70 per cent by 2050,[3] Evernden's statement
questions not only the development of a sense of place in cities but also the
very notion of urban identity. After all, what is meant by an environmental
repertoire if it does not include the actual environment that surrounds us?

New-wave ecocritics, informed by politics of environmental justice
and social ecology, have repeatedly expressed the need to include the study
of the urban environment in ecocriticism. Michael Bennett and David W.
Teague in *The Nature of Cities: Ecocriticism and Urban Environments* point
to the 'self-limiting conceptualizations of nature, culture, and environment
built into many ecocritical projects by their exclusion of urban place'.[4] For
Bennett and Teague, the realization of 'our placement within ecosystems'
is crucial to the understanding of 'urban life and culture'.[5] The reverse
may also be true in understanding our placement within the ecosystem.
William Cronon in 'The Trouble with Wilderness' has equally emphasized
the necessity of moving from 'wilderness fixation' towards seeing 'a natural
landscape that is also cultural, in which the city, the suburb, the pastoral
and the wild each has its proper place'.[6] Lawrence Buell, one of the main
contributors to the development of the Ecocritical School in the nineties,
also distanced himself from the early orientation towards nature writing
and pastoralism in his later work. In *The Future of Environmental Criticism*,
Buell insists on moving towards a more integrated version of environmentalism by including the urban zone.

Nevertheless, acknowledging the absence of urban issues in ecocritical
theory is not a new topic in itself. Decades ago, Bill Devall and George
Sessions mentioned the restrictions of their nature-oriented ideology in
Deep Ecology: Living as if Nature Mattered (1985). Deep ecology was unable to address the serious socio-economic issues of unemployment, urban

---

3   'The European Environment – State and Outlook 2010: Synthesis', *European
    Environment Agency*, <https://www.eea.europa.eu/soer/2010/synthesis/synthe
    sis>, accessed 18 May 2013.
4   Michael Bennett and David W. Teague, *The Nature of Cities: Ecocriticism and
    Urban Environments* (Arizona: The University of Arizona Press, 1999), 4.
5   Bennett and Teague, *The Nature of Cities*, 4.
6   William Cronon, 'The Trouble with Wilderness: Or, Getting Back to the Wrong
    Nature', *Environmental History*, 1/1 (1996), 18.

City Narratives

planning and resource management in cities. Despite this, the movement continued to ignore the urban sphere by insisting that 'nature' alone could provide the experience to foster 'self-realization and biocentric equality'.[7] They believed it was only in the human interaction with wide open spaces that humankind could develop a sense of place, redefine 'the heroic person from conqueror of the land to the person fully experiencing the natural place', cultivate 'the virtues of modesty and humility' and realize 'how the mountains and rivers, fish and bear are continuing their own actualizing processes'.[8] Devall and Sessions's biocentric model was highly problematic. A sense of place, as argued in the previous chapters, is a fluid concept which cannot be easily summarized as a definitive explanation of one's interaction with place in a positive way. We might as well speak of different senses of place which do not necessarily lead to a more or less ecofriendly relationship with our surroundings. Similarly, our experience of nature is always mediated, whether it is due to the physical limitation of human senses and scientific tools used for measurement or the cultural lenses through which sensory data is inevitably processed.

In 'From Wide Open Spaces to Metropolitan Places', Michael Bennett challenges Devall and Sessions's nature-oriented principles. According to him, it is the deep ecology's failure to recognize that these principles 'can easily be found in urban environments' which has led to the restriction of nature to 'wild open spaces'. This nature 'fetishism', as Bennett cites Cronon, has blinded ecocritics 'to the existence of urban environments and the ways in which these metropolitan places challenge an overly narrow conception of ecotheory'.[9] Thereby, Bennett proposes the adoption of a type of ecology that while acknowledging the importance of changing the overly anthropocentric views towards the environment, validates a socially informed perspective. Bennett's social deep ecocriticism has much in common with Murray Bookchin's social ecology, which – as well as offering a critique of urbanization – deals with 'the ongoing social dialectic

---

7   Bill Devall and George Sessions, *Deep Ecology: Living as if Nature Mattered* (Salt Lake City: Peregrine Smith, 1985), 111.

8   Devall and Session, *Deep Ecology*, 110.

9   Bennet, 'From Wide Open Spaces to Metropolitan Places',: The Urban Challenge to Ecocriticism', *Interdisciplinary Studies in Nature and Environment*, 8/1 (2001), 36-7.

146   CHAPTER 5

that weaves together human and nonhuman nature'.[10] In order to 'redeem the city', Bookchin connects the ecology of the wilderness to metropolitan spaces, claiming that this argument 'runs counter to the conventional wisdom that city and countryside, like society and nature, are necessarily in conflict with each other'.[11]

In a sense, social ecocriticism addresses the basic tenets of deep ecology which, as defined by Arne Naess, was initially to move beyond 'pollution and resource depletion' to 'deeper concerns which touch upon principles of diversity, complexity, autonomy, decentralization, symbiosis, egalitarianism, and classlessness'.[12] Addressing these social issues in relation to their impact on the environment and vice versa has proved the interdisciplinarity of ecocriticism and its potential to grow beyond academia. My aim in this chapter is to offer a reading of the modern city from an ecocritical perspective which acknowledges the intricate matrix of natural and cultural forces that construct the urban environment and negotiate urban identity in modern Irish culture. Once again, the literary representations of place are considered in the light of the human-environment relationship and the interconnectivity of place and identity in the Irish cultural repertoire. As the following section will further elaborate, the prejudiced representations of the city in major literary narratives during the Revival were part of the same narrative that misrepresented the country and led to the marginalization of the rural landscape and culture.

'The Rest is Country': Dublin in early Revival literature

The persistence of rural narratives meant that cities were continually neglected in the popular representations of Irish identity and place in

10   Bennet, 'From Wide Open Spaces to Metropolitan Places', 33.
11   Murray Bookchin, Urbanization without Cities: The Rise and Decline of Citizenship (New York: Black Rose, 1992), x.
12   Arne Naess, 'Intuition, Intrinsic Value and Deep Ecology', The Ecologist, 14/5–6 (1973), 95.

City Narratives 147

a country that was soaring towards urbanization. While the post-1960s Ireland saw the emergence of a new urban literature, especially in the North, cities (with few exceptions) made a faint appearance in the works of the nineteenth- and early twentieth-century Irish writers for whom rural Ireland held the key to an authentic version of Irishness. Taking a look at the major literary productions of the period, one comes across the Irish city as an exceptionally restricted geography. More often than not, the city means Dublin, and as far as nineteenth-century fiction is concerned, the 'rest is country'.[13] On the other hand, Dublin was at once the centre and the periphery. While being home to many of the Revival's writers and intellectuals and hosting the key publishing opportunities in Ireland, the city was a less popular subject compared to its counterpart, the country. This lack of reference is especially recognizable in the works of major Irish poets, including W.B. Yeats and George Russell, who spent most of their time in the Dublin.

Dublin and in some cases Galway, Cork and Belfast made an appearance in fiction and drama, especially towards the end of the century; yet, the city often stood for something else. It was either a background for the development of a certain theme, a site for social commentary and satire or represented change and chaos in terms of symbol and allegory. Dublin before the Union, for instance, was a site for nostalgia: The picturesque and ruined cityscapes replicated an urban version of the pastoral in the post-Emancipation city. Maria Edgeworth portrayed post-Union Dublin as a city that had lost its former grandeur and elegance yet acquired a new identity with the emergence of a new class and architecture. Similar to the country in Edgeworthian fiction, the city was predominantly used as a setting where the writer spoke of social reform. Dublin is squeezed into Chapter Six of *The Absentee* where Lord Colombre visits the city swarmed with beggarly appearances in juxtaposition to the *nouveaux riches*. Even though Edgeworth's view of Dublin was generally negative, she did not

---

13   Julian Moynahan, 'The Image of the City in Nineteenth Century Irish Fiction', in Maurice Harmon, ed., *The Irish Writer and the City* (Buckinghamshire: Colin Smythe, 1984), 16.

148   CHAPTER 5

fail to mention the diversity of social class and wit that characterized post-Union Dublin.

Portrayals of Dublin as a ruined city, picturesque and terrifying at once, were seen in the works of Charles Maturin. Dublin, as Moynahan comments, appears as a city of 'Gothic gloom and ruined grandeur'.[14] Maturin explores the city in terms of the picturesque, the same literary technique at work in the pastoral. In *Women; or, Pour et Contre*, Dublin's beauty is described as the 'frightful lifeless beauty of a corpse':

> Its beauty continues [...], but it is the frightful lifeless beauty of a corpse; and the magnificent architecture of its public buildings seems like the skeleton of some gigantic frame, which the inhabiting spirit has deserted; like the vast structure of the bones of the Behemoth, which has ceased to live for ages and around whose remains modern gazers fearfully creep and stare.[15]

Maturin's picturesque and gothic Dublin is a background to the main theme, which concerns the continuing evacuation of the city of its former aristocratic class and its consequent loss of grandeur. As Moynahan observes, this is not 'Rome after its sacking by the Goths, nor is it an interpretation in words of a Piranesi showing picturesque ruins'; it is merely post-Union Dublin after the conversion of the Parliament building to a bank, when the Ascendency left for London and Trinity students transferred to Oxford or Cambridge.[16]

Another popular representation of Dublin in the works of post-Emancipation writers is the depiction of the city in terms of violence. Le Fanu's distrust of the dispossessed Catholic class, who had now reclaimed their land and identity, led to the portrayal of the city as 'the scene of midnight violence and adventure'.[17] In his first novel *The Cock and Anchor*, we come across Dublin as 'the capital of a rebellious and semi-barbarous country – haunted by hungry adventurers, who had lost everything in the

14   Moynahan, 'The Image of the City in Nineteenth Century Irish Fiction', 6.
15   Charles Maturin, *Women; or, Pour et Contre. A Tale* (Edinburgh: James Ballantyne, 1818), 295.
16   Moynahan, 'The Image of the City in Nineteenth Century Irish Fiction', 6.
17   Joseph Sheridan Le Fanu, *The Cock and Anchor: Being a Chronicle of Old Dublin City* (London: Downey, 1896), 52.

City Narratives   149

revolutionary wars, with a most notoriously ineffective police and a rash
and dissolute aristocracy'.[18] The same rebellious Dublin appears as a site of
nostalgia in *The House by the Churchyard*, Le Fanu's more accomplished
novel in terms of plot and characterization. Once again, the sense of place
delivers a mixture of homesickness and nostalgia for a glorious past while
showing contempt for the corrupt and chaotic situation after the dissolution of the Parliament. After Le Fanu, Dublin reappeared in terms of
political violence and Protestant decline in the works of Thomas Moore
and Somerville and Ross, where the city remains a mere setting.

The earliest exception in fiction goes back to John Banim's *The Anglo-
Irish of the Nineteenth Century* (1828). Dublin, while still a platform for

References to Dublin in the pre-1800 and Revival drama did not
present a much different perspective either. Once again, the predominant
image is a 'social rather than a topographical one'.[19] Commenting on the
nineteenth-century Irish drama, Kosok refers to the disappearance of the
city at the beginning of the century, with a growing focus on the more
picturesque vicinity of Dublin as a romantic setting for social melodrama.
These plays were mostly written for the middle-class Londoner for whom
Ireland was an exotic location, no less interesting than any other colony in
the British Empire. Every now and then, however, there is a subtle reference
to the city as a geographical location, a topography made up of various corners, streets, shops and crowds of people. Walter Cox's *The Widow Dempsey's
Funeral* (1822) and John O. Darling's *Grattan: or The Irish Volunteers: A
New National Drama* (1864) were early exceptions produced by amateurs
in Dublin and remained relatively obscure. What differentiated these plays
from the norm was the topographical reference to the cityscapes and locations. In *The Widow Dempsey's Funeral*, for instance, localities, shops,
parks, cemeteries, town quarters and neighbouring villages known at the
time make a solid appearance. Overall, the 'picture is far from realistic'; yet,
'it is a valuable complement to those other artificial images of fashionable
Dublin that were the rule until the turn of the century'.[20]

The earliest exception in fiction goes back to John Banim's *The Anglo-
Irish of the Nineteenth Century* (1828). Dublin, while still a platform for

---

18   Le Fanu, *The Cock and Anchor*, 52.
19   Heinz Kosok, 'The Image of Dublin in Anglo-Irish Drama', in Maurice Harmon,
     ed., *The Irish Writer and the City* (Buckinghamshire: Colin Smythe, 1984), 26.
20   Kosok, 'The Image of Dublin in Anglo-Irish Drama', 26.

criticizing the Ascendency whose conduct while arrogant at home was often servile in England, re-emerges, even if momentarily, as a beautiful city with an organized and accomplished civic structure and architecture. Banim's reference to the Georgian architecture of the city is free from nationalist sentiments that saw in Dublin nothing but an English colonial influence. Even the dissolution of the Parliament did not mean much to the sceptical Catholic writer for whom 'it had never been much of a Parliament anyway'.[21] In the novel, the protagonist's account of a February morning walk in central Dublin reconstructs the city from a fresh vantage point. The former nostalgia and ruined picturesqueness are simply turned into an appreciation of the city streets, river, canal, college and corners through which Gerald strolls without a map. Instead of bewailing the loss of an Irish inheritance, Banim reclaims it through the figure of the walking man who strolls from the Merrion Square area and Royal Exchange building to College Green and from Trinity College towards O'Connell Bridge, where he finally admits that he is standing 'in the centre, of perhaps the most beautiful city-picture in the world'.[22]

Gerald's walk through Dublin took place almost a century ahead of Stephen and Bloom's loitering in Dublin streets in *Ulysses* (1922), which makes John Banim the earliest Irish novelist to have introduced the big city through the vista of the walking figure, hence providing 'walking' as a model for the perception of the modern Irish city. Walking, as Henri Lefebvre claims, is a 'spatial practice';[23] it is not to be mistaken with 'the meaningless status of a repetitive exercise for the sake of stress reduction, calorie expenditure, and cardiovascular fitness' as the change in the significance of walking in modern society indicates.[24] The walking figure, as the following section will further elaborate, becomes the figure in the

---

21 Moynahan, 'The Image of the City in Nineteenth Century Irish Fiction', 11.

22 John Banim, *The Anglo-Irish of the Nineteenth Century: A Novel* (London: Henry Colburn, 1828), 184.

23 Henri Lefebvre, *The Production of Space* (Cambridge, MA: Blackwell, 1991), 38.

24 Garry Roberts, 'London Here and Now: Walking, Street, and Urban Environments in English Poetry from Dunne to Gay', in Michael Bennett and David W. Teague, eds, *The Nature of Cities: Ecocriticism and Urban Environments* (Arizona: University of Arizona Press, 1999), 53.

City Narratives 151

landscape whose view of the urban environment transforms the city into a site of discovery and change. The earlier dichotomous perception of the city as an antidote to the country is pushed aside as the walking figure unveils the range of possibilities for the development of a sense of place in cities.

The poet as *flâneur*: The walking figure in the cityscape

Raymond Williams in 'The Figure in the City' associates the perception of the modern city 'from the beginning, with a man walking, as if alone, in its streets'.[25] This kinetic perception is a response to the city's dynamic flow, its conflicts and complexities and its vice and virtues. The walking figure, a stranger facing a multitude of strangers on his way from one location to another, simultaneously experiences involvement and estrangement. 'Multitude' and 'solitude', according to Baudelaire, whom Williams quotes, are 'equal and interchangeable' terms for 'an active and fertile poet'.[26] What Baudelaire referred to as 'an active and fertile poet', came alive in the figure of the urban poet as a *flâneur* – a role that he himself demonstrated in full and is mostly known for. The *flâneur* was the idler of city streets, the bourgeois dilettante of the nineteenth-century Parisian arcades, the disinterested voyeur and the solitary figure in the crowd. 'Sometimes he is a poet; more often he comes closer to the novelist or the moralist; he is the painter of the passing moment and of all the suggestions of eternity that it contains,' writes Baudelaire in *The Painter of Modern Life and Other Essays*.[27] We come across the character in the erotic voyeur of Baudelaire's *Fleurs du Mal*. He appears in Edgar Allan Poe's 'Man of the Crowd', as well as in the Parisian wilderness of Dumas's *Mohicans de Paris* and Balzac's *Mystère de Paris*.

25 Raymond Williams, *The Country and the City* (London: Chatto and Windus, 1973), 233.
26 Williams, *The Country and the City*, 234.
27 Charles Baudelaire, *The Painter of Modern Life and Other Essays* (London: Phaidon, 1995), 5.

The term '*flâneur*' entered the English language around 1854 in the August edition of Harper's Magazine, which referred to window-shopping in the sunny Metropolitan city as an act of *flânerie*.[28] As a literary device, *flânerie* could be traced back to the survey or urban panorama books in the sixteenth century.[29] William Blake and William Wordsworth's London poems are early examples of reference to the city from the vista of the walking figure in English literature. Charles Dickens and Elizabeth Gaskell used the figure of the walking man for the purpose of social commentary. However, the most famous demonstration of *flânerie* as a cultural practice goes back to the nineteenth-century Parisian arcades and its manifestation in the work of the *flâneur*-poet Charles Baudelaire.

It was Walter Benjamin's study of Paris and Baudelaire that brought *flânerie* to the forefront of literary and critical attention in the twentieth century. In *Charles Baudelaire: A Lyric Poet in the Era of High Capitalism* (1969) and *The Arcades Project* (1982), Benjamin explores *flânerie* as a cultural phenomenon that characterized the Parisian lifestyle in the advent of modernity. For Benjamin, the *flâneur* is quintessentially a Parisian figure, as it was for the anonymous writer of 'Le Flâneur' in *Le livre des cent-et-un*: 'Le flâneur peut naître partout; il ne sait vivre qu'à Paris'.[30] For Baudelaire, 'modernity is the form; Paris is the content. The *flâneur* is the figure and the point of observation that straddles the two and pulls them together into a unity.'[31] But, what made the *flâneur* a Parisian figure?

The emerging consumer capitalism in nineteenth-century Paris, the relevant wealth and education of the bourgeois class who could afford the leisure of walking and idling around the city were important factors in the development of *flânerie* as a Parisian practice. However, besides the socio-economic situation of the nineteenth century that brought with it the

28 Darren Carlaw, *The Flâneur as Foreigner: Ethnicity, Sexuality and Power in Twentieth Century New York Writing* (Newcastle University Library: Unpublished Thesis, 2008), 17.

29 Brand; cited in Carlaw, *The Flâneur as Foreigner*, 17.

30 The *flâneur* can be born anywhere; he does not live but in Paris (*translations mine*). Paris, o *Le livre des cent-et-un* (Paris: Ladvocat Libraire, 1832), 91.

31 Keith Tester, 'Introduction', in Keith Tester, ed., *The Flâneur* (London: Routledge, 1994), 17.

City Narratives 153

wealth and leisure required for *flânerie*, it was the existence of the arcades and the widening of the boulevards by Baron Haussmann that contributed to the iconic practice of the *flâneur*; that is, walking. As Benjamin emphasized, '[s]trolling could hardly have assumed the importance it did without the arcades.'[32] An 1852 illustrated guide to Paris describes the arcades as 'a rather recent invention of industrial luxury. [They] are glass-covered, marble-panelled passageways [...] lined with the most elegant shops, so that such an arcade is a city, even a world, in miniature.'[33] It is in the miniature world of arcades, 'the favourite sojourn of the strollers and the smokers', that the *flâneur* feels most at home, as Ferdinand von Gall writes in *Paris und seine salons*.[34] In other words, the arcades provided the ultimate roaming space and material for what Balzac called 'the gastronomy of the eye'.[35]

The anonymous writer of 'Le Flâneur', who refers to himself as a *flâneur* in *Le livre de cent-et-un*, narrates the story of a stranger who had renounced living in London. He had found it impossible to roam around a city in which the houses are all separated from each other by large blocks, where the passers-by are in constant hurry, the pavements are narrow and there are no quays. He had thus returned to Paris in less than a year to practice what he could not do in London. The dependence of *flânerie* on a particular type of environment makes it a place-conscious practice, such as the classical genres of pastoral and *dinnseanchas*. The city becomes a new landscape in what might be perceived as an urban version of pastoral in an overly man-built environment. Rob Shields refers to the savage and the *flâneur* as distant cousins: one being a connoisseur of the wild, the other of the urban.[36]

32   Walter Benjamin, *Charles Baudelaire: A Lyric Poet in the Era of High Capitalism* (London: Verso, 1983), 36.

33   Walter Benjamin, *The Arcades Project* (Cambridge, MA: Belknap Press of Harvard University Press, 1999), 31.

34   Cited in Benjamin, *Charles Baudelaire*, 36.

35   Physiologie du Mariage 1829; cited in Pierre Larousse, *Grand Dictionnaire Universel du XIXᵉ Siècle* (Paris: Administration du Grand Dictionnaire Universel, 1866), <http://gallica.bnf.fr/ark:/12148/bpt6k205356p/f6.image>, accessed 17 February 2012.

36   Rob Shields, 'Fancy Footwork: Walter Benjamin's Notes on Flânerie', in Keith Tester, ed., *The Flâneur* (London: Routledge, 1994).

154   CHAPTER 5

The arcades, a place between the interior comfort, security and privacy of the houses and the strange, vast exterior of the urban wilderness provided the most suitable landscape for this urban roaming, where the *flâneur* could keep on strolling without being threatened by the unknown and strange sites in the city. Meanwhile, the constant sense of wonder and bewilderment kept him interested in walking and observing. As the arcades lost their glamour and were replaced by shopping galleries, the *flâneur* walked back to the streets where the pavements offered security from the traffic of the road. The overflow of the crowd from one direction to another kept the place a site of flux and multitude, where the indolent walker, demanding elbow room, could continue his leisurely walk and pursue his subject without being recognized.

Benjamin refers to the streets or boulevards as the *flâneur*'s dwelling: 'he is as much at home among the façades of houses as a citizen is in his four walls.'[37] Tied to the place, simultaneously active and passive, walking relates to dwelling in constructing/reconstructing the walker's identity in an ever-changing urban landscape. The *flâneur*'s displaced situation in the city is still tied to the notion of place as dwelling, which he experiences in terms of becoming, a condition that explains his temporary satisfaction when pausing momentarily or sitting down before resuming his walk. 'The ontological basis of the Baudelairean poet', according to Tester, 'resides in *doing* not *being* [...]; the struggle for existential completion and satisfaction requires [...] doing over and over again.'[38] Doing or becoming, in being temporal and dynamic, corresponds to Heidegger and Ingold's notion of dwelling as an ongoing process, which consists of a dynamic relationship between humans and the environment. Hence, *flânerie* can be understood as a constant negotiation of meaning in the quest for dwelling. The cityscape is reconstructed in a continuous act of familiarization/defamiliarization as places, people and objects are noticed and lost in the *flâneur*'s momentary eye contact.

According to Ferguson, '*Flânerie* urbanises observation by making the observer part of the urban scene [...]; the *flâneur* is observed while

37   Benjamin, *Charles Baudelaire*, 37.
38   Tester, *The Flâneur*, 5; original emphasis.

City Narratives

155

observing.'[39] Observation is the *raison d'être* of the *flâneur*,[40] as Auguste de Lacroix referred to the *flâneur* as an observer *par excellence*. He asked: 'qu'est-ce que le flâneur, sinon l'observateur en action, l'observateur dans son expression la plus élevée et la plus éminemment utile?'[41] *Flânerie* is observation in a meaningful context. The *flâneur*'s snapshots of the city streets, shops and passers-by construct a web of memory in a fleeting landscape. *Flânerie* is interpreted as active and cognitive. The constant search for meaning is part of the practice. Only he can read the text that is the city. In other words, the *flâneur* is a semiotician; everything is a sign ready to be deciphered.

The *flâneur* was not the only walking figure in the Parisian cityscape. *L'homme des foules* (the man of the throng), *le badaud* (the onlooker) and the dandy were other nineteenth-century figures whose urban practices were associated with that of walking and observation. While these figures could be interpreted as variant guises under which *flânerie* was practiced, the Baudelairean *flâneur* remains a distinct character. Both *le badaud* and *l'homme des foules* were passive observers who were immersed in the throng; the *flâneur*, on the other hand, was not quite as disinterested or engaged in the life of the crowd as either of them. According to Lacroix, *le badaud* is no thinker. He does not engage, nor is he interested in the crowd: 'Le badaud ne pense pas; il ne perçoit les objets qu'extérieurement. Il n'y a pas de communication entre son cerveau et ses sens. Pour lui les choses n'existent que simplement et superficiellement, sans caractère particulier et sans nuances.'[42] *L'homme des foules*, as described by Baudelaire, seeks to lose all selfhood in 'a quasi-mystic' or 'quasi-orgasmic' fusion with the

---

39   Priscilla Parkhurst Ferguson, 'The *Flâneur* On and Off the Streets of Paris', in Keith Tester, ed., *The Flâneur* (London: Routledge, 1994), 27.

40   Auguste de Lacroix, *Le flâneur*, in *La collection électronique de la Médiathèque André Malraux de Lisieux*, <www.bmlisieux.com/curiosa/lacroi01.htm>, accessed 17 January 2014, (1841), 65.

41   Who is the *flâneur* if not the observer in action, the observer in his most elevated and eminently useful expression? (translation mine). Lacroix, *Le flâneur*, 72.

42   The onlooker does not think; he does not perceive the objects but externally. There is no communication between his mind and his senses. For him, things do not exist but simply and superficially, without any particular character or nuance (translation mine). Lacroix, *Le flâneur*, 66.

mob.[43] The Baudelairean *flâneur*, however, is the man *in* the crowd rather than the man of the crowd. He alone can enjoy bathing in the multitude as Baudelaire mentions in his prose poem 'Les Foules':

> Il n'est pas donné à chacun de prendre un bain de multitude: jouir de la foule est un art; celui-là seul peut faire, aux dépens du genre humain, une ribote de vitalité, à qui une fée a insufflé dans son berceau le goût du travestissement et du masque, la haine du domicile et la passion du voyage.[44]

> [The ability to bathe in the multitude is not given to everyone: Enjoying the crowd is an art; and only he who, at the expense of humanity, has experienced a bout of vitality, is the one a fairy has inspired, in the cradle a taste for dressing up and masques, a taste for hatred from domestic life and a passion for travelling.] (Translation mine.)

Baudelaire's description of the *flâneur* bespeaks the modern conditions of displacement and placelessness. It explains the artist's immersion in the crowd and yet, his or her aversion of conformity. His very role is a discursive practice; his 'leisurely appearance as a personality' is at once a 'protest against the division of labour which makes people into specialists' and 'protest against their industriousness'.[45] In Paul-Ernest de Rattier's hostile description of the *flâneur* in *Paris n'existe pas* (1857), it is the specialization of labour that finally brings about the demise of the *flâneur* in the late nineteenth century:

> The *flâneur* whom we used to encounter on sidewalks and in front of the shop-windows, this nonentity, this constant rubberneck, this inconsequential type who was always in search of cheap emotions and knew about nothing but cobblestones, fiacres, and gas lanterns ..., has now become a farmer, a vintner, a linen manufacturer, a sugar refiner, and a steel magnate.[46]

---

43 Richard D. E. Burton, *The Flâneur and His City: Patterns of Daily Life in Paris 1815–1851* (Durham: University of Durham, 1994), 1.

44 Charles Baudelaire, *Petits Poèmes en Prose (Le Spleen de Paris)* (Paris: Garnier Flammarion, 1967), 61.

45 Benjamin, *Charles Baudelaire*, 54.

46 De Rattier 1857, 74; cited in Benjamin, *Charles Baudelaire*, 54.

City Narratives 157

The kind of relationship the *flâneur* establishes with the public is dependent on a certain degree of freedom from social convention. Once this freedom is taken away, the *flâneur* can no longer continue dawdling in the city. At the heart of this relationship lies an erotic engagement, an empathy with inorganic things that becomes intoxicating, if not narcotic. Empathy, as Benjamin notes, is 'the nature of the intoxication to which the *flâneur* abandons himself in the crowd'.[47] Providing the poet with a sense of inspiration, empathy with inorganic things can be interpreted as a sort of fetish, as the sexualization of commodity and the commodification of sexuality become porous concepts in the modern metropolis.

The *flâneur* was not immune to the overly commodified phenomenon of modernity. Being abandoned in the crowd, yet in a self-conscious and semi-voluntary manner, he 'shares the situation of the commodity'.[48] Like the items on display behind the windows, the *flâneur* is in search of a market for publishing his textual panorama of the city. The commodity, as Baudelaire and Benjamin see it, is not an object of passive gaze; rather, it is the subject. The commodity produced in mass volume is an example of how the labourer is alienated from his labour as the outcome of his labour becomes inaccessible to him once it is presented as commodity in the market. Similarly, the *flâneur* embodies alienation in the increasingly commodified spectacle that is the cityscape.

In the end, the extensive commercialization of the urban sphere and the demolition of the arcades as part of Parisian landscape's modernization during Baron Haussmann brought about the demise of *flâneur* who, from Benjamin's perspective, had become 'little more than a seeker after mystery from banality'. If in the beginning the street had become 'an *intérieur* for him, now this *intérieur* turned into a street, and he roamed through the labyrinth of merchandise as he had once roamed through the labyrinth of the city'.[49] Similar to the consumer, 'duped by the glittering promises of consumerism', the *flâneur* turned into a passive spectator, duped 'by the spectacle of the public'.[50]

47 Benjamin, *Charles Baudelaire*, 55.
48 Benjamin, *Charles Baudelaire*, 55.
49 Benjamin, *Charles Baudelaire*, 54–5.
50 Tester, 'Introduction', 14.

158   CHAPTER 5

While the first half of the nineteenth century saw the summit of *flân-erie* as an urban practice, the second half marked its decline as a Parisian phenomenon. By the time the *Académie Française* gave 'its official appro-bation to the term in 1879', *flânerie* had already lost its vogue.[51] As the arcades were demolished or left to dereliction, the *flâneur* was pushed to the shopping gallery and from there to the streets where his distance was reduced and his leisurely walk gradually turned into an impossibility. Yet, despite the actual disappearance of the *flâneur* as a personality type from the streets of Paris, one can argue that as an artistic practice, *flânerie* has continued to exist in new forms and interpretations. There has been a re-cent proliferation of scholarly articles, books and dissertations that con-sider *flânerie* as an urban phenomenon that is not necessarily linked to the male gaze, the bourgeois class or its original socio-historical context. Considering the origins and influences of *flânerie* out of the nineteenth-century Parisian context, Tester explores the figure of the walking man in relation to the search for identity in urban existence. Post-Baudelairean *flânerie* is understood as,

> the activity of the sovereign spectator going about the city in order to find the things which will occupy his gaze and thus complete his otherwise incomplete identity; satisfy his otherwise dissatisfied existence; replace the sense of bereavement with a sense of life.[52]

Observation and movement remain the basic principles of *flânerie*, and the *flâneur's* engagement with the fundamental question of identity links this historical figure to the contemporary urban society. Extending the role beyond its original framework, *flânerie* continues to negotiate the boundaries of place by redefining a sense of place and identity in terms of movement, flux and change. The *flâneur's* sauntering and his cinematic gaze do not only represent the modern man's interaction with and within the urban environment; rather, his subjective experience of the city, de-centred gaze and constantly moving, unfocused perspective render a

51   Ferguson, 'The *Flâneur* On and Off the Streets of Paris', 32.
52   Tester, 'Introduction', 7.

City Narratives

presencing of the urban landscape with its ironies of situatedness and displacement, belonging and alienation.

Tester's interpretation of the post-Baudelairean *flâneur* applies to the situation of the modern poet in Ireland, a figure in constant movement whose interaction with the city engages with the complex notions of identity and belonging. Luke Gibbons in '"Where Wolfe Tone Statue Was Not": Joyce, Monuments and Memory' contends: 'the inhabitants of Joyce's Dublin enjoy the same marginalized relation to the city as the modernist *flâneur*, at once part of and yet detached from official space.'[53] In the following chapters, I intend to show how the *flâneuresque* view of the Irish city, exemplified in Patrick Kavanagh and Louis MacNeice's urban poetry, helped redefine the identity of the modern Irish poet, who had become an alienated, marginalized figure in the city. This in turn led to a renegotiation of the marginalized role of cities in revivalist narratives and brought the city to the forefront of post-1960 Irish literature.

---

53   Luke Gibbons, '"Where Wolf Tone's Statue Was Not": Joyce, Monuments and Memory', in Ian McBride, ed., *History and Memory in Modern Ireland* (Cambridge: Cambridge University Press, 2001), 140.

CHAPTER 6

Patrick Kavanagh in Dublin: The Irish *Flâneur* and the Big City

Dublin: A site of arrivals and departures

The twentieth century saw a proliferation of Irish fiction and drama produced at home. The foundation of the Irish Literary Theatre, later known as The Abbey Theatre, provided Irish writers with new possibilities for artistic production without depending on the London literary stage. Dublin appeared in various settings, where the city was described in symbolic, realistic and descriptive modes. While for the likes of Seamus de Burca, the choice of a Dublin setting was 'undoubtedly accidental',[1] for the rest, the city regained a new identity. Sean O'Casey's mainly autobiographical *Dublin Trilogy*, for instance, registered the city in terms of both spatial imagery and symbolism. Post-Independence Irish drama represented the formerly glamorous Dublin as 'a crumbling town, of tenements and poverty', replacing the Georgian splendour of the eighteenth-century city with makeshift arrangements in ill-fitted surroundings.[2]

As fiction and drama evolved towards embracing the urban culture, there was still an apparent lack of reference to the city in poetry. Dublin-born poets, from James Clarence Mangan and Thomas Moore in the nineteenth century to the Revivalists W. B. Yeats and George Russell, did not write of Dublin. It was James Joyce, an expatriate Dubliner, who brought

---

1   Heinz Kosok, 'The Image of Dublin in Anglo-Irish Drama', in Maurice Harmon, ed., *The Irish Writer and the City* (Gerrards Cross: Colin Smythe, 1984), 33.
2   Kosok, 'The Image of Dublin in Anglo-Irish Drama', 33.

the city to the forefront of Irish literature in fiction and, to a lesser extent, in poetry. Thomas Kinsella in 'The Irish Writer' called James Joyce the father of modern Irish poetry.[3] By inscribing the city rather than the country as a central theme and substituting the rural Irish landscape with the urban cityscape of Dublin city, Joyce paved the way for the exploration of Irish sense of place and identity in terms of urban poetics. This poetics, as described by Kennedy-Andrews, is concerned with the 'understanding of alienation, fragmentation and discontinuity as the essential features of the modern Irish condition.'[4]

Post-Revival Dublin was, for the first time, elevated to the popularity of the historical cities of Troy and Babylon in Classical literature. Joyce's memorable portrayals of the city in *Dubliners* (1914), *Ulysses* (1922) and, to some extent, *The Portrait of the Artist as a Young Man* (1916) projected Dublin as a city that offered its streets to the walking idlers who were ready to negotiate the meaning of modern urban life in the fashion of Stephen Dedalus and Leopold Bloom. The Joycean Dublin is not merely a background to the development of a particular theme. Dublin *is* the theme. In *Dubliners*, perhaps the most significant post-Revival portrait of Dublin, the city emerges through a framework of fifteen short stories that narrate the account of Dubliners from three perspectives: childhood, adolescence and adulthood. Joyce's descriptions of Dublin – its various locations, streets and back alleys – became an integral part of understanding life in Dublin city at the beginning of the twentieth century. The stories are modernist in tone and capture both the social and political stasis of the city while showcasing the significant changes that were taking place in pre-independence Ireland. According to Augustine Martin, the city in *Dubliners* is no longer 'a story but presented as foreground, theme and heroine of the fictional enterprise.'[5] In fact, Joyce's reference to the 'continuous movement of bodies – human,

3   Thomas Kinsella, 'The Irish Writer', in Thomas Kinsella and William Butler Yeats, eds, *Davis, Mangan, Ferguson? Tradition and the Irish Writer* (Dublin: Dolmen Press, 1967).

4   Elmer Kennedy-Andrews, *Writing Home: Poetry and Place in Northern Ireland, 1968–2008* (Cambridge: D.S. Brewer, 2008), 11.

5   Agustin Martin, 'Novelist and City: The Technical Challenge', in Maurice Harmon, ed., *The Irish Writer and the City* (Buckinghamshire: Colin Smythe, 1984), 42.

Patrick Kavanagh in Dublin 163

embryonic, marine, celestial, inanimate, mineral, organic, animal'[6] rescued the city from the stasis of former representations. Dublin turned into an ever-changing organic body, a site of flux, multitude and diversity, hence invoking a sense of place that challenged the nationalist stereotypes of belonging to an unchanging and stagnant notion of place in Irish Revival literature.

Representations of Dublin in terms of flux and movement corresponded with the city's role as a port of arrivals and departures in the twentieth century. Dublin was the major literary centre from 1921 up to the period just before the outbreak of the Second World War in 1939. The literary and cultural institutions in Dublin at the time included 'The National Library of Ireland, The National Museum, The National Gallery, The Royal Irish Academy, and The Royal Hibernian Academy'.[7] However, London and New York remained the first publishing markets during the thirties as a result of the 'Censorship of Publications Act, 1929', which led to an approximate number of 120 books being banned each year, including the works of James Joyce, Samuel Beckett, William Faulkner and Ernest Hemingway. Censorship remained the main cause of tension between writers and society in the Republic prior to 1957.[8] Patrick Kavanagh's 'The Wake of the Books: A Mummery', published for the first time in the *Bell* in 1947, is a satire directed at the Censorship Act and the resulting conflicts among writers and publishers. Following the Free State's turbulent and unstable political atmosphere of post-1922, Dublin witnessed an emerging realism after a bitter disillusionment. Frank O'Connor, Francis Stuart and Peadar O'Donnell were imprisoned while Liam O'Flaherty and Sean O'Faolain left the country.

The tension between the writers and Ireland eased during the war. They became less exile-prone after 1940, for both 'psychological and economic' reasons.[9] Little by little, the atmosphere became one of support. As

6 Martin, 'Novelist and City: The Technical Challenge', 48.
7 Vivian Mercier, 'Literature in English, 1921–84', in Jacqueline R. Hill, ed., *A New History of Ireland, VII: Ireland 1921–1984* (Oxford: Oxford University Press, 2003), 487.
8 Mercier, 'Literature in English, 1921–84', 505.
9 Mercier, 'Literature in English, 1921–84', 503.

164   CHAPTER 6

the foreign markets for the publication of Irish works were diminishing, those who had remained in Ireland found themselves indebted to their country, which had now turned to be their 'alternative source of income'. Radio Éireann, *The Irish Times* and other Dublin papers as well as The Abbey Theatre among others tended to help the 'prose writers' – and sometimes poets too.[10] While the likes of Joyce left Dublin for cities in Europe and North America, a growing number of writers arrived in Dublin in search of an audience and a publishing agent. The lack of printing and publishing industries and a coherent literary intelligentsia in industrial Belfast also drew many of the Ulster-born poets to Dublin and London, among whom was Patrick Kavanagh who had already appealed to Dublin's literary market as the 'ploughboy poet'. Gradually, Dublin turned into Kavanagh's second parish, where his earlier love/hate relationship was replaced with an equally complicated relationship with the big city. Dublin offered Kavanagh a site for self-discovery while Kavanagh provided Dublin with its first poet-*flâneur*.

From the peasant bard of County Monaghan to Dublin's best-known *Flâneur*: Patrick Kavanagh in Dublin

After his first visit to Dublin in 1931, to meet his mentor George Russell (AE), Patrick Kavanagh left behind his sixteen-acre farm in Inniskeen, Monaghan to reside permanently in Dublin at the dawn of the Second World War. Kavanagh's recognition both before and after his move to the city was primarily due to his rural origins. On his arrival in Dublin, the ploughboy poet 'was immediately fitted to be the authentic peasant bard of the Irish Literary Revival'.[11] Irishness in the late thirties was still heavily influenced by the ethos of the Irish Literary Renaissance, which the young poet had come to despise by then.

10   Mercier, 'Literature in English, 1921–84', 503.
11   Rosemarie Rowley, 'Patrick Kavanagh: An Irish Pastoral Poet in the Cit', *Journal of Ecocriticism*, 1/2 (2009), 94.

Patrick Kavanagh in Dublin 165

In 'Self-Portrait', Kavanagh expressed his early disillusionment with moving to Dublin and confronting a literary intelligentsia under the influence of Yeats and his school: 'When I came to Dublin in 1939 the Irish Literary affair was still blooming. It was the notion that Dublin was a literary metropolis and Ireland, as invented and patented by Yeats, Lady Gregory and Synge, a spiritual entity.'[12] Later on, he referred to the move as 'the worst mistake' of his life. Kavanagh's frustration with Dublin's literary society resonated through most of his early works in the capital, especially those written from 1947 until his lung operation in 1955. 'The Wake of the Books', 'The Paddiad', 'Leave them alone', 'Bank Holiday' and 'Adventures in Bohemian Jungle' carry a strong sense of irony and sarcasm. The poet's disillusionment and frustration with the Irish literati in Dublin and the Irish society in general add a certain bitterness to the rather lengthy poems written in this period.

According to Antoinette Quinn, moving to Dublin was 'disastrously mistimed'.[13] The outbreak of the war and the resulting consequences such as 'paper rationing' in Ireland, the Censorship of Publication Act, the hostility of the Irish literary market towards the Irish poets and the preoccupation of the foreign market with revivalist stereotypes were among the reasons Kavanagh regretted his decision. Furthermore, his rather singular and uncouth manners alienated him from the Irish literati, whom he satirized in various poems, including 'Paddiad', published in *Horizon* in August 1949. In the prefatory note to the poem in *Come Dance with Kitty Stobling and Other Poems* (1960), he particularly mentioned his 'infected' youth under the influence of 'Ireland as a spiritual entity'[14] and wished 'to dramatise his own emancipation from what he perceived as a tame, scholarly, clerkly approach to literature and life'.[15] 'Paddiad' draws a loose comparison with Alexander Pope's *Dunciad*, which was published anonymously in Dublin

12 Patrick Kavanagh, *A Poet's Country: Selected Prose*, ed. Antoinette Quinn (London: Penguin Books, 2003), 307.
13 Antoinette Quinn, *Patrick Kavanagh: A Biography* (Dublin: Gill and Macmillan, 2001), ix–x.
14 Patrick Kavanagh, *Come Dance with Kitty Stobling and Other Poems* (London: Longmans, 1960), 42.
15 Quinn, *Patrick Kavanagh: A Biography*, 286.

166   CHAPTER 6

and dealt with the subject of English poetasters in Queen Anne's reign. The Irish literati in 'Paddiad' are compared to Dunces in Pope's satire, and Pearl Bar, 'Where the bards of Ireland are'[16] replaces Grub Street in London. Kavanagh projects the literary establishment in Dublin 'as a business cooperative, oblivious to standards of excellence, preoccupied with marketing and advertising strategies and mutual promotion'. The Paddies are composite characters of 'Austin Clarke, Robert Farren, Smyllie, MacManus, and Maurice Walsh', who are set against Paddy Conscious, who represents 'Yeats, Sean O'Casey, James Joyce' and Kavanagh himself.[17]

A comparison between *The Great Hunger* (1942) and 'Paddiad' (1949) shows a gradual change in Kavanagh's outlook towards his role as a poet in Irish society. The 'social critic and spokesman of the oppressed' in *The Great Hunger* gradually changed to the 'self-promoting literary and cultural critic' in later poems.[18] Post-war period philistinism, snobbery, provincialism and the flaws of a money-grubbing people in a country moving towards consumer capitalism continued to be criticized by Kavanagh, whom Quinn justly credits as Dublin's 'best-know *Flâneur*'[19] in the post-war period.

More than being an honorary title, *flânerie* as a literary practice clarifies Kavanagh's situation in the capital and his special treatment of Dublin city as a focal point in subverting the metanarratives of Irishness. Just as Paris had turned into Baudelaire's subject matter for lyric poetry, Dublin became Kavanagh's subject and ultimate source of inspiration. His love/hate relationship with Dublin, expressed time and again in his poems and essays, is characteristic of the *flâneur's* relationship with the city, namely that of Baudelaire with Paris and Benjamin with Berlin. Being enticed and profoundly disturbed by the city, Baudelaire and Benjamin felt neither 'at home in it nor content away from it', as Graeme Gilloch points out in *Myth and Metropolis*.[20] Dublin was caught between Kavanagh's adoration

---

16   Patrick Kavanagh, 'The Paddiad', in *Collected Poems* (London: Penguin Books, 2005), 154.
17   Quinn, *Patrick Kavanagh: A Biography*, 286.
18   Quinn, *Patrick Kavanagh: A Biography*, 287.
19   Quinn, *Patrick Kavanagh: A Biography*, x.
20   Graeme Gilloch, *Myth and Metropolis: Walter Benjamin and the City* (Oxford: Polity, 1997), 139.

Patrick Kavanagh in Dublin

and detestation in a similar fashion. His prose essays refer to the city as 'malignant Dublin';[21] Dubliners are seen as 'heartless philistines'.[22] At the same time, Dublin turned into Kavanagh's second parish where the poet's daily walk from Pembroke Road to Baggot Street Bridge wove a new wave of memory around its streets. In a way, Kavanagh created a new map of Dublin, yet this mapping, as Gary Roberts refers to the walking map of the city, 'is not a mere reflection of an unproblematic and static arrangement of physical space; it is an active linguistic construction of that space every time that it is performed'.[23]

Kavanagh's impatience with the city resulted from his search for self-satisfaction and artistic triumph. As Tester remarks, the *flâneur* always wishes to be somewhere else, in search of satisfying his gaze and his 'dissatisfied existence'.[24] For him, satisfaction is only temporal, summarized between those short intervals when he is not walking. Dublin was a site of exploration, a site of self-recovery and redemption as Kavanagh's famous Canal Bank sonnets remind the reader. The Canal Bank seat, where Kavanagh used to convalesce in the summer of 1955, was the physical locus of this transitory satisfaction, where he claimed to have been born a second time in the sonnet 'Canal Bank Walk', published in May 1958 in *Encounter*.

The transitory nature of satisfaction pushes the *flâneur* back to the streets. Referring to Roquentin in Sartre's *Nausea*, Tester points to the urban landscape as 'a place of dissatisfaction, of searching not finding. For the *flâneur*, satisfaction could be anywhere; but that only means that satisfaction is most certainly not here'.[25] It is the *flâneur's* urge to move and constant change of focus that best describe urban life as a dynamic phenomenon. According to Gilloch, 'the city creates and demands a new mode

21   Kavanagh, *A Poet's Country*, 307.
22   Quinn, *Patrick Kavanagh: A Biography*, xi.
23   Gary Roberts, 'London Here and Now: Walking, Street, and Urban Environments in English Poetry from Dunne to Gay', in Michael Bennett and David W. Teague, eds, *The Nature of Cities: Ecocriticism and Urban Environments* (Arizona: University of Arizona Press, 1999), 48.
24   Keith Tester, 'Introduction', in Keith Tester, ed., *The Flâneur* (London: Routledge, 1994), 7.
25   Tester, 'Introduction', 10.

168   CHAPTER 6

of representation, a new artistic sensibility and practice corresponding to the transformed perception of the urban environment.'[26] Kavanagh's contribution to this new aesthetics starts from the streets of Dublin, where walking transforms the romantic nostalgia of the city's past to the *flâneur's* fleeting and somatic memory, where the city is born anew in each encounter.

'The life of a street': Walking and urban identity

Kavanagh's poetry is full of references to walking and observation. 'Leaves of Grass', 'October', 'Is', 'Canal Bank Walk', 'Song at Fifty', 'Yellow Vestment', 'Living in the Country', 'New Item', 'The Poet's Ready Reckoner', 'A Summer Morning Walk', 'Jungle', 'Tale of Two Cities' and 'Auditors In' are instances of Kavanagh's mature poetry which set the poet at the heart of the urban existence; that is, the streets. The *flâneur's* walk, while embodying dynamism, is a discursive practice in resisting the automated speed and movement of the modern city and in defying social norm and conformity. The movement of the ordinary city dweller from home to work and to the shopping centre is hurried; it lacks the contemplative and observatory nature of the *flâneur's* sauntering. Furthermore, the *flâneur's* detached attitude is 'a short step away from isolation and alienation',[27] which makes him immune to the imposed memory of the city's memorial sites and parades. In his study of Joyce's *Dubliners*, Bonafous-Murat discusses how the 'involuntary memory' frozen in Dublin's memorials and ceremonial parades 'induces habit and "predisposition", depriving the characters of agency in their relationship to the past', which makes it impossible 'to wander around a town fraught with memories.'[28]

26   Gilloch, *Myth and Metropolis*, 133.
27   Tester, 'Introduction', 6.
28   Carle Bonafous-Murat; cited in Gibbons, '"Where Wolf Tone's Statue Was Not": Joyce, Monuments and Memory', in Ian McBride, ed., *History and Memory in Modern Ireland* (Cambridge: Cambridge University Press, 2001), 157.

Patrick Kavanagh in Dublin 169

Dublin streets were a site of encounter, shock and disillusionment for Kavanagh. Yet, before anything else, it was Kavanagh's philosophy of 'not caring' and his freedom from the romantic nostalgia of the past that equipped him with the *blasé* attitude that is prerequisite to the *flâneur's* survival in the metropolis. In the 'Author's Note' to *Collected Poems* (1964), Kavanagh summarized his response to the negative and harsh criticism directed at his poetry at the time: 'I have never been much considered by the English critics. I suppose I shouldn't say this. But for many years I have learned not to care.'[29] The *blasé* attitude describes Kavanagh's new relationship with the big city, a mixture of concern and disinterest; in other words, the ebb and flow of the city reaches the poet-*flâneur* but does not drown him. Similar to the Baudelairean *flâneur*, Kavanagh is 'the man *of* the crowd as opposed to the man *in* the crowd.'[30]

The streets of Dublin turned into Kavanagh's dwelling and provided him with a new subject matter for his urban brand of 'epic' poetry. Kavanagh's portrayals of Dublin correspond to Baudelaire's poetry on Paris, which, according to Benjamin, was not a commemoration or a 'hymn to the homeland', but bespoke 'the gaze of the allegorist [...], the gaze of the alienated man [...], the gaze of the *flâneur*.'[31] As mentioned earlier, Kavanagh had repeatedly denounced any belief in 'the virtue of a place.'[32] His urban lyrics, though highly place-conscious, should not be categorized under the same class of poetry that aimed at representing Ireland for the purpose of implementing a certain identity pattern, for example, the myth of 'Irishness'. As Heaney argued, '[t]he "matter of Ireland", mythic, historical or literary, forms no significant part of [Kavanagh's] material.'[33] Kavanagh's poetry recreates a dwelling devoid of 'cultural anxiety',[34] where

29   Patrick Kavanagh, 'Appendix A: Author's Note to Collected Poems (1964)', in *Collected Poems* (London: Penguin Books, 2005), 291.

30   Tester, 'Introduction', 3.

31   Walter Benjamin, *The Arcades Project* (Cambridge, MA: Belknap Press of Harvard University Press, 1999), 10.

32   Kavanagh, *A Poet's Country*, 309.

33   Seamus Heaney, *Preoccupations: Selected Prose, 1968–1978* (New York: Farrar, Straus, and Giroux, 1981), 115.

34   Seamus Heaney, 'The Placeless Heaven: Another Look at Kavanagh', *The Massachusetts Review*, 28/3 (1987), 376.

170   CHAPTER 6

the fleeting and transitory scenes of the urban environment become part
of the Irish cultural scene.

The *flâneur's* ephemeral and transitory sketches of the city correspond to what Baudelaire calls modernity: 'La modernité, c'est le fugitif, le
transitoire, le contingent, la moitié de l'art, dont l'autre moitié est l'éternel
et l'immuable.'[35] Kavanagh's poem 'Is', which depicts the 'life of a street' –
to quote a line from the poem – expresses his belief in the essence and importance of 'watching' as an end in itself: 'The only true teaching / Subsists
in watching / Things moving or just colour / Without the comment from
the scholar.'[36] Kavanagh's 'casual' gaze preserves a panoramic view of an
ordinary urban scene for the future:

> Casually remark
>
> On a deer running in a park;
>
> [...]
>
> Name for the future
>
> The everydays of nature
>
> [...]
>
> Girls in red blouses,
>
> Steps up to houses,
>
> Sunlight round gables,
>
> Gossip's young fables,
>
> The life of a street.[37]

The *collage* of these casually observed subjects (deer, girls, steps, sunlight, etc.) resembles Benjamin's technique of literary montage in *The
Arcades Project*, where fragments of critical analysis, literary texts and

35   Modernity is that which is fleeting, transitory, contingent; it is half of the art, the
     other half being eternal and immutable (*translation mine*). Charles Baudelaire, *Les
     Fleurs du Mal* (Paris: Gallimard, 1996), 13.
36   Kavanagh, 'Is', *Collected Poems* 222.
37   Kavanagh, 'Is', 222.

Patrick Kavanagh in Dublin 171

commentary are put together to recreate a panorama of the nineteenth-century Parisian arcades and boulevards, portraying the spirit of the age and Benjamin's artistic sensibility. The seemingly random juxtaposition of the items in Kavanagh's poem creates a plurality of interpretation as the viewing eye shifts focus from one vantage point to another. Meaning becomes fleeting and transitory, reflecting Baudelaire's interpretation of modernity as fleeting, transitory and contingent.

Love at last sight: Encounters in the city

The *flâneur's* outlook is a mixture of disinterestedness and shock at viewing the unfamiliar urban landscape. Kavanagh was a stranger in Dublin; his first-hand experiences belonged to the country. The city was a site of momentary encounters and shock, of intoxication and, consequently, of boredom. Kavanagh's encounter with the crowd, as in the poems 'On Raglan Road', 'The Rowley Mile' and 'Cyrano de Bergerac', echoes the impression of 'love at last sight' in the city: a notion that we come across in Baudelaire's famous poem in *Tableaux Parisiens*: 'À Une Passante'. The poem is about a momentary encounter between the persona (the *flâneur*) and a stranger: 'Une femme [...]/ Agile et noble'.[38] Their eyes meet and a momentary connection is made before she is lost in the crowd again. This is the last time the poet ever sees the woman, hence love at *last*, rather than first, sight.

> Un éclair ... puis la nuit! – Fugitive beauté
>
> Dont le regard m'a fait soudainement renaître,
>
> Ne te verrai-je plus que dans l'éternité?
>
> Ailleurs, bien loin d'ici! trop tard! *jamais* peut-être!
>
> Car j'ignore où tu fuis, tu ne sais où je vais,

---

38 Baudelaire, *Les Fleurs du Mal*, 134.

172   CHAPTER 6

Ô toi que j'eusse aimée, ô toi qui le savais![39]

[A flash of lightning ... then darkness! Fleeting beauty

By whose glance I was suddenly reborn,

Will I see you no more for eternity?

Elsewhere, very far from here! Too late! *Never* perhaps!

For I am oblivious to where you flee, you know not where I go,

O you whom I would have loved, O you who knew it!] (*Translation mine.*)

Such fleeting encounters characterize the chaotic experience of an individual lost in the multitude of passers-by in the city. A single moment creates for the poet the first and last impression of being allured and disappointed at the same time. Love, as Benjamin comments, is 'being stigmatized by the big-city'.[40] The ephemeral moments of intoxication and stimulation, which embodied the essence of *modernité* for Baudelaire, are elusive. The crowd provides and takes away the object of desire. The look of love at last sight is 'alluring and wistful', yet 'rooted in denial and frustration'.[41] As Gilloch points out, 'the erotic becomes a momentary act of seeing, of voyeurism. The glimpsed figure of the urban crowd may awaken sexual desire, but it remains unfulfilled.'[42]

For Kavanagh, it is the magic and ruination of love at last sight that constructs the image of the city as a sight of temptation and disappointment. In 'On Raglan Road', one of Kavanagh's most memorable poems, the poet foresees the disappointment following an encounter on what was then an ordinary street: 'On Raglan Road on an autumn day I met her first and knew / That her dark hair would weave a snare that I might one day rue.'[43] What remains of this momentary encounter is a street name: the site

39   Baudelaire, *Les Fleurs du Mal*, 134.
40   Walter Benjamin, *Charles Baudelaire: A Lyric Poet in the Era of High Capitalism* (London: Verso, 1983), 46.
41   Gilloch, *Myth and Metropolis*, 145–6.
42   Gilloch, *Myth and Metropolis*, 145–6.
43   Kavanagh, 'On Raglan Road', *Collected Poems* 130.

Patrick Kavanagh in Dublin 173

of a memory and a memory of a site in the metropolis. In a way, the urban space is rebuilt through the walking poem, where the poet *presences* the urban landscape through the articulation of a kinetic experience embedded in time and place. According to Gary Roberts, 'The walking poem allows the city dweller to represent the city by simultaneously engaging mind and body and their relationships to the structures of the environment.' As such, 'the poetics of walking reveal, as the philosopher Maurice Merleau-Ponty explains, a phenomenology of experience.'[44]

Unlike the Baudelairean persona, the walking figure in Kavanagh often comes across the woman again; yet, what makes the poem an expression of love at last sight is Kavanagh's ability to present a fresh image of each encounter, which ultimately leads to estrangement as the object of love disappears, always walking away:

> On a quiet street where old ghosts meet I see her walking now
>
> Away from me so hurriedly my reason must allow
>
> That I had wooed not as I should a creature made of clay –
>
> When the angel woos the clay he'd lose his wings at the dawn of day.[45]

Regardless of the various rendezvous, the *flâneur* remains a stranger in a city full of strangers. 'The Rowley Mile' and 'Cyrano de Bergerac', published in 1954 under the title of 'Two Sentimental Songs' in *The Bell*, embody another Baudelairean example. The first poem starts with the account of a sudden encounter: 'As I was walking down a street / Upon a summer's day / A typical girl I chanced to meet.'[46] The unexpectedness of the situation turns a 'typical' Dublin girl – a stranger bereft of the agility and nobility of Baudelaire's 'fugitive beauté' – into an object of desire, whom the poet pursues in vain. What is left behind from this momentary crossing of the paths and the few words exchanged thereafter is, once again, the memory of love at last sight encrypted in a single street name. The Rowley Mile becomes a site of shock and allurement (meeting the

44 Roberts, 'London Here and Now', 48.
45 Kavanagh, 'On Raglan Road', 130.
46 Kavanagh, 'The Rowley Mile', *Collected Poems* 193.

174   CHAPTER 6

girl), of multitude ('The street was full of eyes that stared') and, finally, of disappointment ('As I walked down that sunny street / I was a broken man').[47]

'Cyrano de Bergerac' is different from both poems in expressing not only the poet's shock and disappointment at encountering a stranger, but also of introducing the stranger, an equally deprived figure, as a *flâneuse*. The *flâneuse's* moment of erotic encounter is being transformed to a similar state of unfulfillment: 'She *was* in love and worried / About someone who was not'.[48] The alluring 'passante' in Baudelaire's poem turns into an idle figure who avoids direct contact in Kavanagh's poem: 'She kicked a pebble with her toe, / She tapped a railing idly – and when we met she swerved and took / The corner very widely'.[49] Unlike the object of desire that remains mute at the male gaze, the *flâneuse* narrates the story of her own encounter in the city. *Flânerie* in the nineteenth-century Paris was quintessentially a male occupation. A woman without company could not have loitered in the streets or dawdled in the arcades without attracting negative attention. Immunity from the public is the first condition for the *flâneur's* existence in the city. The male gaze in the nineteenth-century Paris would have eventually labelled a potential *flâneuse* as a prostitute, a figure that encompassed the sexualization of commodity and the commodification of sexuality.

From pastoral to post-pastoral and the creation of urban epic

Kavanagh's poetics evolved alongside his role as a *flâneur* in Dublin from a rural-pastoral tradition to what might be called 'urban pastoral' or 'post-pastoral' in Terry Gifford's and Rowley's terms, respectively.[50] His minute attention to detail and power of observation in encounters with rural loci were re-enacted in his treatment of the urban subject matter in Dublin.

47   Kavanagh, 'The Rowley Mile', 194.
48   Kavanagh, 'Cyrano de Bergerac', *Collected Poems* 195.
49   Kavanagh, 'Cyrano de Bergerac', 195.
50   Rowley, 'Patrick Kavanagh', 92.

Patrick Kavanagh in Dublin 175

While *flânerie* is first and foremost associated with the metropolis, it could be argued that Kavanagh's first apprenticeship as a *flâneur* commenced in the country where, despite the familiarity of faces and scenes in everyday rural life, the characters still come across new scenes and encounters. Kavanagh's rural landscape has a recognizable social dimension where meaning is negotiated through narratives similar to those of the urban environment. The countryside held for Kavanagh a peculiar mixture of wonder, novelty and boredom.

According to Benjamin, the shock of encountering unnoticed, strange and new urban phenomena and people wears away almost immediately as the *flâneur* faces the 'new' as 'always-the-same',[51] which finally leads to discovering the repetitive pattern of urban life amidst the hustle and bustle of the streets. Kavanagh's familiarization of the unfamiliar in the city turns into a defamiliarization of the familiar in the country. Just as the reader is immersed in the repetitive rhythm of country life, a sense of novelty, beauty and wonder is introduced in a momentary encounter between the persona and a familiar scene, place or person, transformed under the *flâneur's* gaze. Kavanagh often describes the landscape in perspectives. The poet's cinematic gaze moves from a nearby object or point of focus to elements emerging from a distance in the landscape, a technique he might have developed from his role as a film critic for an Irish newspaper at the time. Tarry's moment of epiphany while catching the girth strap under the belly of the horse in the second chapter of *Tarry Flynn* is one of those instances where the observer's moving lens is at work. Through Tarry's point of view, the close-up scene gives way to what is happening at a distance. The beauty of the landscape in perspective brings Tarry to a realization of the beauty and meaning in everyday rural life:

> He stooped down under the belly of the animal to catch the girth strap and as he did he caught a glimpse of the morning sun coming down the valley; it glinted on the swamp and the sedge and flowers caught a meaning for him. That was his meaning. Having found it suddenly, the tying of the girth and the putting of the mare in the cart and every little act became a wonderful miraculous work. It made

51 Cited in Gilloch, *Myth and Metropolis*, 121.

him very proud too and in some ways impossible. Other important things did not seem important at all.[52]

Through Tarry's *flâneuresque* observation in the novel, Kavanagh provides the reader with a fresh account of the quotidian rural environment, its people and beauties amongst the ordeals of farm life. Tarry is not a passive observer; he is in constant search for meaning and, interestingly, finds it in odd places.

Such appreciation of beauty and finding importance in ordinary things is reminiscent of poems written after Kavanagh's lung surgery in 1955, including the poems 'Auditors In', 'Is' and 'The Hospital'. Like Tarry who finds beauty and meaning under the belly of a horse, Kavanagh finds importance and beauty in 'unpoetic' places in the city. In 'The Hospital', the poet expresses empathy towards 'the functional ward in a chest hospital'.[53] The cubicles, washbasins, the staircase, the gravelled yard and all that might be called 'an art lover's woe' are viewed as valid subjects for poetry:

> But nothing whatever is by love debarred,
>
> The common and banal her heat can know.
>
> The corridor led to a stairway and below
>
> Was the inexhaustible adventure of a gravelled yard.
>
> This is what love does to things: the Rialto Bridge,
>
> The main gate that was bent by a heavy lorry,
>
> The seat at the back of a shed that was a suntrap.
>
> Naming these things is the love-act and its pledge;
>
> For we must record love's mystery without claptrap,
>
> Snatch out of time the passionate transitory.[54]

52 Patrick Kavanagh, *Tarry Flynn* (London: Penguin Books, 1978), 38.
53 Kavanagh, 'The Hospital', *Collected Poems* 217.
54 Kavanagh, 'The Hospital', 217.

Patrick Kavanagh in Dublin

The *flâneur's* ability to empathize with inorganic things finds an example in this sonnet. The 'inexhaustible adventure of a gravelled yard' indicates the possibility of finding novelty in the seemingly 'common and banal' scenes of urban life, be it a street, a park, a canal bank or a hospital chest ward in Dublin. Once again Kavanagh is a 'namer'; only in this case, the hills and valleys of Shancoduff are replaced by a gate 'bent down by a heavy lorry' and a 'seat at the back of a shed'.[55] The 'passionate transitory' corresponds to Kavanagh's interpretation of beauty 'as not being first and foremost linked to the land, but as being rather primordially tied to the suchness of things'.[56] In Rowley's words, the 'innocent celebrant of nature and her beauties' in Monaghan countryside becomes a 'wry observer' of human nature and urban landscapes in Dublin.[57]

In 'Question to Life', Kavanagh clearly states the importance of ordinary urban phenomena, commodities and people to Irish poetry, which are no less relevant than 'the passion of primrose banks in May'.[58] Kavanagh's 'urban epic', a term he uses in 'Auditors In' and 'Is', indicates the continuation of a post-pastoral tradition, where the ordinary scenes from a street or a local feud in the country become the main theme. In 'Auditor's In', the apparently insignificant occurrences of everyday rural life, such as the mass going of 'a young girl' and 'dandelions at Willie Hughes's', are named as 'equally valid' for the creation of 'urban epic, peasant ballad'.[59]

In 'Epic', a fourteen-line sonnet published in 1951, Kavanagh writes about having almost 'lost his faith in Ballyrush and Gortin' until he realizes the importance of the local and parochial in poetry:

> I have lived in important places, times
>
> When great events were decided: who owned
>
> That half a rood of rock, a no-man's land
>
> Surrounded by our pitchfork-armed claims.

---

55 Kavanagh, 'The Hospital', 217.
56 Rowley, 'Patrick Kavanagh', 98.
57 Rowley, 'Patrick Kavanagh', 94.
58 Kavanagh, 'Questions to Life', *Collected Poems* 220.
59 Kavanagh, 'Auditors In', *Collected Poems* 181.

178 CHAPTER 6

> I heard the Duffys shouting 'Damn your soul'
>
> And old McCabe, stripped to the waist, seen
>
> Step the plot defying blue cast-steel –
>
> 'Here is the march along these iron stones'.
>
> That was the year of the Munich bother. Which
>
> Was most important? I inclined
>
> To lose my faith in Ballyrush and Gortin
>
> Till Homer's ghost came whispering to my mind.
>
> He said: I made the *Iliad* from such
>
> A local row. Gods make their own importance.[60]

The poem is a fine explanation of Kavanagh's parochial vision which lies at the opposite end to provincialism. According to him, 'The provincial has no mind of its own'; his eyes are turned towards 'the metropolis'. It is the popular trend in the metropolis that defines the provincial mentality. 'The parochial mentality, on the other hand, is never in doubt about the social and artistic validity of his parish.'[61] The provincial attitude would have dismissed the relevance of local places, Ballyrush and Gortin, as subject matter for poetry in time of war. The Second World War, referred to as 'The Emergency' in Ireland, was one of the gravest Irish concerns since independence from Britain. To not write of war was considered a lack of sensibility among the literary intelligentsia in Dublin. Yet, for Kavanagh, the parochial ethics held the key to 'sensitive courage and the right kind of sensitive humility', in his own words.[62]

The parochial was not necessarily bound to Kavanagh's local Parish. As his later poetry shows, Dublin turned into Kavanagh's second parish, where writing about the mundane urban life grew an importance of its own, in contrast to the lack of interest among the Irish literary circle in Dublin inclined towards London as a literary metropolis. Kavanagh's relationship

---

60 Kavanagh, 'Epic', *Collected Poems* 184.
61 Kavanagh, *A Poet's Country*, 10.
62 Kavanagh, *A Poet's Country*, 237.

with Dublin, characteristic of the *flâneur's* relationship to the city, was that of a perpetual discovery. While early poems characterized the stranger's state of shock and disappointment, the later poems are about consolation, familiarity and repose.

A change of setting is perhaps the most recognisable element in Kavanagh's treatment of the parochial in this period. The scenery is urban yet tranquil, beautiful but moderate, mixing the elements of the city and the country, that of culture and nature, respectively. A comparison with 'Shancoduff' (1934), published with Kavanagh's mature poetry in *Come Dance with Kitty Stobling and Other Poems* (1962), highlights the evolution from pastoral to post-pastoral. The Inniskeen local placenames, Shancoduff, Glassdrummond and Rocksavage, are now replaced with Dublin placenames, Raglan Road, Grafton Street, Pembroke Road, Pearl Bar, The Palace and Baggot Street, which are more familiar to the urban audience. The mood is no longer elegiac and melancholic; 'No time for self-pitying melodrama', writes Kavanagh in 'Auditors In'.[63]

Kavanagh's valorization of his parish contributed to 'the devolution of Irish culture'[64] by elevating the parochial to the level of the universal. According to Tomaney, both views share a 'concern with fundamentals'.[65] Kavanagh's most characteristically *flâneuresque* portrayal of Dublin took place after his operation in 1955. The short period of convalescence at the Grand Canal banks enabled him to reconstruct a new Dublin, immersed in the banal and habitual. The city in later poems does not stand for anything other than what it communicates to the poet in a single moment of encounter. It is not a symbol or allegory; nor is it a site for nostalgia or utopia. Kavanagh's post-Canal aesthetics define the final stages of reconciliation with a lifelong struggle for self-satisfaction and literary recognition, characterized in the poet's love/hate relationship to place.

Kavanagh's routine walks from Baggot Street to Pembroke Road became a 'setting for the final development of the parochial ethic'.[66] In terms

---

63   Kavanagh, 'Auditors In', 182.
64   John Tomaney, 'Parish and Universe: Patrick Kavanagh's Poetic of the Local', *Environment and Planning: Society and Space*, 28 (2010), 322.
65   Kavanagh, *A Poet's Country*, 27.
66   Tomaney, 'Parish and Universe: Patrick Kavanagh's Poetic of the Local', 321.

180 CHAPTER 6

of *flânerie*, Kavanagh had turned into a 'walking encyclopaedia, the literal embodiment of shifting signifiers', as Gibbons refers to the walking figure in Irish literature.[67] The *flâneur*'s map of Dublin extended from the Grand Canal to Raglan Road, passing through Pembroke Road and Baggot Street. Gradually, Baggot Street Bridge and the Grand Canal in Dublin replaced Kavanagh's rural landscape. In 'If Ever You Go to Dublin Town', Kavanagh asks the posterity to look for him not in the countryside but on Baggot Street or Pembroke Road and in a pub rather than a farm.

Kavanagh's post-Canal aesthetics is an example of Dublin's status as a local subject matter under parochial ethics. 'Canal Bank Walk' and 'Lines Written on a Seat on the Grand Canal, Dublin', published in *Come Dance with Kitty Stobling and Other Poems* (1960), are examples of this urban aesthetics. Abundant in water-redemption imagery, they insist on tranquillity and immersion in common everyday life: wallow in the habitual, the banal / Grow with nature again as before I grew'.[68] At this point, the shock and wonder of earlier encounters does not take the poet by surprise; rather, the *flâneur* has reached a point where every new object and spectacle in the city becomes pleasantly familiar, even if momentarily. The more familiar Kavanagh becomes with the urban landscape, the more weightless his portraits of the city become. His mature poetry is not weighed down by sarcasm and irony. He finds in Dublin, not in Monaghan, an ultimate location for his Parnassus:

> O commemorate me where there is water,
>
> Canal water preferably, so stilly
>
> Greeny at the heart of summer. Brother
>
> Commemorate me thus beautifully
>
> Where by a lock Niagarously roars
>
> The falls for those who sit in the tremendous silence
>
> Of mid-July. No one will speak in prose

---

67   Gibbons, '"Where Wolf Tone's Statue Was Not"', 151.
68   Kavanagh, 'Canal Bank Walk', *Collected Poems* 224.

Patrick Kavanagh in Dublin 181

Who finds his way to these Parnassian islands.[69]

Once located in the country, Kavanagh's sense of place and inspiration is now predominantly urban. His Parnassus is Dublin-bound, located on the banks of the Grand Canal, where the poet wishes to be commemorated in both sonnets. His reunion with nature ('Grow with nature again as before I grew') takes place by the Canal, where the water is still and green in the mid-summer heat. The nature in the city is of a different kind from the countryside, yet both are mediated through the poet's perspective. Once, nature in Monaghan had him under a spell ('Stony Grey Soil', *Tarry Flynn*, *The Green Fool*), now, the less natural environment in Dublin holds the key to his poetic inspiration and peace.

Kavanagh's treatment of the city turned ordinary and unknown city locations and streets such as Raglan Road into contemporary Irish landmarks. Yet, in contrast to the monolithic, monumental memory of statues and ceremonial parades, the *flâneur's* somatic memory provided a space for dialogue and negotiation between people and places. By choosing Dublin as his subject matter, Kavanagh liberated Irish poetry from the romantic nostalgia of the previous generations and their dramatized Irishness under the influence of the Irish Literary Revival. His aesthetics as a Dubliner was the ultimate evolution of his rural-pastoral tradition, as cityscapes replaced the rural landscape, bringing the city to the forefront of Irish cultural imagination in the twentieth century.

---

69   Kavanagh, 'Lines Written on a Seat on the Grand Canal, Dublin', *Collected Poems* 227.

CHAPTER 7

Louis MacNeice's North: The 'Incorrigibly Plural' Sense of Place in Modern Irish Poetry

Introduction

In comparison to Dublin, Belfast made a far less significant appearance in poetry, prose and drama during the Revival period up to the 1960s, when the city became a major source of inspiration for the new generation of Irish poets including Paul Muldoon, Derek Mahon, Seamus Heaney, Michael Longley and Ciaran Carson, to name a few. Mahon, for instance, mentioned the secluded status of Protestant Belfast in the Irish literary imagination:

> The suburbs of Belfast have a peculiar relationship to the Irish cultural situation inasmuch as they're the final anathema for the traditional Irish imagination. A lot of people who are important in Irish poetry cannot accept that the Protestant suburbs in Belfast are a part of Ireland. At an aesthetic level they can't accept that.[1]

As an industrial city, Belfast was often aligned with industrial cities in England. According to Edna Longley, the image of Belfast in literature 'through most of its history, has combined Philistia with its other possible aspects as "Bigots-borough" (James Douglas's coinage) or

---

1   Derek Mahon, in an interview with Harriet Cooke, the *Irish Times* (17 January 1973); cited in George Watson, 'Landscape in Ulster Poetry', in Gerald Dawe and John Wilson Foster, eds, *The Poet's Place: Ulster Literature and Society* (Belfast: Institute of Irish Studies, 1991), 11.

Cokestown-across-the-water'.[2] Furthermore, Belfast was the biggest Protestant region in Ireland, making it twice removed from the dominant Catholic influence in the country. It was not until the late thirties that some Northern writers, such as the novelists Forrest Reid in *Peter Waring* (1937) and Michael McLaverty in *Call My Brother Back* (1939), turned to their native Belfast for a chance to explore a sense of divided identity and seclusion from the mainstream literary intelligentsia centred in Dublin. Once again the city – now Belfast – was viewed as the embodiment of violence, cruelty and corruption, set against the serene and romantic countryside – rural Ulster – in Irish literature. These aspects made their way through fiction in works such as Brian Moore's *The Emperor of Ice-Cream* (1965), which focused on the city's sense of doom, violence and sectarianism reinforced by the air raids which targeted Belfast during the Second World War. Janet MacNeill's *Maiden Dinosaur* (1964), however, was among the few novels that revealed a different Belfast. Hers was the city of the comfortable, well-to-do Protestant class, in contrast to the typical violent and sectarian Belfast of Northern Irish poetry and drama.[3]

Although Belfast's appearance in literature was still subtle in comparison to Dublin's, it was Belfast, more than any other city in Ireland, that helped to move the centre of gravity in Irish literature from the country to the city and from the 'rooted' representations of Irishness to multiple, diasporic and dynamic perceptions of Irish identity and place. The Partition, while increasing the gap that already existed between the Protestant and Catholic classes, created a state of inbetweenness that influenced the first and second generation of Irish writers, who experienced what Stephen Gwynn in *Experiences of a Literary Man* (1926) famously termed as a 'spiritual hyphenation':

> I was brought up to think myself Irish, without question or qualification; but the new nationalism prefers to describe me and the like of us, as Anglo-Irish. A.E. has

---

2   Edna Longley, 'The Writer and Belfast', in Maurice Harmon, ed., *The Irish Writer and the City* (Buckinghamshire: Colin Smythe, 1984), 65.

3   Agustin Martin, 'Novelist and City: The Technical Challenge', in Maurice Harmon, ed., *The Irish Writer and the City* (Buckinghamshire: Colin Smythe, 1984), 50.

Louis MacNeice's North

even set me down in print as [...] the typical Anglo-Irishman. So all my life I've been spiritually hyphenated without knowing it.[4]

While the likes of the Ulster poet John Hewitt found new ways of negotiating their identity as an equally valid version of Irishness, the Partition played a far more troubled and confusing role for the Belfast-born poet Fredrick Louis MacNeice. MacNeice's reception as an 'Irish' poet was obscured until the publication of major academic scholarship, most notably that of Edna Longley and the works of the late Northern poets Mahon, Montague and Carson, who acknowledged the pivotal influence of MacNeice in their poetry. MacNeice's association with the Auden Group, his residence outside Ireland and the thin bulk of poems about Ireland, plus his BBC career, Oxford education as a classicist and critique of Ireland's neutrality during the Second World War were reasons to question whether or not his poetry made a contribution to the ongoing question of Irishness. Reviewing MacNeice's *Collected Poems* in the winter edition of *Rann* (1940), Roy McFadden dismissed the poet's Irishness due to a lack of a sense of place:

> The only uneasy ghost in Mr. MacNeice's mind is his place of origin. From time to time the poet reverts to Ireland, nostalgically, impatiently, contemptuously – only to set his face firmly again towards the English scene. This retreat from childhood is a pity for, in the absence of any *spiritual roots*, Mr. MacNeice might well have strengthened his work by *allegiance to place* ... Allegiance to something beyond one's immediate time is a valuable asset in poetry. Mr. MacNeice is to apply for membership for Mr. Hewitt's school of regionalism, and studying the superstitions and sagas of the forefathers, discover Louis MacNeice.[5]

McFadden's reference to MacNeice's lack of 'spiritual roots' and the necessity of 'allegiance to place' proves the strong influence of the metanarrative of Irishness well into the 1940s and 1960s, which Hewitt, for instance, responded to by invoking a sense of place rooted in the Ulster countryside. Aiming at legitimizing the planters' Irishness through a spiritual

---

4   Stephen Gwynn, *Experiences of a Literary Man* (London: Butterworth, 1926), 11.

5   Roy McFadden, 'Review of *Collected Poems* by Louis MacNeice and *The Edge of Being* by Stephen Spender', *Rann*, 7 (Winter 1949–1950), 11; *my emphasis*.

186   CHAPTER 7

connection to the land, Hewitt's allegiance to Ulster could also be interpreted as part of the same Anglo-Irish rhetoric of compensation exercised
by Yeats and his contemporaries.

MacNeice's version of Irishness, on the other hand, was not a matter
of rootedness or allegiance to a certain locale. In fact, his poetry was predominantly tied to places; yet, it was his subversive connection to place,
rather than a lack of connection, that dismissed his poetry as 'unIrish'. It
is true that MacNeice had an uneasy relationship with his place of origin,
just like his other northern contemporaries, namely Cecil D. Lewis, Samuel
Becket and even Patrick Kavanagh, whom Neil Corcoran has considered
'a kind of honorary Ulsterman'.[6] For instance, Patrick Kavanagh's constant
repudiation of the myth of Irishness and disbelief in the virtue of a place
did not correspond to Hewitt's school of regionalism, either. Although in
comparison to MacNeice's urban, English connections, Kavanagh's rural,
Catholic background automatically qualified him as a legitimate Irish bard.

Louis MacNeice's love/hate relationship with his birthplace had its
roots in the poet's troubled childhood. In an early autobiographical essay,
he mentions his disapproval of the North which, he insists, was due to
personal reasons:

> I have always had what may well be a proper dislike and disapproval of the North of
> Ireland but largely as I find on analysis for improper i.e. subjective reasons. A harassed
> and dubious childhood under the hand of a well-meaning but barbarous mother's
> help from County Armagh led me to think of the North of Ireland as prison and
> the South as a land of escape. Many nightmares, boxes on the ears, a rasping voice
> of disapproval [...] sodden haycocks, fear of hell-fire, my father's indigestion – these
> things [...] bred in me an almost fanatical hatred for Ulster. [...] Everything had its
> sinister aspect – milk shrinks the stomach, lemon thins the blood. Against my will
> I was always given sugar in my tea. The north was tyranny.[7]

MacNeice's mother had unexpectedly died in a nursing home for the
mentally ill when the poet was a young boy. He also had a brother that
suffered from Dawn syndrome, and his father, who was an Anglican min-
ister, was often remote. The young MacNeice regarded the South with its

6   Cited in Stan Smith, ed., *Patrick Kavanagh* (Dublin: Irish Academic Press, 2009), 8.
7   Louis MacNeice, *Zoo* (London: Michael Joseph, 1938), 79.

Louis MacNeice's North

mythical charm as an escape from the North's hardness and determinism. As a member of the Anglo-Irish Ascendency, privileged by the rights of birth and ancestry, he was aware of the complicated and troublesome question of belonging to an Ireland divided by religious sectarianism and political dispute. Yet, rather than seeking poetic refuge in the idyllic South of his childhood, the majority of his poems about Ireland offer an honest, hence troubled relationship, with his homeland. In his introduction to *Autumn Journal*, he wrote: 'Poetry in my opinion must be honest before anything else and I refuse to be "objective" or clear-cut at the cost of honesty.'[8]

The sense of place in MacNeice's poetry delivers trauma, anxiety and displacement as much as affiliation and attachment. As such, it shares a similarity with Kavanagh's resistance to the metanarrative of Irishness. MacNeice's nightmarish accounts of the North and his sceptical view of Ireland as a commodity for sale equally subverted the myth of place which had played such an important role in the poetry of W. B. Yeats and his generation. While Kavanagh and MacNeice are seldom regarded as contemporaries and less often included in comparative studies, their subversion of the myth of Irishness and their influence on the next generation of Irish poets are quite similar. As much as Kavanagh empowered Heaney to write of humble backgrounds, MacNeice enabled the likes of Muldoon and Mahon to write of exilic and mobile senses of Irishness. MacNeice's receptivity to the city, according to Kennedy-Andrews, 'is part and parcel of a vision of the world perceived as "flux" and "incorrigibly plural".'[9] This new perception of Irishness may be MacNeice's biggest contribution to modern Irish poetry. Furthermore, his allegorical use of the genre of travel writing negotiated the role of movement and technology in Irish narratives while his *flâneuresque* perspective turned the focus towards the commodification of Ireland during the Revival and its impact on both the marginalized environment and people of Northern Ireland.

---

8   MacNeice, 'Note to Autumn Journal', in Eric Robertson Dodds, ed., *The Collected Poems of Louis MacNeice* (London: Faber and Faber, 1966), 791.

9   Elmer Kennedy-Andrews, *Writing Home: Poetry and Place in Northern Ireland, 1968–2008* (Cambridge: D.S. Brewer, 2008), 11.

188   CHAPTER 7

A modern aesthetics: MacNeice and cities

In 'Modern Poetry', a short essay included in Oliver Sayler's symposium 'Revolt in the Arts' (1929), the American poet Hart Crane pointed out the importance of forming a poetic language that can at once relate to and absorb the machine age and urban experience 'as naturally and casually as trees, cattle, galleons, castles and all other human associations of the past'.[10] Unless it is able to form a spontaneous 'terminology of poetic reference as the bucolic world of pasture, plow, and barn', modern poetry – Crane believed – had failed its 'full contemporary function'.[11] Crane's emphasis on the responsibilities of the modern poet in internalizing the machine age in poetry was soon to become a poetic doctrine embraced by poets on both sides of the Atlantic, including the Thirties generation in Great Britain. The new poetic language was not only to rescue modern poetry from the outmoded pastoral forms that had dominated English and Anglo-Irish poetry for the last century but also helped to develop a medium to explore and explain modern urban experience.

In 'What am I doing here? MacNeice and Travel', Terence Brown gave Louis MacNeice, rather than any other poet of the era, the credit of bridging the gap between modern urban experience and poetic language with his peculiar treatment of urban subject matter in such poems as 'Bluebells', *Autumn Journal*, 'Birmingham', and 'Belfast'.[12] MacNeice opened modern poetry to new interpretations, including questions of identity and place in Ireland. If Kavanagh revolutionized the entire mode of understanding rural Irish identity through paying attention to mundane and so-called 'unpoetic' details of rural life, MacNeice reflected on aspects of modern Irish experience, such as urban ennui, exile, displacement and industrial

---

10   Hart Crane, *The Complete Poems of Hart Crane* (New York: Liveright Publishing, 1958), 181.
11   Crane, *The Complete Poems*, 182.
12   Terence Brown, 'What Am I Doing Here? MacNeice and Travel', in Fran Brearton and Edna Longley, eds, *Incorrigibly Plural: Louis MacNeice and His Legacy* (Manchester: Carcanet, 2012).

Louis MacNeice's North 189

exploitation, which were often ignored, underestimated or peripheralized in the Revival and post-Independence narratives.

Like Kavanagh, MacNeice had a keen eye for observation. At times, his poems become a menagerie of peculiarly mismatched items. In 'Birmingham', from the 'Chromium dogs on the bonnet' and 'Cubical scent-bottles [,] artificial legs [,] arctic foxes and electric mops' to the relaxed faces of 'shopgirls' during the lunch hour, no single detail is left out.[13] Yet, there is a method to the madness of accumulating details and constant repetition in MacNeice's poetry. The ordering, juxtaposing and comparing of the seemingly unrelated items reflect the experience of modernity as a constant process of familiarization and defamiliarization of objects, people and encounters in the modern industrial city. Like Walter Benjamin in *The Arcades Project*, MacNeice conveys the experience of 'the new in the context of the always-the-same'.[14] In the words of Graeme Gilloch:

> The definitive experience of the metropolitan environment is the never-ending encounter with the nothing-new, *ceaseless repetition*. It is the fundamental basis of the mythic character of modernity. The fetishization of the commodity and the charm of fashion are the key elements of the spell that holds the modern metropolis in thrall, half-dormant, half-bored.[15]

Repetition alone is one of the most noticeable literary techniques in MacNeice's urban poetics. In fact, the enlarged 1974 edition of *Princeton Encyclopedia of Poetry and Poetics* places MacNeice's poetry under the 'entry for repetition'.[16] Repetition takes various forms and functions in MacNeice's poetry. In 'Leaving Barra' and 'Autobiography', it is 'thematically, emotionally or psychologically functional'; in other poems, such as 'Trains to Dublin', it takes a more political significance as shown in the 'explicit political refusal' of the line: 'But I will not give you any idol

---

13   Louis MacNeice, 'Birmingham', in *The Collected Poems of Louis MacNeice* (London: Faber and Faber, 1966), 17, 18.

14   Graeme Gilloch, *Myth and Metropolis: Walter Benjamin and the City* (Oxford: Polity, 1997), 121.

15   Gilloch, *Myth and Metropolis*, 121; my emphasis.

16   Neil Corcoran, 'The Same Again? MacNeice's Repetitions', in Fran Brearton and Edna Longley, eds, *Incorrigibly Plural: Louis MacNeice and His Legacy*, 257.

or idea, creed or King'.[17] On the other hand, the repetition of patterns, objects and cycles in his urban poems deliver a critique of modernity, of the ennui of urban life that characterized Northern Ireland. His treatment of the urban subject matter delivers the 'half-dormant, half-bored' yet shocking experience of modernity that the Benjaminian *flâneur* faces. His odd comparisons – trams moving like sarcophagi ('The Glaciers'), the traffic policeman 'with his figure of a monolith Pharaoh' ('Birmingham'), 'zeppelin clouds and Pentecost-like cars' headlights' ('Birmingham') and traffic crawling and 'Carrying its dead boulders down a glacier wall' ('The Glacier') – represent modernity in terms of myth. The recurrence of tedious industrial patterns, mass production, consumerism and constant circulation of commodities announce the new as the ever-the-same.

The organic/inorganic play in MacNeice's 'urban sublime'

For MacNeice, as for Kavanagh, the view of the figure in the landscape is the vista from which the poet represents the environment. The figure and the environment, in other words, are disclosed through one another. In 'Belfast', the exploited man is camouflaged in a landscape of exploitation as MacNeice ties descriptions of the Northerner to his/her immediate geological and geographical environment:

> The hard cold fire of the northerner
>
> Frozen into his blood from the fire in his basalt
>
> Glares from behind the mica of his eyes
>
> And the salt carrion water brings him wealth.
>
> Down there at the end of the melancholy lough
>
> Against the lurid sky over the stained water
>
> Where hammers clang murderously on the girders

---

17 Corcoran, 'The Same Again? MacNeice's Repetitions', 261.

Louis MacNeice's North

> Like crucifixes the gantries stand.
>
> And in the marble stores rubber gloves like polyps
>
> cluster; celluloid, painted ware, glaring
>
> Metal patents, parchment lampshades, harsh
>
> Attempts at buyable beauty.[18]

This early oxymoronic description gives way to a bold juxtaposition of the organic geology of salt and basalt with the inorganic cluster of 'celluloid, painted ware, glaring / Metal patents, parchment lampshades.'[19] Such juxtaposition is vexing to the reader; it demands an 'awakening from the dream-state of commodity capitalism'[20] by displacing things from their original utility environments. Gathering these seemingly unrelated objects together and placing the natural and the artificial side by side, the poem disturbs the dream-state of the metropolis, just as Benjamin's literary montage in *The Arcades Project* blasts 'the phantasmagoria of urban modernity, offering a "profane illumination" that holds out the possibility of transformative meaning.'[21]

Commenting on Benjamin's displacing and emplacing of the various left-overs of modernity in *The Arcades Project*, Terry Eagleton points to Benjamin's 'constellatory method' as redrawing 'the relationship between the part and the whole', destroying 'the assumed and habitual place of the thing in the historical logic of commodity fetishism and showing the arrested object as the embodiment of history itself: "dialectics at a standstill".'[22] According to Hannah Arendt, once things are brought to a standstill, they are enabled to 'shine by themselves, to speak their own essences

---

18 MacNeice, 'Belfast', *Collected Poems* 17.

19 MacNeice, 'Belfast', 17.

20 Catriona Sandilands, 'Green Things in the Garbage: Ecocritical Gleaning in Walter Benjamin's Arcades', in Axel Goodbody and Kate Rigby, eds, *Ecocritical Theory: New European Approaches* (Charlottesville: University of Virginia Press, 2011), 31.

21 Sandilands, 'Green Things in the Garbage', 31.

22 Terry Eagleton, *The Ideology of the Aesthetic* (Oxford: Blackwell, 1990), 329.

[...] in the right company of other things'.[23] Hence, it could be inferred that the gathering of the organic and artificial elements in MacNeice's poem converts the inert commodified 'nature' to a dialectical one, where there is a possibility of dialogue and negotiation.

The notion of 'dialectics at a standstill' also recurs in Heidegger's philosophy of *Dasein* (being-in-the-world), where the natural is often disclosed in juxtaposition to the artificial. In his description of the Greek temple in 'The Origin of the Work of Art', Heidegger refers to the built monument as a *clearing* that discloses the earth, that is, the material from which the temple, the artwork and the like are built. Nature is hidden in the tool, in the monument, in the bridge: 'forgotten and lost', yet existing potentially.[24] Once looking at the instrument, bridge or monument from a non-instrumental perspective, we provide an outlet, a *clearing* through which the earth or the natural presence invested in things becomes manifest.

Poetic language, as Heidegger argues, is one such *clearing*. Rather than being a mere vehicle for representing an external physical reality (Aristotle's *mimesis*) or a pre-formed idea (Plato's *eidos*), poetry offers disclosure 'in its attention to the singularity of beings in appearance, to the relatedness of the seemingly unrelated, and in its emphasis on the play of indeterminacy, uncertainty, enigma, and revelation'.[25] In MacNeice's poetry, the North is a land/cityscape of exploitation where nature and culture meet. The material and the artificial replace the natural and claim an organic life of their own. Referring to phrases such as 'screened face', 'the heart's funfair', 'fidgety machines', 'proud glass' and the like in 'Birmingham', Edna Longley mentions the 'inorganic "organism"' in MacNeice's poetry: '[b]y a process of alarming exchange here the inorganic eats into the organic or assumes an oppressive life of its own'.[26] In 'Belfast', MacNeice blends in, blurs and subverts the

---

23   Hannah Arendt, 'Introduction: Walter Benjamin 1892–1940', in Hannah Arendt, ed., *Walter Benjamin: Illuminations* (New York: Schocken, 1967), 11.

24   Michael Haar, *The Song of the Earth: Heidegger and the Grounds of the History of Being* (Bloomington: Indiana University Press, 1993), 59.

25   Trevor Norris, 'Martin Heidegger, D. H. Lawrence, and Poetic Attention to Being', in Axel Goodbody and Katherine E. Rigby, eds, *Ecocritical Theory: New European Approaches* (Charlottesville: University of Virginia Press, 2011), 124.

26   Michael Longley, *Louis MacNeice: A Study* (London: Faber and Faber, 1988), 47–8.

Louis MacNeice's North

natural/artificial elements of his surrounding landscape, where one can no longer draw a line of distinction between the natural and the artificial. The poem becomes a site of disclosure, a *clearing* that discloses the social and natural elements in dialectic. Rather than ignoring the strong presence of an industrial landscape, MacNeice's poetry invokes a sense of place that is inseparable from and dependent on it. By juxtaposing the natural elements of the Northern landscape with the artificial elements of the industrial cityscape, he brings to light the formerly unrepresentable in the Irish Revival literature; that is, a sense of plurality, confusion, cruelty and alienation.

Drawing on ideas from Edmund Burke, Jean-François Lyotard in his famous essay 'The Sublime and the Avant-Garde' referred to the presentation of the unrepresentable as characteristic of modern art. By no longer 'bending itself to models' and presenting 'the fact that there is an unrepresentable', modern art actualizes 'a figure potentially there in the language'.[27] MacNeice's representation of the natural landscape through the artificial and vice versa discloses the hidden possibilities of meaning and identity in the North. The outcome is the creation of 'urban sublime'; through a shocking combination of the organic and the inorganic, the poem creates an intensified experience. This intensified experience is what Burke calls 'the sublime'. Rather than focusing on the natural and beautiful alone, MacNeice's poetry creates a state of shock. The grand dimension of erect mills and gantries in juxtaposition to the hills and mountains of the rough Ulster landscape creates an intensified experience, which is a mixture of admiration and awe. Lyotard states,

> The arts, whatever their materials, pressed forward by the aesthetics of the sublime in search of intense effects, can and must give up the imitation of models that are merely beautiful, and try out surprising, strange, shocking combinations. Shock is, *par excellence*, the evidence of (something) *happening,* rather than nothing, suspended privation.[28]

---

27   Jean-François Lyotard, *The Inhuman: Reflections on Time* (Cambridge: Polity Press, 1991), 101.

28   Lyotard, *The Inhuman*, 100; *original emphasis.*

194   CHAPTER 7

What is *happening* through MacNeice's creation of the urban sublime is the possibility of interpretation, of acknowledging the plurality of sense of place and identity, of *disclosing* rather than *concealing*. 'Carrickfergus' is one fine example where the poet sets the tone for plurality and indicates a state of inbetweenness from the very first line: 'I was born in Belfast between the mountain and the gantries'.[29] MacNeice's hometown Carrick is a divided landscape of the natural and artificial, of poverty and prosperity, of religious sects and identities, not formerly represented, at least not at this level of clarity:

> The scotch Quarter was a line of residential houses
>
> But the Irish Quarter was a slum for the blind and halt.
>
> [...]
>
> The Norman walled this town against the country
>
> To stop his ears to the yelping of his slave.[30]

The divided landscape of County Antrim echoes the poet's sense of division from the poorer sections of the Irish society: 'I was the rector's son, born to the Anglican order, / Banned for ever from the candles of the Irish poor.'[31] He later draws further attention to the social disorder and inequality of the war years and regional conflict, to which he had said goodbye as a child, in his words, joining the 'puppet world of sons' away from the realities of the North:

> I went to school in Dorset, the world of parents
>
> Contracted into a puppet world of sons
>
> Far from the mill girls, the smell of porter, the salt-mines
>
> And the soldiers with their guns.[32]

29   MacNeice, 'Carrickfergus', *Collected Poems* 69.
30   MacNeice, 'Carrickfergus', 69.
31   MacNeice, 'Carrickfergus', 69.
32   MacNeice, 'Carrickfergus', 70.

Louis MacNeice's North 195

MacNeice's account of Carrickfergus does not end here. The poet revisits the notions of home and dwelling almost eight years later in 'Carrick Revisited' (1945). The poem may be called a Wordsworthian Prelude, yet of a considerably shorter length and situated in a different setting from the surroundings of the Lake District. Reflecting on his childhood in Carrick, MacNeice refers to the interconnectedness of his existence and the land upon which it becomes manifest in an act of *dwelling*: 'Who was – and am – dumbfounded to find myself / In a topographical frame – here, not there'?[33] The 'random chemistry of soil and air' has determined the poet's identity as a displaced Anglo-Irishman, where 'neither western Ireland nor southern England / cancels' what he calls 'this interlude'.[34] Whether it is set in Carrick or Belfast, Dublin or Galway, MacNeice's Irishness remains a mixture of belonging and displacement, as the following excerpts from 'The Closing Album' and 'Valediction' indicate:

This was never my town,

I was not born nor bred

Nor schooled here and she will not

Have me alive or dead

But yet she holds my mind

With her seedy elegance.[35]

***

I cannot deny my past to which my self is wed,

The woven figure cannot undo its thread.[36]

He is neither 'Free of all roots nor yet a rooted peasant'. The urban civilization has bastardized him 'Out of the West',[37] where he could only

33   MacNeice, 'Carrick Revisited', *Collected Poems* 224.
34   MacNeice, 'Carrick Revisited', 225.
35   MacNeice, 'The Closing Album', *Collected Poems* 163.
36   MacNeice, 'Valediction', *Collected Poems* 53.
37   MacNeice, 'Western Landscape', *Collected Poems* 257.

196   CHAPTER 7

reminisce the memories of his childhood or return as a tourist. Both out-
looks consist of a degree of disinterestedness and engagement, required
of a *flâneur's* 'pre-habitual' gaze, which becomes more pronounced in
MacNeice's representations of the industrial North.

The Industrial North: Consumer capitalism and socio-environmental inequalities

MacNeice was a poet of cities. Belfast, Galway, Dublin, Barcelona,
London and Birmingham are some of the most popular places MacNeice
explored in his poetry. His encounter with cities can, in many instances, be
compared to Benjamin's treatment of the metropolis either as a foreigner
or a child, which gave him the vantage point of a *flâneur's* disinterested
outlook towards people and places. The gaze of the child or foreigner is
'pre-habitual'; it has not yet been 'unobscured by familiarity and habit', as
Gilloch states in relation to Benjamin's view of Moscow and Berlin:

> In Moscow, Benjamin becomes a 'child' in a foreign city. In Berlin, he becomes a 'for-
> eigner' in the city of his childhood. He transforms the urban setting by presenting
> it to the reader as it is perceived 'at first sight'.[38]

Once again, perception 'at first sight' becomes one of ultimate importance. By distancing himself either in time or space, if not both, the *flâneur*
configures the city as a sight of novelty, shock and bewilderment in each
encounter; in other words, a place worth observing and exploring. Similar
to Kavanagh, MacNeice registers a *flâneuresque* technique in his portrayal
of cities, evident in his treatment of the North, where the poet's childhood memories were formed. In 'Valediction', he encounters the place
through an act of remembrance; yet, in being distanced temporarily/spa-
tially from the present time and societal norms – hence, uncontaminated
by habit – the child's memory gives the poet agency in his relationship to

38   Gilloch, *Myth and Metropolis*, 61.

Louis MacNeice's North 197

the past. What MacNeice sees in Ireland of his childhood as a *flâneur* is a commercialized commodity, claiming people's 'individuality':

> On a cardboard lid I saw when I was four
>
> Was the trade-mark of a hound and a round tower,
>
> And that was Irish glamour, and in the cemetery
>
> Sham Celtic crosses claimed our individuality.[39]

By going back in time and reflecting on the once novel scene of Irish life, MacNeice is able to dig out the 'drug-dull fatalism'[40] of a country fetishized during the Revival and presented in terms of myth in literature, tourism and politics. The repetition of the same old patterns claims the individuality of the emerging identities and perceptions of Irishness among the new generation. The 'drug-dull fatalism' that MacNeice associates with Irish stereotypes echoes Marx and Benjamin's reference to the narcotic effects of consumer capitalism, stigmatizing the city since the industrial revolution in the nineteenth century.

The industrialization and modernization of Ireland, as mentioned earlier, was a relatively late and uneven phenomenon. The sudden proliferation of linen export in the Irish economy converted the rural northern landscape of nineteenth-century Ireland into a gradual conglomerate of linen mills, factories and shipyards. The industrialization of linen and the rise of cotton production in Belfast alone centralized the Ulster economy around itself and pushed Dublin's hinterlands to a periphery.[41] By the 1930s, the Northern landscape was predominantly urban and industrialized. In order to arrive at a sense of continuity and tradition through focusing on the landscape, Irish writers had continually ignored or compensated the urban and industrial with the rural and pastoral. MacNeice, however, discloses the North through a subversion of the former dichotomies of city

---

39   MacNeice, 'Valediction', 53.
40   MacNeice, 'Valediction', 52.
41   Kevin Whelan, 'Settlement and Society in Eighteenth-Century Ireland', in Gerald Dawe and John Wilson Foster, eds, *The Poet's Place: Ulster Literature and Society* (Belfast: Institute of Irish Studies, 1991), 57.

198   CHAPTER 7

versus country and nature versus culture. Juxtaposing the natural and the artificial in such poems as 'Belfast', MacNeice brings about the possibility of disclosure as the poem provides a *clearing* for bringing-forth the bitter socio-ecological realities in Northern Ireland. For MacNeice, the North represents a state of inbetweenness ('I was born in Belfast between the mountain and the gantries'[42]); it embodies industrialism, poverty and social inequality ('The Scotch Quarter was a line of residential houses / But the Irish Quarter was a slum for the blind and halt'[43]); it stands for religious sectarianism and prejudice ('See Belfast, devout and profane and hard'[44]).

Belfast is a cityscape of gantries, shipyards and linen mills, where 'hammers clang murderously on the girders', and gantries are a reminder of crucifixes.[45] The factory worker, linen girl and shipyard labourer are the scapegoats of this industrial city, where the labourer is alienated from the product of his or her labour. In *Autumn Journal,* MacNeice clearly refers to the infected consumer culture in Belfast and the exploitation of labour in the foreign market:

> But they make their Ulster linen from foreign lint
>
> And the money that comes in goes out to make more money
>
> A city built upon mud;
>
> A culture built upon profit.[46]

He had elsewhere shown his disappointment and estrangement with commercialized Ireland. His reference to Irish linen in several poems hints at the alienating result of industrialism in the North. For the expatriate poet abroad, the Irish linen should be a sign of affection, comfort and home: 'And the linen which I lie on came from Ireland / In the easy days / When all I thought of was affection and comfort, / Petting and praise.'[47] Yet, behind this apparent sense of homeliness and belonging,

42   MacNeice, 'Carrickfergus', 69.
43   MacNeice, Carrickfergus', 69.
44   MacNeice, 'Valediction', 52.
45   MacNeice, 'Belfast', 17.
46   MacNeice, 'Note to Autumn Journal', 132.
47   MacNeice, 'Note to Autumn Journal', 110.

Louis MacNeice's North 199

there is a sense of alienation, represented in the luxury product which remains inaccessible to those who have produced it. Linen, which had turned into one of major Irish exports besides beef and butter since the late seventeenth century, was 'cheaper to produce in a low labour cost environment'; moreover, 'the link to Dublin-London financial services plus their custom-free status in Britain gave them a competitive advantage'.[48] The fact that the North offered a lower labour cost environment is indicative of its less advantageous status in the Irish cultural repertoire, justifying not only the exploitation of its inhabitants (human resources) in terms of cheap labour but also the environmental degradation of the Ulster landscape through the excessive use of natural resources. The link between environmental and social justice concerns becomes evident in the poem, as MacNeice reminds the reader that the profit made from this industry does not return to the labourer.

Walter Benjamin's critique of industrial progress as an exploitation of nature and human labour *for gratis* applies to Northern Ireland, where exploitation, poverty and alienation were but side effects of excessive industrialization. Nature-as-commodity equalled Ireland-as-commodity. The exploited wilderness of post-Conquest Ireland had therefore turned into a cityscape of exploitation, an urban wilderness under consumer capitalism, which alienated man not only from nature, but also from the product of his own labour; in other words, from himself. The object of exploitation is once again man-plus-the-environment. The environment, more than ever before, becomes a *standing-reserve*, a commodity reserved for exchange, as explained in Heidegger's view of technology.

Viewed from an ecojustice perspective, which studies the possible links between environmental problems and social justice issues, the vices of an industrial economy – including its negative impact on the environment as in the line 'The brook ran yellow from the factory stinking of chlorine'[49]– expose the poorer sections of society, often directly, to the effects of environmental degradation. In the same section of *Autumn Journal*, MacNeice points to the unfavourable living and working conditions in an

48   Whelan, 'Settlement and Society in Eighteenth-Century Ireland', 57.
49   MacNeice, 'Carrickfergus', 69.

environment exploited since his childhood and the sharp contrast that exists between the poor and affluent areas of the city, where the smoke from the chimneys reminds of a prosperity that is always 'round the corner', but never close enough:

> And the North, where I was a boy,
>
> Is still the North, veneered with the grime of Glasgow,
>
> Thousands of men whom nobody will employ
>
> Standing at the corners, coughing.
>
> And the street-children play on the wet
>
> Pavement – hopscotch or marbles;
>
> And each rich family boast a sagging tennis-net
>
> On a spongy lawn beside a dripping shrubbery.
>
> The smoking chimneys hint
>
> At prosperity round the corner.[50]

Once again, we are reminded of how culture and environment are closely interconnected; how pollution, unemployment and poverty are intertwined in a culturally marginalized landscape, thus making the study of environmental degradation relevant to cultural studies and adding an environmental dimension to the latter.

MacNeice and trains: A *Flâneur* on board?

As mentioned earlier, the Benjaminian *flâneur* was either a child or tourist whose view was not spoilt by habit. MacNeice's return to Ireland as a tourist was a self-conscious act in his poetry. His journeys by train represent his *flâneuresque* view of place and identity; he remains distanced, yet

---

50   MacNeice, 'Note to Autumn Journal', 133.

Louis MacNeice's North

not detached. While Kavanagh's poetry makes frequent references to acts of walking, MacNeicean observations of the urban scene often take place through the windows of a train in movement. In fact, he uses the genre of travel writing as an allegory for his displaced position as an Anglo-Irish poet torn between places and identities.

The quest for belonging continued almost throughout the entire length of MacNeice's prolific vocation, as he frequented locations in and outside Ireland. He was particularly interested in small insular countries like Iceland – islands where a sense of community was believed to be present. However, he questioned the sense of community embraced in revivalist narratives as indicative of a 'genuine' Irish culture. In part XVI of *Autumn Journal*, he asks: 'Why do we like being Irish?' and responds:

> And partly because Ireland is small enough
>
> To be still thought of with a family feeling,
>
> And because the waves are rough
>
> That split her from a more commercial culture;
>
> And because one feels that here at least one can
>
> Do local work which is not at the world's mercy
>
> And that on this tiny stage with luck a man
>
> Might see the end of one particular action.
>
> *It is self-deception of course;*
>
> *There is no community in this island either.*[51]

As the ironical turn of the last two lines indicates, Ireland is no different from the rest of the modern world (especially England) in being commercialized. It is infected by the stereotypes of martyrdom, Gaelicism and pastoralism, while censorship, unemployment, pollution and inequality feature the country. MacNeice's sense of Irishness remains in and outside Ireland at the same time. There is a sense of attachment that he cannot shun ('The woven figure cannot undo its thread'); yet for him, it is not the

51   MacNeice, 'Note to Autumn Journal', 133; *my emphasis*.

idea of belonging to a fixed location but the quest for belonging that constructs a sense of place and becomes his situation of belonging. Therefore, the poet dwells in between places rather than being tied to a fixed locality or the idea of a certain place.

MacNeice's frequent references to cars, trains, buses and airplanes were not to overload his poetry with a modernist, technological jargon. Rather, the recurrence of such terminology as skidding, clutching, reversing and gearing was a direct response to the 1930s – the age of travel and technology. According to Valentine Cunningham in *British Writers in the Thirties* (1988), '[t]he new age of easy transport for the upper middle classes, for the *déraciné* intelligentsia and the bohemian, brought most of Europe and other parts of the world within the ambit of the literary imagination.'[52] MacNeice was a frequent visitor to cities in Europe and across the continent. Writing of road traffic and the passing of vehicles and trains conveyed an antipastoral dimension to the sense of place that very much characterized the spirit of the age. In 'Trains in the Distance', he wrote of trains as part of his childhood memories: 'Trains came threading quietly through my dozing childhood, / Gentle murmurs nosing through a summer quietude.'[53]

Trains continued to be part of MacNeice's experience as an urban poet, traveller and journalist. Leonita Flynn calls him a 'poet of trains.'[54] As a poetic metaphor, trains embody the poet's panoramic gaze and indicate the passage of time in a dynamic land/cityscape. Flynn points to the train journeys as both 'an interregnum in the day and an event in themselves'; in possessing 'the right quality of active passivity (or passive activity)', they are a source of poetic 'inspiration.'[55] This passive activity/active passivity, the constant movement of the train and the panoramic gaze give the audience an opportunity to view MacNeice's experience on the train as a *flâneur*. As his constant movement

---

52   Valentine Cunningham, *British Writers in the Thirties* (1988); cited in Brown, 'What Am I Doing Here? MacNeice and Travel', 77.

53   MacNeice, *Collected Poems*, 3.

54   Leonita Flynn, 'On MacNeice on Trains', in Fran Brearton and Edna Longley, eds, *Incorrigibly Plural: Louis MacNeice and His Legacy* (Manchester: Carcanet, 2012), 70.

55   Flynn, 'On MacNeice on Trains', 70.

Louis MacNeice's North 203

quickens to that of a train's speed, the scenery stretches from the streets to the land/cityscapes between destinations. His gaze is barred by the window, but the window offers him security from the crowd and a freedom to gaze while escaping the gaze of strangers outside.

Nevertheless, in its distance from the actual landscape, the view from the train might be charged with superficiality and incomprehension, characteristics that are often ascribed to a tourist's perspective. MacNeice, however, was not ignorant of the accumulated wealth and consumer capitalism of the modern city that made travelling a frequent possibility. In *Out of the Picture* (1937), he satirized how the decade's prosperity had turned the world into an oyster, offering 'miles and miles of distance for your money'.[56] Viewed as a tourist in his own country, he had, nevertheless, a truer-to-life way of looking at the ordinary urban sights that he encountered on his trips. Hessel refers to the *flâneur's* preference of '*site* to *sight*-seeing', which helps to unearth 'the hidden histories and unexplained details of what is presented to him'.[57] MacNeicean 'sight-seeing' is equally subversive. In 'Valediction', he parodies the perception of Ireland as a commodified tourist attraction:

Park your car in Killarney, buy a souvenir

Of green marble or black bog-oak, run up to Clare,

Climb the cliff in the postcard, visit Galway city,

Romanticise our Spanish blood.

And pay for the trick beauty of a prism

In drug-dull fatalism.

I will exorcise my blood

And not to have my baby-clothes my shroud

I will acquire an attitude not yours

And become as one of your holiday visitors,

56 Louis MacNeice, *Out of the Picture* (London: Faber and Faber, 1937), 49.
57 Cited in Gibbons, '"Where Wolf Tone's Statue Was Not": Joyce, Monuments and Memory', in Ian McBride, ed., *History and Memory in Modern Ireland* (Cambridge: Cambridge University Press, 2001), 149.

204   CHAPTER 7

And however often I may come

Farewell, my country, and in perpetuum;[58]

This is not a mere nostalgic or contemptuous return to the past, as McFadden
would have claimed. According to Brown, 'this long poem confronts Ireland
as a country that reveals its beauty to the eye of a tourist but which holds its
children in an iron grip, imprisoning them in their personal lives and in the
public constraints of an implacable history.'[59] MacNeice's travelling persona,
like Kavanagh's, has an eye for spontaneous encounters with the banal. The
seemingly unimportant details of everyday urban life construct for MacNeice
what they represented for Kavanagh in Dublin: that is, the landmarks of a
contemporary urban landscape.

Travel poems such as *Autumn Journal* enabled MacNeice 'to situate himself in a landscape or topography that bespeaks significant social realities.'[60]
In 'Trains to Dublin', he insists on offering the reader not 'any idol or idea /
Creed or king', but instead 'incidental things which pass / Outward through
space exactly as each was':

I give you the disproportion between labour spent

And joy at random; the laughter of the Galway sea

Juggling with spars and bones irresponsibly,

I give you the toy Liffey and the vast gulls,

I give you fuchsia hedges and whitewashed walls.

I give you the smell of Norman stone, the squelch

Of bog beneath your boots, the red bog-grass,

The vivid chequer of the Antrim hills, the trough of dark

Golden water for the cart-horses, the brass

Belt of serene sun upon the lough.

58   MacNeice, *Collected Poems* 53.
59   Terence Brown, 'Louis MacNeice's Ireland', in Terence Brown and Nicholas
     Grene, eds, *Tradition and Influence in Anglo-Irish Poetry* (Hampshire: MacMillan,
     1989), 83.
60   Brown, 'What Am I Doing Here? MacNeice and Travel', 81.

Louis MacNeice's North 205

And I give you the faces, not the permanent masks,

But the faces balanced in the toppling wave -

His glint of joy in cunning as the farmer asks

Twenty per cent too much, or a girl's, forgetting to be suave,

A tiro choosing stuffs, preferring mauve.[61]

The kinetic energy of the moving train runs through the poet's mobile gaze from Galway sea to Antrim hills, rebuilding a scenery of organic and inorganic phenomena, as in the line 'the fuchsia hedges and white-washed walls'. The relentless rhythm takes the poet on a journey, not only through space but also through time, bringing together past, present and future at a glance. Counting the buttons on the seat, the persona observes the scenery while moving back and forth between past and future sights. Furthermore, MacNeice's invocation of place happens through a mixture of visual, olfactory, tactile and auditory senses, as the following line indicates: 'the smell of Norman stone, the squelch / Of bog beneath your boots, the red bog-grass.'[62]

According to Brown, the *oeuvre* of travel writing suggests that 'for MacNeice, life is experienced as if by a traveller who suffers the wearing ennui of belonging nowhere'.[63] Later poems 'report on a variety of such frames until journeying itself becomes an alienating condition of being'.[64] As the novelty of visiting new places wears off, journeying reinforces a perpetual state of inbetweenness, of departing from a place but never arriving at a new destination, of the tediousness of the trip itself. The constant movement of the wiper, 'clearing, blurring, clearing'[65] and the monotony of the road ahead exemplify the ennui of modern life, of belonging nowhere, of wandering from place to place, as 'trains carry us about'.[66] In the end, places turn into topographical frames, the multiplicity of which point to

---

61   MacNeice, 'Trains to Dublin', *Collected Poems* 28.
62   MacNeice, 'Trains to Dublin', 28.
63   Brown, 'What Am I Doing Here? MacNeice and Travel', 82.
64   Brown, 'What Am I Doing Here? MacNeice and Travel', 83.
65   MacNeice, 'The Wiper', *Collected Poems* 505.
66   MacNeice, 'Trains to Dublin', 27.

the multiplicity of experience, of plurality and mutability. Eventually, constant travelling exhausts the possibility of encountering new places; hence, the travel mode becomes 'a metonymy of a restless, *déraciné* modernity (mobile but futile)',[67] representing more than ever the elusive question of identity in modern Ireland, North and South.

---

67   Brown, 'What Am I Doing Here? MacNeice and Travel', 83.

Conclusion

The study of place and place attachments has been a staple subject of enquiry in the field of Irish Studies, which ever since the emergence of an Irish ecocritical scholarship in the early 2000s has acquired a new depth. Whereas earlier works focused on historical, geographical or socio-political considerations of place and identity, recent publications have integrated an environmental dimension that connects literary analyses to wider cultural and global concerns such as deforestation, urban sprawl, immigration, climate change and so on. Building on the existing scholarship, the present study offered readings from modern Irish verse in the light of Ireland's natural and cultural landscapes. Simply put, *From Landscapes to Cityscapes* should be viewed as a minor ecocritical exercise in the field of Irish Studies, hoping to inspire new perspectives that arise out of an environmental scrutiny of the same old questions of place and identity in Irish literature.

Each chapter addressed a different aspect of the human-environment relationship through an analysis of a variety of narratives that represent or deal with a certain type of environment, from the wilderness to the country to the city. While also considering examples from earlier Irish literary history, the period under investigation started with *fin de siècle* Ireland, when an emphasis on authenticity and returning to the so-called native values of the past was on top of Ireland's literary and political agenda up to the 1960s, when the enduring presence of an idealistic interpretation of Irishness – described by J. J. Lee as a 'supreme imaginative achievement' – began 'to dissolve'.[1] Perhaps the term that best describes this period is 'change'; the partition of Ireland, the foundation of the Free State and later on the official independence of the Republic transformed not only the political fate of the island but also revolutionized its economy and social system. The

---

1   John Joseph Lee (1989, 648); cited Brian Graham, *Ireland and Irishness: Place, Culture and Identity* (London: Routledge, 2002).

ongoing emigration and poverty resulted in the constant depopulation of Ireland. Industrialization and urbanization were other influential factors in the literary and political narratives. Last, but not least, the formation, summit and gradual decline of the Irish Literary Revival was contemporaneous with these changes.

The Irish sense of place, as promoted during the Revival, was synonymous with the idea of a homogenous national identity based on a secure and stable relationship with place, while place was often interpreted in terms of an idealized rural landscape west of Shannon. Initially developed as a counterpart to the hostile British stereotyping, the Revival's version of Irishness turned into a metanarrative of identity which neglected the nature of difference and heterogeneity on the island of Ireland. The emphasis on creating a unified sense of place – hence a unified sense of identity – created a sterile version of an imagined space; in other words, a *heterotopia* that hovered between the two extreme poles of illusion and compensation. What the Irish Literary Revival had created was a potent mindscape, a cultural image disconnected from the physical landscape it was meant to represent. As such, it relied on attachment to stories about place rather than the place itself, hence replacing *genius loci* with *genius fabulae*. The various examples of environmental neglect in Ireland, including the construction of the M3 Motorway near the Valley of Tara or the ongoing Shell to Sea campaign in County Mayo, not to mention the late or unsuccessful implications of EU environmental directives such as sustainable development in Ireland prove that at least in these cases, the Irish sense of place has not been realized in any material way. As Patrick Sheeran pointed out, a sense of place is 'not just a matter of semantics' but 'is first and foremost an experience. It is also the result of pragmatic considerations, of cost benefit analysis, of pure thoughtlessness and greed.'[2]

William Butler Yeats, the most influential figure of the Revival, played an important role in contributing to the narrative construction of place. Yeats's early poetry created an imagined topography where 'nature' merged with 'super-nature'. His invocation of a sense of place in this period reached

---

2   Patrick Sheeran, 'Landscape and Literature', in *Journal of the Galway Archaeological and Historical Society*, 5 (2003), 153.

Conclusion 209

beyond the physical significance of the landscape to deliver a symbolic/eso-
teric connection to the 'authentic' Irish culture before the Conquest. The
middle poems encompassed, however, a more personal and realistic representation that arose out of an acknowledgement of his Anglo-Irish heritage,
embedded in the topography of the area, namely that of the Anglo-Irish
demesne. Reference to the Big House and the cultivated gardens emphasized the Ascendancy's right of belonging to Ireland through building and
cultivating its landscape, which from a Heideggerian perspective translates
into a form of dwelling. Yeats's emphasis on grounding Irishness continued
throughout the length of his prolific career, where the last poems established his constant presence in the landscape through an invocation of a
funerary sense of place, itself a configuration of the earlier place-conscious
tradition of *dinnseanchas*.

For Patrick Kavanagh, a sense of place was first and foremost a matter
of direct engagement with land, in all its beauties and hardships. Kavanagh's
poetry presented the rural landscape as a dwelling rather than a cultural
mindscape dealing with unrealistic images and ideals. From the type of soil
to the seasonal changes that determined the agricultural economy of the
region, Kavanagh's rural portrayals intertwined daily social activities in the
parish with the region's topography. His panoramic views of the landscape
in conjunction with detailed descriptions of the taskscapes – Ingold's terminology for the activities that take place in a given region – presented
an environment that, despite its relative social stasis in comparison with
the city, remained in constant flow, a reminder of the complex interplay
of place and identity in the countryside.

The insider's perspective, exemplified in Kavanagh's parochial aesthetics, points to the necessity of addressing environmental issues and
campaigns from a local perspective. As discussed in Chapter three, the
rural community is both the addresser and addressee of environmental
issues; therefore, an ecological perspective that fails to acknowledge and
prioritize the role of the rural community is destined to fail. Kavanagh's
poetics of dwelling suggests the possibility of developing a degree of environmental awareness through a realization of a sentient and intuitive
understanding of our interconnectedness to the ecology of our region.
In contrast to the rationalistic and dichotomous perception of human

beings as separate from 'nature', a sentient ecology embeds them as organisms-in-their-environment.[3]

This type of ecology is not restricted to the rural landscapes, per se. As the analysis of Kavanagh's urban poetry in Chapter six showed, not only is it possible to develop a sense of place in cities, but an understanding of the urban sphere and its complex network of socio-environmental relations are a prerequisite to developing a comprehensive perception of our surrounding environment. Such a perception embraces rather than rejecting the multiplicity of experiences and identities in the modern world. Kavanagh's appreciation of the parks and the surroundings of the Grand Canal in Dublin reminds us of the possibility of viewing the city in positive terms. Mirroring the dynamic nature of the city, his *flâneuresque* portrayals of Dublin defined Irishness in terms of movement and change. Thus, the under- or misrepresented city, mostly viewed as an antidote to the country, emerged as perhaps the most important landscape in defining a sense of place and identity in modern Ireland.

Patrick Kavanagh's contemporary Louis MacNeice was another influential figure in subverting the metanarrative of Irishness by writing first and foremost of cities. With MacNeice as with Kavanagh, 'nature' found significance beyond its former romanticized appropriation in Irish Celtic Renaissance. Both poets shared a distrust of the earlier narratives and employed an aesthetics that was attuned to the suppressed social reality of their marginalized landscapes. MacNeice's 'uneasy' sense of place was as much about love and attachment as it was about detachment and alienation. His 'Northern' poems disclosed a socio-environmental reality whereby the harsh social life in post-Partition Ulster mirrored the geological harshness of its landscape. Ulster's industrial economy 'grimed' the city – to use MacNeice's own words – with pollution, inequality and poverty. Representations of Belfast and Carrick, in particular, implied the correspondence of marginalized land/cityscapes with marginalized identities. Just as the Northern identity – itself multiple and problematic – was often overlooked or misrepresented in previous narratives, the politically partitioned landscape of Ulster was ecologically prone to deterioration as a

---

3   Tim Ingold, *The Perception of the Environment: Essays on Livelihood, Dwelling and Skill* (London and New York: Routledge, 2000).

Conclusion

result of cultural neglect and political violence. In Cronon's view, the negative or indifferent attitude towards a landscape often justifies its modification and destruction. In this case, the least favourite part of the Irish landscape was highly industrialized or, from a Heideggerian perspective, challenged/manipulated beyond its intrinsic value to render greater economic profit.

The profit, on the other hand, was not shared by the people who laboured in factories, mills and mines but alienated them from their own labour, which in return led to an alienation of the people from the very landscape upon which they relied for procurement. Furthermore, the partitioned landscape implied a state of inbetweenness that MacNeice particularly engaged with on a personal level due to his privileged Protestant upbringing. In fact, the very awareness of his distance as an outsider/traveller emancipated his poetry from the anxiety of representation shared by many of the Revival poets and his contemporaries in Ireland.

Irish poetry has undergone tectonic changes since the 1960s. The new generation of Irish poets, including Seamus Heaney, Paul Muldoon, Michael Longley, Ciaran Carson, Eavan Boland, Eiléan Ní Chuilleanáin and Medbh McGuckian, to name a few, contested the hegemonic understanding of Irishness and raised their voices to speak of the multiplicity of the Irish experience on the island of Ireland. Given the interconnected nature of global emergencies – political, economic and environmental – Irish writers, scholars and researchers have a great task ahead of them, one that asks for a higher level of engagement with the local in the context of the global in other words, a greater degree of environmental commitment.

Perhaps ecocriticism has not lived up to its ambition of joining together the sciences and humanities in the hope of solving our planet's ecological crises; yet, one cannot overlook the greater environmental interest that it has inspired, especially in literary and cultural studies. On the other hand, when it comes to implementing environmental laws, scientists and policymakers have become more receptive to considering the voice of local populations. Nevertheless, there is still a long path ahead. While the more scientifically - oriented disciplines, including urban studies and ecology, can benefit from the interdisciplinary interaction with literary scholarship, this interdisciplinarity can help rescue literary studies and ecocriticism from their insular position as academic, textual fields.

Bibliography

Aalen, Fredrick, 'Imprint of the Past', in Desmond Gillmor, ed., *The Irish Countryside: Landscape, Wildlife, History, People* (New York: Barnes and Noble, 1989).

'Annual Review and Outlook for Agriculture, Food and the Marine 2019', Department of Agriculture, Food, and the Marine, Forest Statistics, 41, <https://assets.gov.ie/97198/bed066d2-194c-4645-81cd-8e7ba2a3448e.pdf>, accessed 28 December 2022.

Arendt, Hannah, 'Introduction: Walter Benjamin 1892–1940', in Walter Benjamin, *Illuminations* (New York: Schocken, 1967).

Baker, Susan, 'The Evolution of the Irish Ecology Movement', in Wolfgang Rudig, ed., *Green Politics One* (Edinburgh: Edinburgh University Press, 1990).

Banim, John, *The Anglo-Irish of the Nineteenth Century: A Novel* (London: Henry Colburn, 1828).

Barnes, Trevor J. and James S. Duncan, eds, *Writing Worlds: Discourse, Text and Metaphor in the Representation of Landscape* (London: Routledge, 1992).

Barry, John and Pat Doran, 'Environmental Movements in Ireland: North and South', in John McDonagh et al., eds, *A Living Countryside? The Politics of Sustainable Development in Rural Ireland* (Surrey: Ashgate).

Baudelaire, Charles, *Les Fleurs du Mal* (Paris: Gallimard, 1996).

_____, *The Painter of Modern Life and Other Essays* (London: Phaidon, 1995).

_____, *Petits Poèmes en Prose* (*Le Spleen de Paris*) (Paris: Garnier Flammarion, 1967).

Behrendt, Stephen C., *British Women Poets and the Romantic Writing Community* (Baltimore: Johns Hopkins University Press, 2009).

Benjamin, Walter, *The Arcades Project* (Cambridge, MA: Belknap Press of Harvard University Press, 1999).

_____, *Charles Baudelaire: A Lyric Poet in the Era of High Capitalism* (London: Verso, 1983).

_____, *Illuminations* (New York: Schocken, 1967).

Beckett, James Camlin, *The Anglo-Irish Tradition* (London: Faber and Faber, 1976).

Bennet, Michael, 'From Wide Open Spaces to Metropolitan Places: The Urban Challenge to Ecocriticism', *Interdisciplinary Studies in Literature and Environment*, 8/1 (2001), 31-52

214   *Bibliography*

Bennett, Michael and David Warfield Teague, eds, *The Nature of Cities: Ecocriticism and Urban Environments* (Arizona: The University of Arizona Press, 1999).

Bookchin, Murray, *Urbanization without Cities: The Rise and Decline of Citizenship* (New York: Black Rose, 1992).

Brearton, Fran and Edna Longley, eds, *Incorrigibly Plural: Louis MacNeice and His Legacy* (Manchester: Carcanet, 2012).

'Brief History of Coole Park', *An Roinn*, Department of Agriculture, Fisheries and Food, <http://coolepark.ie/location/index.html>, accessed 14 January 2013.

Brihault, Jean, 'Lady Morgan: Deep Furrows', in Jacqueline Genet, ed., *Rural Ireland, Real Ireland?* (Buckinghamshire: Colin Smythe, 1996), 71.

Brown, Terence, *The Literature of Ireland: Criticism and Culture* (Cambridge: Cambridge University Press, 2010), 22.

———, 'Louis MacNeice's Ireland', in Terence Brown and Nicholas Grene, eds, *Tradition and Influence in Anglo-Irish Poetry* (Hampshire: MacMillan, 1989).

——— and Nicholas Grene, eds, *Tradition and Influence in Anglo-Irish Poetry* (Hampshire: MacMillan, 1989).

———, 'What Am I Doing Here? MacNeice and Travel', in Fran Brearton and Edna Longley, eds, *Incorrigibly Plural: Louis MacNeice and His Legacy* (Manchester: Carcanet, 2012).

Buell, Lawrence, *The Environmental Imagination: Thoreau, Nature Writing, and the Formation of American Culture* (London: Belknap, 1996).

Burton, Richard D. E., *The Flâneur and His City: Patterns of Daily Life in Paris 1815–1851* (Durham: University of Durham, 1994).

Buttimer, Anne and Luke Wallin, eds, *Nature and Identity in Cross-Cultural Perspective* (The Netherlands: Kluwer Academic Publishers, 1999).

Byrd, Thomas L., *The Early Poetry of W. B. Yeats: The Poetic Quest* (New York: Kennikat Press, 1978).

Cambrensis, Giraldus, *The Topography of Ireland* (Cambridge: In parentheses, 2000).

Carlaw, Darren, *The Flâneur as Foreigner: Ethnicity, Sexuality and Power in Twentieth Century New York Writing* (Newcastle University Library: Doctoral Thesis, 2008).

Carleton, William, *The Black Prophet* (Shannon: Irish University Press, 1972).

———, *The Ned M'Keown Stories* (Frankfurt am Main: Outlook Verlag GmbH, 2018).

———, *Tales and Sketches Illustrating the Character of the Irish Peasantry* (New York: Garland, 1980).

———, *Traits and Stories of the Irish Peasantry*, 3rd edn (Dublin: William Fredrick Walkman, 1843).

Bibliography

Cawley, Mary, 'Rural People and Services', in Desmond Gillmor, ed., *The Irish Countryside: Landscape, Wildlife, History, People* (New York: Barnes and Noble Books, 1989), 197–225.

Clark, Timothy, *The Cambridge Introduction to Literature and the Environment* (Cambridge: Cambridge University Press, 2011).

Cloke, Paul and Owain Jones, 'Dwelling, Place, and Landscape: An Orchard in Somerset', *Environment and Planning A: Economy and Space*, 33/4 (2011), 649–66.

Connolly, Claire, *A Cultural History of the Irish Novel, 1790–1829* (Cambridge: Cambridge University Press, 2011).

———, 'Irish Romanticism, 1800–1830', in Margaret Kelleher and Philip O'Leary, eds, *The Cambridge History of Irish Literature* (Cambridge: Cambridge University Press, 2006), 407–48.

Crane, Hart, *The Complete Poems of Hart Crane* (New York: Liveright Publishing, 1958).

Cronon, William, 'A Place for Stories: Nature, History, and Narrative', in Anne Buttimer and Luke Wallin, eds, *Nature and Identity in Cross-Cultural Perspectives* (Dordrecht: Kluwer Academic Publishers, 1999), 201–34.

———, 'The Trouble with Wilderness: Or, Getting Back to the Wrong Nature', *Environmental History*, 1/1 (1996), 7–28.

Crozier, Maurna, ed., *Cultural Tradition in Northern Ireland* (Belfast: Institute of Irish Studies, 1989).

Corcoran, Neil, 'The Same Again? MacNeice's Repetitions', in Fran Brearton and Edna Longley, eds, *Incorrigibly Plural: Louis MacNeice and His Legacy* (Manchester: Carcanet, 2012), 257–73.

Cunningham, Valentine, *British Writers in the Thirties* (Oxford: Oxford University Press, 1988).

Cusick, Christine, ed., *Out of the Earth: Ecocritical Readings of Irish Texts* (Cork: Cork University Press, 2010).

Dauksta, Dainis, 'Landscape Painting and the Forest – The Influence of Cultural Factors in the Depiction of Trees and Forests', in Eva Ritter and Dainis Dauksta, eds, *New Perspectives on People and Forests* (Dordrecht: Springer, 2011), 119–38.

Dawe, Gerald and John Wilson Foster, eds, *The Poet's Place: Ulster Literature and Society* (Belfast: Institute of Irish Studies, 1991).

Devall, Bill and George Sessions, *Deep Ecology: Living as if Nature Mattered* (Salt Lake City: Peregrine Smith, 1985).

Duff, David, ed., *The Oxford Handbook of British Romanticism* (Oxford: Oxford University Press, 2018).

Duffy, Charles Gavan, *Conversations with Carlyle* (London: Forgotten Books, 2013).

Duffy, Patrick J., 'Writing Ireland: Literature and Art in the Representation of Irish Place', in Brain Graham, ed., *In Search of Ireland: A Cultural Geography* (London: Routledge, 1997), 64–84.

Eagleton, Terry, *The Ideology of the Aesthetic* (Oxford: Blackwell, 1990).

Edgeworth, Maria, *Castle Rackrent* (Auckland: The Floating Press, 2010).

Ellmann, *Identity of Yeats* (London: Macmillan, 1954).

'The European Environment – State and Outlook 2010: Synthesis', *European Environment Agency*, <https://www.eea.europa.eu/soer/2010/synthesis/synthesis>, accessed 18/05/2013.

Evernden, Neil, 'Beyond Ecology: Self, Place, and Pathetic Fallacy', in Cheryll Glotfelty and Harold Fromm, eds, *The Ecocriticism Reader: Landmarks in Literary Ecology* (Athens: University of Georgia Press, 1996), 92–104.

Felton, Robert Todd, *A Journey into Ireland's Literary Revival* (Sydney: ReadHowYouWant, 2007).

Ferguson, Priscilla Parkhurst, 'The *Flâneur* on and off the Streets of Paris', in Keith Tester, ed., *The Flâneur* (London: Routledge, 1994), 22–43.

Flower, Robin, *The Irish Tradition* (Oxford: Clarendon Press,1966).

Flynn, Brendan, 'Environmental Lessons for Rural Ireland from the European Union: How Great Expectations in Brussels get Dashed in Bangor and Belmullet', in John McDonagh et al., eds, *A Living Countryside? The Politics of Sustainable Development in Rural Ireland* (Farnham: Ashgate, 2009), 53–68.

Flynn, Leonita, 'On MacNeice on Trains', in Fran Brearton and Edna Longley, eds, *Incorrigibly Plural: Louis MacNeice and His Legacy* (Manchester: Carcanet, 2012).

Fierobe, Claude, 'The Peasantry in the Irish Novels of Maria Edgeworth', in Jacqueline Genet, ed., *Rural Ireland, Real Ireland?* (Buckinghamshire: Colin Smythe, 1996), 59–70.

'Forest Statistics Ireland 2022', <https://www.gov.ie/en/collection/15b56-forest-statistics-and-mapping/#annual-forest-sector-statistics>, accessed 28 December 2022.

'Forest Statistics Ireland 2020', <https://www.teagasc.ie/media/website/crops/forestry/advice/Forest-Statistics-Ireland-2020.pdf>, accessed 28 December 2022.

Foster, John Wilson, 'Encountering Traditions', in John Wilson Foster and Helena C. Chesney, eds, *Nature in Ireland: A Scientific and Cultural History* (Dublin: The Lilliput Press, 1997), 23–70.

Foster, John Wilson and Helena C. Chesney, eds, *Nature in Ireland: A Scientific and Cultural History* (Dublin: The Lilliput Press, 1997).

Foster, Robert Fitzroy, 'Varieties of Irishness', in Maurna Crozier, ed., *Cultural Tradition in Northern Ireland* (Belfast: Institute of Irish Studies, 1989).

Bibliography

227

_____, *Words Alone: Yeats and His Inheritances* (Oxford: Oxford University Press, 2011).

Foucault, Michel, 'Of Other Spaces: Utopias and Heterotopias', in *Architecture/ Mouvement/Continuité*, 1984, <https://web.mit.edu/allanmc/www/foucaultı.pdf>, accessed 1 April 2023.

Frawley, Oona, *Irish Pastoral: Nostalgia and Twentieth-Century Irish Literature* (London: Irish Academic Press, 2005).

_____, 'Kavanagh and the Irish Pastoral Tradition', in Stan Smith, ed., *Patrick Kavanagh* (Dublin: Irish Academic Press, 2009), 92.

'Forest Resources Assessment Working Paper', *FRA 2015 – Terms and Definitions*, <https://www.fao.org/3/ap862e/ap862e.pdf>, accessed 12 January 2023.

Garrard, Greg, *Ecocriticism* (New York: Routledge, 2004).

Genet, Jacqueline, *Rural Ireland, Real Ireland?* (Buckinghamshire: Colin Smythe, 1996).

_____, 'Yeats and the Myth of Rural Ireland', in Jacqueline Genet, ed., *Rural Ireland, Real Ireland?* (Buckinghamshire: Colin Smythe, 1996), 139–58.

Gibson, Walter S., *Bruegel* (London: Thames and Hudson, 1977).

Gibbons, Luke, '"Where Wolf Tone's Statue Was Not": Joyce, Monuments and Memory', in Ian McBride, ed., *History and Memory in Modern Ireland* (Cambridge: Cambridge University Press, 2001), 139–59.

Gillmor, Desmond, ed., *The Irish Countryside: Landscape, Wildlife, History, People* (New York: Barnes and Noble, 1989).

_____, 'Land, Work and Recreation', in Desmond Gillmor, ed., *The Irish Countryside: Landscape, Wildlife, History, People* (New York: Barnes and Noble, 1989), 161–96.

Gilloch, Graeme, *Myth and Metropolis: Walter Benjamin and the City* (Oxford: Polity, 1997).

Glacken, Clarence, 'Reflections on the History of Western Attitudes to Nature', in Anne Buttimer and Luke Wallin, eds, *Nature and Identity in Cross-Cultural Perspectives* (Dordrecht: Kluwer Academic Publishers, 1999), 1–18.

Glancy, Ruth, *Thematic Guide to British Poetry* (Connecticut: Greenwood Press, 2002).

Glotfelty, Cheryll and Harold Fromm, eds, *The Ecocriticism Reader: Landmarks in Literary Ecology* (Athens: University of Georgia Press, 1996).

Graham, Brian, 'Ireland and Irishness: Place, Culture and Identity', in Brian Graham, ed., *In Search of Ireland* (London: Routledge, 1997), 1–16.

_____, *In Search of Ireland* (London: Routledge, 1997).

_____, *Ireland and Irishness: Place, Culture and Identity* (London: Routledge, 2002).

218   *Bibliography*

Graham, Colin, *Deconstructing Ireland: Identity, Theory, Culture* (Edinburgh: Edinburgh University Press, 2001).

Green, Miranda, *Animals in Celtic Life and Myth* (London: Routledge, 1992).

Gregory, Augusta, *Coole* (Dublin: The Cuala Press, 1931).

Griffin, Carl J., 'Space and Place – Popular Perceptions of Forests', in Eva Ritter & Dainis Dauksta, eds, *New Perspectives on People and Forests* (Dordrecht: Springer, 2011), 139–58.

Guignon, Charles B., ed., *The Cambridge Companion to Heidegger* (Cambridge: Cambridge University Press, 1999).

Gwynn, Edward John, *The Metrical Dindshenchas* (Dublin: Hodges, Figgis, and Co.; London: William and Noegate, 1924), <http://archive.org/stream/met ricaldindsenc04royauoft/metricaldindsenc04royauoft_djvu.txt>, accessed 12 April 2013.

Gwynn, Stephen, *Experiences of a Literary Man* (London: Butterworth, 1926).

―――, *Irish Books and Irish People* (Dublin: Talbot Press, 1919).

Haar, Michel, *The Song of the Earth: Heidegger and the Grounds of the History of Being* (Bloomington: Indiana University Press, 1993).

Harmon, Maurice, ed., *The Irish Writer and the City* (Gerrards Cross: Colin Smythe, 1984).

Harris, Daniel A., *Yeats: Coole Park and Ballylee* (Baltimore: John Hopkins University Press, 1974).

Heaney, Seamus, 'The Placeless Heaven: Another Look at Kavanagh', *The Massachusetts Review*, 28/3 (1987), 371–80.

―――, *Preoccupations: Selected Prose, 1968–1978* (New York: Farrar, Straus, and Giroux, 1989).

Heidegger, Martin, *Basic Writings*. Rev. and expanded edn, ed. David F. Krell (London: Routledge, 1993).

―――, *Poetry, Language, Thought* (New York: Harper & Row, 1975).

Herron, Thomas, '"Goodly Woods": Irish Forests, Georgic Trees in Books 1 and 4 of Edmund Spenser's *Faerie Queene*', *Quidditas: Journal of the Rocky Mountain Medieval and Renaissance Association*, 19 (1998), 97–122, <https://scholarsarch ive.byu.edu/cgi/viewcontent.cgi?article=1288&context=rmmra>, accessed 21 March 2023.

Hirsch, Edward, 'The Imaginary Irish Peasant', *PMLA*, 106/5 (1991), 116–133.

'History of Forestry in Ireland', Forest Service Department of Agriculture, Fisheries and Food, 2008, <https://www.agriculture.gov.ie/media/migration/forestry/ forestservicegeneralinformation/abouttheforestservice/IrishForestryAbriefhi story200810.pdf>, accessed 23 June 2013.

Bibliography

Holliday, Shawn, 'Patrick Kavanagh (1904–1967)', in Alexander G. Gonzalez, ed., *Modern Irish Writers: A Biocritical Source Book* (Westport: Greenwood Press, 1997), 138–43.

Ingold, Tim, *The Perception of the Environment: Essays on Livelihood, Dwelling and Skill* (London: Routledge, 2010).

'Ireland's Environment: An Integrated Assessment 2020', *Environmental Protection Agency*, <https://www.epa.ie/our-services/monitoring--assessment/assessment/irelands-environment/state-of-environment-report-/>, accessed 23 June 2022.

'Ireland's Environment – An Assessment, 2016', *Environmental Protection Agency*, <https://epawebapp.epa.ie/ebooks/soe2016/files/assets/basic-html/page-1.html#>, accessed 2 February 2018.

'Ireland's Forests – Statistics 2020', <https://www.teagasc.ie/media/website/crops/fores try/advice/Forest-Statistics-Ireland-2020.pdf>, accessed 28 December 2022.

'Ireland's Lost Glory', *Birds and All Nature*, 7/4 (1900).

'Ireland's National Inventory Report', *Environmental Protection Agency*, 2022, <https://www.epa.ie/publications/monitoring--assessment/climate-change/air-emissions/Ireland-NIR-2022_%Merge_v2..pdf>, accessed 27 December 2022.

'Irish Forests – Annual Statistics 2019', <https://www.teagasc.ie/media/webs ite/crops/forestry/advice/Forest-Statistics-Ireland-2022.pdf>, accessed 28 December 2022.

Jackson, John Brinckerhoff, *A Sense of Place, A Sense of Time* (New Haven: Yale University Press, 1994).

Jackson, Roy, 'Overcoming Physicophobia – Forests as Sacred Source of Our Human Origins', in Eva Ritter and Dainis Dauksta, eds, *New Perspectives on People and Forests* (Dordrecht: Springer, 2011), 29–40.

Jeffares, Alexander Norman, *A Commentary on the Collected Poems of W. B. Yeats* (London: Macmillan, 1968).

Owain Jones, 'Materiality and Identity – Forests, Trees and Senses of Belonging', in Eva Ritter and Dainis Dauksta, eds, *New Perspectives on People and Forests* (Dordrecht: Springer, 2011), 159–78.

Kavanagh, Patrick, 'Appendix A: Author's Note to Collected Poems (1964)', in *Collected Poems* (London: Penguin Books, 2005).

———, *Collected Poems* (London: Penguin Books, 2005).

———, *Come Dance with Kitty Stobling and Other Poems* (London: Longmans, 1960).

———, *The Green Fool* (London: Penguin Books, 2001).

———, 'The Paddiad', in *Collected Poems* (London: Penguin Books, 2005).

———, 'Ploughman', in *Collected Poems* (London: Penguin Books, 2005).

———, *A Poet's Country, Selected Prose*, ed. Antoinette Quinn (London: Penguin Books, 2003).

_____, *Tarry Flynn* (London: Penguin Books, 1978).

Kelleher, Margaret, 'Famine and Ecology, 1750–1900', in Malcolm Sen, ed., *A History of Irish Literature and the Environment* (Cambridge: Cambridge University Press, 2022).

_____ and Philip O'Leary, eds, *The Cambridge History of Irish Literature* (Cambridge: Cambridge University Press, 2006).

Kelly, Jim, 'Ireland and Union', in David Duff, ed., *The Oxford Handbook of British Romanticism* (Oxford: Oxford University Press, 2018), 137–56.

Kelly, Mary et al., *Cultural Sources of Support Upon Which Environmental Attitudes Draw: Second Report of National Survey Data*, 52, <www.ucd.ie/environ/repo rts/envirattitudessecondrept.pdf#search='environmental%20attitudes%20 in%20Ireland>, accessed 6 April 2013.

Kennedy-Andrews, Elmer, *Writing Home: Poetry and Place in Northern Ireland, 1968–2008* (Cambridge: D.S. Brewer, 2008).

Kennedy-O'Neill, Joy, 'Sympathy between Man and Nature: Landscape and Loss in Synge's Riders to the Sea', in Christine Cusick, ed., *Out of the Earth: Ecocritical Readings of Irish Texts* (Cork: Cork University Press, 2010), 36–49.

Kiberd, Declan, *Inventing Ireland: The Literature of the Modern Nation* (London: Vintage, 1995).

Kinsella, Thomas, 'The Irish Writer', in Thomas Kinsella and William Butler Yeats, eds, *Davis, Mangan, Ferguson? Tradition and the Irish Writer* (Dublin: Dolmen Press, 1967).

_____, *The New Oxford Book of Irish Verse* (Oxford: Oxford University Press, 1989).

_____ and William Butler Yeats, eds, *Davis, Mangan, Ferguson? Tradition and the Irish Writer* (Dublin: Dolmen Press, 1967).

Kosok, Heinz, 'The Image of Dublin in Anglo-Irish Drama', in Maurice Harmon, ed., *The Irish Writer and the City* (Gerrards Cross: Colin Smythe, 1984), 18–36.

Lacroix, Auguste, *Le flâneur*, in *la collection électronique de la Médiathèque André Malraux de Lisieux* (1841), <www.bmlisieux.com/curiosa/lacroi01.htm>, accessed 17 January 2014.

Larousse, Pierre, *Grand Dictionnaire Universel du XIXᵉ Siècle* (Paris: Administration du Grand Dictionnaire Universel, 1866), <http://gallica.bnf.fr/ark:/12148/ bpt6k205356p/f6.image>, accessed 17 February 2012.

Leerssen, Joseph Theodoor, *Remembrance and Imagination: Patterns in the Historical and Literary Representation of Ireland in the Nineteenth Century* (Indiana: University of Notre Dame Press, 1997).

Le Fanu, Joseph Sheridan, *The Cock and Anchor: Being a Chronicle of Old Dublin City* (London: Downey, 1896).

Lefebvre, Henri, *The Production of Space* (Cambridge, MA: Blackwell, 1991).

Bibliography

Leonard, Liam, *Green Nation: The Irish Environmental Movement from Carnsore Point to the Rossport Five* (Dundalk: Choice Publishing, 2006).

Leopold, Aldo, *A Sand County Almanac* (New York: Oxford University Press, 1949).

Longley, Edna, 'The Writer and Belfast', in Maurice Harmon, ed., *The Irish Writer and the City* (Buckinghamshire: Colin Smythe, 1984), 65–89.

Longley, Michael, *Louis MacNeice: A Study* (London: Faber and Faber, 1988).

Lyons, Francis Stewart Leland, *Culture and Anarchy in Ireland 1890–1939* (Oxford: Oxford University Press, 1979).

Lyotard, Jean-François, *The Inhuman: Reflections on Time* (Cambridge: Polity Press, 1991).

McDonagh, John et al., eds, *A Living Countryside? The Politics of Sustainable Development in Rural Ireland* (Surrey: Ashgate, 2009).

————, 'The Great Pyramids of Carlingford Lough: John Hinde and the De Valerian Utopia', in Alison O'Malley-Younger and Frank Beardow, eds, *Representing Ireland: Past, Present and Future* (Sunderland: University of Sunderland Press, 2005), 37–46.

MacNeice, Louis, 'Birmingham', in *The Collected Poems of Louis MacNeice* (London: Faber and Faber, 1966).

————, *The Collected Poems of Louis MacNeice* (London: Faber and Faber, 1966).

————, 'Note to Autumn Journal', in Eric Robertson Dodds, ed., *The Collected Poems of Louis MacNeice* (London: Faber and Faber, 1966).

————, *Out of the Picture* (London: Faber and Faber, 1937).

————, *Zoo* (London: Michael Joseph, 1938).

Maignant, Catherine, 'Rural Ireland in the Nineteenth Century and the Advent of the Modern World', in Genet, *Rural Ireland, Real Ireland?* (Buckinghamshire: Colin Smythe, 1996), 21–9.

McAreavey, Ruth et al., 'Conflicts to Consensus: Contested Notions of Sustainable Rural Tourism on the Island of Ireland', in John McDonagh et al., eds, *A Living Countryside? The Politics of Sustainable Development in Rural Ireland* (Surrey: Ashgate, 2009), 219–36.

McBride, Ian, ed., *History and Memory in Modern Ireland* (Cambridge: Cambridge University Press, 2001).

McElroy, James, 'Ecocriticism and Irish Poetry: A Preliminary Outline', *Estudios Irlandeses*, 6 (2011), 54–69.

McFadden, Roy, 'Review of *Collected Poems* by Louis MacNeice and *The Edge of Being* by Stephen Spender', *Rann*, 7 (Winter 1949–1950).

Martin, Thomas Augustine, 'Novelist and City: The Technical Challenge', in Maurice Harmon, ed., *The Irish Writer and the City* (Buckinghamshire: Colin Smythe, 1984), 37–51.

Marx, Karl and Fredrich Engels, *The Communist Manifesto* (Oxford: Oxford University Press, 1997 [1848]).

Maturin, Charles, *Women; or, Pour et Contre. A Tale* (Edinburgh: James Ballantyne, 1818).

Meir, Colin, *The Ballads and Songs of W. B. Yeats: The Anglo-Irish Heritage in Subject and Style* (London: Macmillan, 1979).

Mercier, Vivian, 'Literature in English, 1921–84', in Jacqueline R. Hill, ed., *A New History of Ireland, VII: Ireland 1921–1984* (Oxford: Oxford University Press, 2003), 487–537.

Mitchell, Fraser J. G., 'The Dynamics of Irish Post-Glacial Forests', in J. R. Pilcher and S. S. Mac an T-Saoir, eds, *Wood, Trees and Forests* (Dublin: Royal Irish Academy, 1995), 13–22.

Montague, John, *The Figure in the Case and Other Essays* (New York: Syracuse University Press, 1989).

Moynahan, Julian, 'The Image of the City in Nineteenth Century Irish Fiction', in Maurice Harmon, ed., *The Irish Writer and the City* (Buckinghamshire: Colin Smythe, 1984), 1–17.

Mulligan, Amy C., 'Landscape and Literature in Medieval Ireland', in Malcolm Sen, ed., *A History of Irish Literature and the Environment* (Cambridge: Cambridge University Press, 2022), 33–51.

Naess, Arne, 'Intuition, Intrinsic Value and Deep Ecology', *The Ecologist*, 14/5–6 (1973), 201–3.

'National Forest Inventory 2022', <https://www.gov.ie/en/collection/15b56-forest-statistics-and-mapping/#annual-forest-sector-statistics>, accessed 28 December 2022.

'Nature and Wildlife', *An Roinn*, Department of Agriculture, Fisheries and Food, <http://coolepark.ie/location/index.html>, accessed 14 January 2013.

Neeson, Eoin, 'Woodland in History and Culture', in John Wilson Foster and Helena C. Chesney, eds, *Nature in Ireland: A Scientific and Cultural History* (Dublin: Lilliput Press, 1997), 133–56.

Norberg-Schulz, Christian, *Genius Loci: Towards a Phenomenology of Architecture* (New York: Rizzoli, 1980).

Nordin, Irene Gilsenan, 'The Place of Writing in the Poetry of W. B. Yeats and Patrick Kavanagh', *Nordic Journal of English Studies*, 2 (2014), 43–56.

Norris, Trevor, 'Martin Heidegger, D. H. Lawrence, and Poetic Attention to Being', in Axel Goodbody and Katherine E. Rigby, eds, *Ecocritical Theory: New European Approaches* (Charlottesville: University of Virginia Press, 2011), 113–25.

Norton, Brian, *Toward Unity Among Environmentalists* (New York: Oxford University Press, 1991).

Bibliography

Ó Fathartaigh, Mícheál, *Developing Rural Ireland: A History of the Irish Agricultural Advisory Services* (Dublin: Wordwell Books, 2022).

O'Brien, Conor Cruise, ed., *The Shaping of Modern Ireland* (Toronto: University of Toronto Press, 1960).

O'Dowd, Anne, 'Folklife and Folk Traditions', in Desmond Gillmor, ed., *The Irish Countryside: Landscape, Wildlife, History, People* (New York: Barnes and Noble Books, 1989), 121–60.

O'Hanlon, Richard, 'Forestry in Ireland: The Reforestation of a Deforested Country', *The Forestry Source*, 17/6–7 (2012), <http://www.rohanlon.org/downloads/O'Hanlon%20Forestry%20Source%20June%202012.pdf>, accessed 17 February 2013.

O'Malley-Younger, Alison and Frank Beardow, eds, *Representing Ireland: Past, Present and Future* (Sunderland: University of Sunderland Press, 2005).

O'Toole, Fintan, *The Lie of the Land: Irish Identities* (London: Verso, 1997).

Otway-Ruthven, Annette Jocelyn, *A History of Medieval Ireland* (London: E. Benn, 1968).

'Our Rural Future: Rural Development Policy 2021–2025', <https://www.gov.ie/en/publication/4c236-our-rural-future-vision-and-policy-context/>, accessed 1 August 2022.

Owenson, Sydney, *Lady Morgan's Memoirs: Autobiography, Diaries and Correspondence*, ed. William Hepworth Dixon (London: William H. Allen, 1862).

————, *O'Donnel: A National Tale* (London: H. Colburn, 1814).

Pierce, Joanna Tapp, '"Nothing can happen Nowhere": Elizabeth Bowen's Figures in Landscape', in Christine Cusick, ed., *Out of the Earth: Ecocritical Readings of Irish Texts* (Cork: Cork University Press, 2010), 50–65.

Pilz, Anna, 'Narratives of Arboreal Landscapes', in Malcolm Sen, ed., *A History of Irish Literature and the Environment* (Cambridge: Cambridge University Press, 2022), 97–114.

Proudfoot, Bruce, 'The Economy of the Irish Rath', *Medieval Archaeology*, 5/1 (1961), 94–122.

'Provisional Woodland Statistics 2022', <https://www.forestresearch.gov.uk/tools-and-resources/statistics/statistics-by-topic/woodland-statistics/#:~:text=Key%20findings,and%209%25%20in%20Northern%20Ireland>, accessed 27 December 2022.

Quinn, Antoinette, *Patrick Kavanagh: A Biography* (Dublin: Gill and Macmillan, 2001).

————, *Patrick Kavanagh: Born-Again Romantic* (Dublin: Gill and Macmillan, 1991).

Reeves-Smyth, Terence, 'The Natural History of Demesnes', in John Wilson Foster and Helena C. G. Chesney, eds, *Nature in Ireland: A Scientific and Cultural History* (Dublin: Lilliput Press, 1997), 549–74.

Ritter, Eva and Dainis Dauksta, eds, *New Perspectives on People and Forests* (Dordrecht: Springer, 2011).

Roberts, Gary, 'London Here and Now: Walking, Street, and Urban Environments in English Poetry from Dunne to Gay', in Michael Bennett and David W. Teague, eds, *The Nature of Cities: Ecocriticism and Urban Environments* (Arizona: University of Arizona Press, 1999), 33–54.

Ross, Andrew, 'The Social Claim on Urban Ecology', in Michael Bennett and David W. Teague, eds, *The Nature of Cities: Ecocriticism and Urban Environments* (Arizona: The University of Arizona Press, 1999), 15–32.

Rowley, Rosemarie, 'Patrick Kavanagh: An Irish Pastoral Poet in the Cit', *Journal of Ecocriticism*, 1/2 (2009), 92–103.

Rudig, Wolfgang, ed., *Green Politics One* (Edinburgh: Edinburgh University Press, 1990).

Sandilands, Catriona, 'Green Things in the Garbage: *Ecocritical Gleaning in Walter Benjamin's Arcades*', in Axel Goodbody and Kate Rigby, eds, *Ecocritical Theory: New European Approaches* (Charlottesville: University of Virginia Press, 2011), 30–42.

Scannell, Yvonne and Sharon Turner, 'A Legal Framework for Sustainable Development in Rural Areas of the Republic of Ireland and Northern Ireland', in John McDonagh et al., eds, *A Living Countryside? The Politics of Sustainable Development in Rural Ireland* (Surrey: Ashgate, 2009), 25–52.

Sessions, George, ed., *Deep Ecology for the Twenty-First Century: Readings on the Philosophy and Practice of the New Environmentalism* (London: Shambhala, 1995).

Sidnell, Michael J., 'The Allegory of Yeats's "The Wanderings of Oisin"', *Colby Library Quarterly*, 15/2 (1979), 137–51.

Sheeran, Patrick, '*Genius Fabulae*: The Irish Sense of Place', *Irish University Review*, 18/2 (1988), 191–206.

———, 'The Narrative Creation of Place: Yeats and West of Ireland Landscapes', in Anne Buttimer and Luke Wallin, eds, *Nature and Identity in Cross-Cultural Perspective* (The Netherlands: Kluwer Academic Publishers, 1999), 287–300.

Sen, Malcolm, 'Introduction', in Malcolm Sen, ed., *A History of Irish Literature and the Environment* (Cambridge: Cambridge University Press, 2022), 1–32.

Shields, Rob, 'Fancy Footwork: Walter Benjamin's Notes on Flânerie', in Keith Tester, ed., *The Flâneur* (London: Routledge, 1994), 61–80.

Spenser, Edmund, *A View of the Present State of Ireland* (Oregon: University of Oregon Press, 1997).

Bibliography

Smith, Stan, ed., *Patrick Kavanagh* (Dublin: Irish Academic Press, 2009).

————, 'Introduction: Important Places, Times', in Stan Smith, ed., *Patrick Kavanagh* (Dublin: Irish Academic Press, 2009), 1–19.

Smyth, Gerry, 'Shite and Sheep: An Ecocritical Perspective on Two Recent Irish Novels', *Irish University Review*, 30/1 (2000), 163–78, <https://www.jstor.org/stable/25517132>, accessed 21 March 2023.

————, *Space and Irish Cultural Imagination* (Hampshire: Palgrave, 2001).

Snyder, Gary, *Practice of the Wild* (San Francisco: North Point Press, 1990).

Squire, Charles, *Celtic Myth and Legend: Poetry and Romance* (London: Gresham Publishing Company, 1905).

Sullivan, Kelly, 'The Ecology of the Irish Big House, 1900–1950', in Malcolm Sen, ed., *A History of Irish Literature and the Environment* (Cambridge: Cambridge University Press, 2022), 173–89.

Tester, Keith, *The Flâneur* (London: Routledge, 1994).

————, 'Introduction', in Keith Tester, ed., *The Flâneur* (London: Routledge, 1994), 1–21.

Tomaney, John, 'Parish and Universe: Patrick Kavanagh's Poetic of the Local', in *Environment and Planning: Society and Space*, 28 (2010), 311–25.

'Tourism and the Environment', *Fáilte Ireland's Environmental Action Plan 2007–2009*, 9, <https://discomap.eea.europa.eu/map/Data/Milieu/OURCOAST_103_IE/OURCOAST_103_IE_Doc6_EnvironmentTourism.pdf>, accessed 1 April 2023.

'Tourism Recovery Plan 2020–2023', prepared by the *Tourism Recovery Taskforce* (2020), <https://www.gov.ie/pdf/?file=https://assets.gov.ie/90006/80801 fc3-a69b-4faf-843b-be9bff4d6a0f.pdf#page=null>, accessed 21 March 2023.

Tovey, Hilary, 'Environmentalism in Ireland: Modernisation and Identity', in Patrick Clancy et al., eds, *Ireland and Poland: Comparative Perspectives* (Dublin: University College Dublin, 1992), 275–87.

————, 'Managing Rural Nature: Regulation, Translation and Governance in the Republic of Ireland and Northern Ireland', in John McDonagh et al., eds, *A Living Countryside? The Politics of Sustainable Development in Rural Ireland* (Surrey: Ashgate, 2009), 107–22.

'UNFCCC Marrakesh Accords', 2001, <https://unfccc.int/resource/docs/cop7/13a01.pdf>, accessed 12 January 2023.

Varley, Tony, 'The Politics of Rural Sustainability', in John McDonagh et al., eds, *A Living Countryside? The Politics of Sustainable Development in Rural Ireland* (Surrey: Ashgate, 2009), 1–24.

————, 'Populism and the Politics of Community Survival in Rural Ireland', in John McDonagh et al., eds, *A Living Countryside? The Politics of Sustainable Development in Rural Ireland* (Surrey: Ashgate, 2009), 341–60.

Wade, Allan, ed., *The Letters of W. B. Yeats* (London: Rupert Hart-Davis, 1954).

Wall, Eamonn, *Writing the Irish West: Ecologies and Traditions* (Indiana: University of Notre Dame Press, 2011).

Watson, George, 'Landscape in Ulster Poetry', in Gerald Dawe and John Wilson Foster, eds, *The Poet's Place: Ulster Literature and Society* (Belfast: Institute of Irish Studies, 1991), 1–15.

Whelan, Kevin, 'Settlement and Society in Eighteenth-Century Ireland', in *The Poet's Place: Ulster Literature and Society* (Belfast: Institute of Irish Studies, 1991), 45–62.

Wenzell, Tim, *Emerald Green: An Ecocritical Study of Irish Literature* (Newcastle upon Tyne: Cambridge Scholars Publishing, 2009).

Williams, Raymond, *The Country and the City* (London: Chatto and Windus, 1973).

_____, *Culture and Society 1780–1950* (Harmondsworth: Penguin, 1961).

_____, *Keywords: A Vocabulary of Culture and Society* (New York: Oxford University Press, 1976).

Witoszek, Nina, 'Ireland: A Funerary Culture', *Studies: An Irish Quarterly Review*, 76/302 (1987).

_____ and Patrick Sheeran, *Talking to the Dead: A Study of Irish Funerary Tradition* (Amsterdam: Editions Rodopi, 1998).

Yeats, William Butler, 'Anashuya and Vijaya', in Peter Allt and Russell K. Alspach, eds, *The Variorum Edition of the Poems of W. B. Yeats* (New York: The Macmillan Company, 1957).

_____, *Autobiographies* (London: MacMillan Press, 1973).

_____, *The Collected Poems of W. B. Yeats* (London: Macmillan, 1967).

_____, *Essays and Introductions* (New York: MacMillan, 1961).

_____, *Explorations* (London: MacMillan, 1962).

_____, 'Fergus and the Druid', in Peter Allt and Russell K. Alspach, eds, *The Variorum Edition of the Poems of W. B. Yeats* (New York: Macmillan, 1966).

_____, 'Introduction', in William Carleton, *Stories from Carleton with an Introduction from W. B. Yeats* (London: Walter Scott; New York: W. J. Gage and Co., 1889).

_____, *Memoirs of W. B. Yeats*; trans. and ed. Denis Donoghue (London: Macmillan, 1972).

_____, 'Municipal Gallery Revisited', in Peter Allt and Russell K. Alspach, eds, *The Variorum Edition of the poems of W. B. Yeats* (New York: Macmillan, 1966).

_____, *Mythologies* (London: MacMillan, 1962).

_____, *Representative Irish Tales* (G.P. Putnam's Sons, 1891).

_____, *Uncollected Prose*, ed. John. P. Frayne and Colton Johnson (London: Macmillan, 1975).

Bibliography

_____, *The Variorum Edition of the Poems of W. B. Yeats*, ed. Peter Allt and Russell K. Alspach (New York: Macmillan, 1966).

_____, *The Wanderings of Oisin*, in Peter Allt and Russell K. Alspach, eds, *The Variorum Edition of the Poems of W. B. Yeats* (New York: The Macmillan Company, 1957).

Zima, Peter V., *Deconstruction and Critical Theory* (London: Continuum, 2002).

Zimmerman, Michael E., 'Heidegger, Buddhism, and Deep Ecology', in Charles B. Guignon, ed., *The Cambridge Companion to Heidegger* (Cambridge: Cambridge University Press, 1999), 240–69.

_____ et al., eds, *Environmental Philosophy: From Animal Rights to Radical Ecology*. 3rd edn (New Jersey: Prentice Hall, 2001).

Index

absentee landlordism 18, 50, 71, 98, 100
Act of Union 18, 41, 49, 51, 72, 95
    post-Union Ireland 42, 147–8
    unionism 98, 99, 229
aesthetics 43, 45, 61, 65, 86, 87, 107, 112,
    168, 179–81, 183, 188, 193, 209, 210
agriculture 18, 21, 24–6, 28, 82–3, 100,
    120–2, 209
    see also farming
alienation 8, 18, 27, 49, 108, 109, 114, 157,
    159, 162, 165, 168, 169, 193, 198–9,
    205, 210, 211
animals 2, 13, 14, 26, 29, 38, 46, 59, 97, 98,
    120, 140, 163, 175
Anglo-Irishness 8, 51, 57, 68–74, 99, 149,
    184, 185, 186, 187, 195
    Anglo-Irish demesne 10, 19, 43–4,
      66–70, 74, 209
    Anglo-Irish heritage 69, 70, 71, 209
    Anglo-Irish tradition 9, 51, 104, 188
    Anglo-Irish writers 50, 52–3, 57,
      61, 200
    Gardens, the (cultivated) 10, 43–5,
      68, 71, 75, 97, 209
    see also Ascendency
an Gorta Mór see Famine, great Irish (the)
Anwesen 15, 28, 29, 159, 172
arcades 151–4, 157, 158, 170, 171, 174
architecture 69, 74, 97, 147, 148, 150,
aristocracy 72, 73, 79, 148, 149
arrivals and departures 16, 17, 57, 161, 163
artificiality 120, 149, 189, 191–4, 197
Ascendency, the (Protestant) 51–2, 58,
    70, 72, 74, 103, 148, 150, 187
    see also Anglo-Irishness

attachment(s) 8–10, 46, 49, 67, 70, 74,
    76, 86, 114, 117, 135, 139, 143, 187,
    201, 208, 210
    place attachments 2–3, 8, 207
authenticity 5, 42, 75, 95, 103, 129,
    141, 207
auto-exoticism 53, 64

badaud, le 155
banality 109, 114, 116, 121, 124–6, 132, 133,
    157, 176, 177, 179, 180, 204
Banim, John 149–50
    Anglo-Irish of the Nineteenth Century,
      The 149
Bards 47, 48, 49, 68, 166, 186
    bardic tradition 9, 32, 35, 41, 44, 56,
      107, 113
    peasant bard, figure of 10, 104, 108,
      111, 129, 164
Baudelaire, Charles 61, 151–2, 155, 156,
    157, 166, 170, 172
    Fleurs du Mal 151
    Painter of Modern Life and Other
      Essays, The 151
Becket, James Camlin 3, 51
Belfast 10, 11, 147, 164, 183–5, 188, 193,
    195, 196–8, 210
belonging, sense of 10, 48–9, 52, 55, 66,
    76, 79, 86, 159, 163, 187, 195, 198,
    200–1, 205, 209
    see also rootedness
Ben Bulben 60, 77, 78–9
Benjamin, Walter 152, 153, 154, 156–7,
    166, 169, 172, 175, 189, 196
    Arcades Project, The 152, 170, 189, 191

230   *Index*

*Charles Baudelaire: A Lyric Poet in
      the Era of High Capitalism* 152
Bestand see standing-reserve
Big House 10, 43–4, 53, 65, 71–2, 97, 209
   see also Anglo-Irish demesne
biocentrism 145
Brehon laws 9, 16, 17, 26, 29
Brexit 22, 82
Bruegel, Pieter 120
   Harvesters, The 120
Building, act of 9, 20, 24, 29–30, 62, 71,
      74, 75, 85, 86–7, 126, 209
   see also dwelling

cahirs (cathairs) 30, 33
capitalism 91, 152, 166, 191, 196, 197,
      199, 202
   see also consumer capitalism
Carleton, William 95, 100–4, 107,
      123, 128
   *Black Prophet, The: A Tale of the Irish
      Famine* 101–2
   Ned M'Keown Stories, The 103
   Parra Sastha 102
   *Tales and Sketches Illustrating
      the Character of the Irish
      Peasantry* 104
   *Traits and Stories of the Irish
      Peasantry* 71, 101, 102
Carrick 140, 194–5, 210
Catholic Emancipation 42, 50, 52, 72, 95,
      99, 147, 148
celibacy 105, 112, 124, 133
Celtic Revival *see* Irish Literary Revival
Celtic Tiger 8, 20, 82, 85, 91
Censorship of the Publication Act,
      1929 163, 165
Christianity 8, 16, 23, 27, 30–2, 34–9, 46,
      56, 60, 95, 106, 123
   Christian scribes 37, 39

   see also catholic emancipation;
      Protestant Ascendency
cities 10–11, 62, 84–5, 91, 110, 116, 133–4,
      146–55, 157–9, 161–4, 166 –76,
      178–81, 183–4, 187, 189, 196–9,
      203, 207, 209–10
cityscapes 2, 5, 7, 11, 117, 137, 147, 149, 151,
      154, 155, 157, 162, 181, 192, 193, 198,
      199, 202, 203, 207, 210
civilizations 14, 25–6, 63, 83, 95, 130, 195
classes (social) 50–1, 69, 92–3, 95, 97,
      110, 131, 148–9, 152, 158, 184
clay 31, 62, 79, 116, 123, 125, 127–9, 132,
      134–5, 173
   see also soil
clearings 15, 192, 197
colonization 7, 16, 19, 23, 24, 27, 34, 83
   colonial period 25, 28, 34, 49
commercialization 58, 90, 157, 201
commodity 157, 174, 187, 189, 191,
      196, 199
   commodification 157, 174, 187,
      192, 203
   see also consumer culture
Commonwealth, the (period) 18
communities 11, 29, 49, 86, 87, 80–90,
      92–4, 96, 109, 118, 129, 201
   land community 29, 55
   rural community 10, 87, 94, 116, 122,
      127, 128, 141, 209
   textual community 70
consumerism 157, 190
   consumer capitalism 152, 166, 196,
      197, 199, 202
   consumer culture 198
Conquest, the (Norman) 9, 16, 17, 23,
      24, 25, 29, 34, 43, 52, 83, 106–6,
      113, 114, 199, 209
Coole 68–9, 70, 72, 76, 77, 137
   Coole House 68, 70, 73, 77, 44
   Coole Park 20, 46, 65, 70, 73

Index

231

countryside, the 10, 18, 20, 42, 61–4, 71, 77, 78, 81–3, 85–7, 88–91, 93–8, 104–7, 109, 110, 111, 113, 114, 115, 116–7, 118–9, 120, 122–3, 124, 127, 129–31, 138, 141, 146, 175, 177, 180, 181, 184, 185, 209
    see also rurality
COVID 19 (pandemic) 22, 82, 85
Crops 83, 117, 119, 121
    crop failure 83, 84
    single crop system 83, 101
cultivation 10, 21, 23, 24, 25, 26, 28, 43, 44, 47, 65, 71, 74, 97, 209
culture(s) 1, 2, 6–7, 8, 9, 13, 14, 16, 23, 27, 28, 43, 52, 86, 88, 95, 96, 97, 102, 105–8, 113, 114, 118, 128–30, 144, 146, 161, 179, 192, 197–8, 200–1, 209
Celtic culture(s) 16, 37
early Irish culture 9, 28, 29, 30

Dasein 115, 192
death 19, 32, 50, 53, 57, 74, 76–9, 84, 95, 101, 115, 121, 123, 133–5
defamiliarization 128, 154, 175, 189
deforestation 2, 7, 13, 14, 17–19, 23, 35, 44, 207
    afforestation 20–1
    reforestation 19–20
desacralization 32, 34, 35
detachment 8, 10, 49, 135, 139, 168, 200, 210
determinism 84, 187
de Valera, Eamon 3, 128
dialectics 191, 192
dichotomies 6, 7, 14, 26, 27, 45, 62, 75, 84, 102, 109, 116, 151, 197, 209
dinnseanchas 46–7, 52, 153, 209
disclosure 28, 68, 114, 118, 190, 192, 193, 197, 210
discrimination 11, 50, 52, 53, 72

disillusionment 133, 163, 164, 165, 168
disinterestedness 151, 155, 169, 171, 195, 196
displacement 11, 49, 53, 54, 156, 159, 187, 188, 195
dispossession 44, 51–2, 57, 58, 59, 148
distance 7, 63, 85, 98, 102, 104, 107, 109, 118, 120, 130, 141, 144, 158, 175, 196, 200, 202, 203, 211
divinity 7, 38, 39
drama (Irish) 147, 149, 161, 183, 184
Dublin 9–11, 50, 51, 69, 71, 83, 104, 110–11, 113, 117, 119, 122, 130, 136, 146–50, 159, 161–7, 108–9, 171, 173–4, 175, 177–81, 183, 184, 189, 195, 196, 198, 204, 210
duns 30, 33
dwelling 9, 18, 29–31, 32–4, 35–7, 39, 44, 54, 56, 58, 59, 62–4, 65–7, 68, 70, 71, 74–7, 79, 87, 96, 111, 114–5, 116, 120, 121, 126, 139, 141, 154, 169, 194, 195, 209
    dwellers 10, 30, 33, 58, 68, 70, 77, 79, 84, 86, 87, 94, 95, 104, 106, 110, 126, 141, 168, 173
    see also poetics of dwelling

ecocriticism 1–2, 5, 14, 27, 44, 54, 62, 143–6, 207, 211
    Irish ecocriticism 1–2, 4, 207
    urban ecocriticism 10, 143
ecojustice 93–4, 144, 199
ecology 2, 116, 137, 140, 141, 143, 145, 146, 209–11
    deep ecology 144, 146
    social ecology 144, 145
economy 22, 28, 81, 82, 85, 87, 91, 94, 197, 199, 207, 209, 210
Edgeworth, Maria 41, 51, 71, 95, 97–9, 100, 103–4, 147
    Absentee, The 98, 147

Castle Rackrent 71, 97, 98, 104
Ormond 98
emigration 19, 50, 81, 95, 96, 112, 208
ennui 11, 188, 190, 205
environment(s) 2, 4, 6–9, 11, 14, 16, 17,
  20, 23–4, 25, 27, 29–33, 35, 36,
  37, 38–9, 41, 42, 43, 47, 60, 74,
  75, 79, 81, 83, 84, 85–7, 90, 91,
  93, 102, 106, 108, 113, 115–21, 123,
  126–7, 131, 133, 135, 138, 140–1,
  143–6, 151, 153–4, 159, 167, 169,
  173, 175, 181, 187, 189, 190, 198–
  200, 207, 209–10
environmental awareness 8, 93,
  140, 209
environmental campaigns 87, 88, 90,
  93, 208, 209
environmental criticism *see*
  ecocriticism
environmental directives 82, 89, 208
environmental discourse 1, 14, 91
environmental ethics 1, 29
environmental issues 10, 89, 91–2,
  94, 209
environmental justice *see* ecojustice
environmental laws 88–9, 93, 211
environmentality 1, 5
Environmental Protection Agency (EPA),
  Ireland 88
esoterism *see* occult, the
estrangement *see* alienation
European Union 20, 82, 89
exile 8, 163, 188
exploitation 6, 9, 14, 19, 23, 24, 26, 27,
  28, 34, 35, 72, 90, 128, 189–90,
  192, 198–9

faeries 45, 46, 52, 57, 58, 63–64, 83
Famine, the Great Irish 19, 72, 83, 95, 97,
  105, 126, 129

famine 2, 19, 52, 53, 83–4, 95, 97,
  101, 127
farming 14, 18, 23–4, 81, 83, 86–7, 90,
  114, 118, 119, 121–3, 128, 131, 136
farm(land)s 20–1, 83, 112, 114, 122,
  132, 133, 136, 137, 139–40, 164,
  176, 180
farmers 10, 17, 19, 20, 21, 89, 90, 102,
  105, 115, 116, 121, 123, 156, 204
fields 25, 67–8, 83, 100, 112, 118–20,
  126, 129, 130, 132, 133, 134, 136–7,
  139, 207
see also agriculture
fatalism 197, 203
fetish 145, 157, 189, 191, 197
fiction 10, 52–3, 100, 108, 147, 149,
  161–2, 184,
fin de siècle 70, 207
flânerie 11, 151–9, 161, 164, 166–71, 173–6,
  178–81, 187, 190, 195–6, 200, 202,
  203, 210
Flights of the Northern Earls 35
flora and fauna 16, 25, 46, 69, 78, 138
flux 154, 158, 163, 187
folklore 9, 43, 53, 58–9, 62, 63, 68, 94, 95
forests 9, 13–16, 17–23, 24–8, 33–6, 37–8,
  44, 55, 59, 65
forestry 19–20, 22–3, 74, 81, 87, 90
timber 14, 17, 18, 20, 21, 24, 28,
  86, 139
fragmentation 162

gaze 100, 148, 157–8, 167, 169–70, 174–5,
  195, 196, 202, 205
Genet, Jacqueline 98, 106, 107, 108, 109
genius fabulae 47, 208
genius loci 32, 47, 208
gentry 19, 71
geography 27, 52, 65, 79, 147
geology 190, 191, 210
geopiety 16, 29

Index 233

see also tree veneration
georgic (mode) 114
Giraldus Cambrensis (Gerald of
    Wales) 24–6, 83
    Expugnatio Hibernica 25
    Topographia Hibernica 24, 25
Globalization 85, 87, 90
Gothic (genre) 41, 53, 148
Great Frost, the 4
Green Movement, the 92–3
Gregory, Lady 44, 54, 65–7, 69, 70, 72–
    4, 76, 95, 108, 165
guilt 44, 52, 72, 134
Gwynn, Edward J. 46
    Temair Breg 46, 47, 79
Gwynn, Stephen 50, 103, 184
    *Experiences of a Literary
      Man* 184, 185
    Irish Books and Irish People 50, 104

habitats 18, 65, 89, 138
habits 24–5, 50, 53, 108, 109, 168,
    196, 200
Heaney, Seamus 48, 49, 114, 117, 123, 129,
    136, 137, 139, 141, 169, 173, 187, 211
hegemony 8, 49, 50, 211
Heidegger, Martin 9, 15, 28–30, 33, 54,
    62, 66, 67, 68, 115, 154, 192, 199,
    209, 211
hermits 34, 36–9, 108
    hermit poetry 9, 11, 44
    hermit's hut 36–7
heroes 43, 48, 79, 95, 97, 104, 107, 109,
    114, 127, 129, 145, 162
heterotopia 65, 96, 208
historiography 3, 47
homme des foules, le 155

identities 2, 4, 8–9, 10, 11, 41, 48–9, 52,
    53, 78, 87, 92, 108, 111, 117, 144,
    146–8, 154, 158–9, 161, 162, 168,

    169, 184–5, 188, 193, 195, 200,
    205, 207–10
    national identity 16, 42, 53, 58, 96,
    131, 208
imagery 9, 41, 44–5, 64, 75, 97, 112–13,
    161, 180
inbetweenness 49, 63, 184, 193, 197,
    205, 211
Independence, the (Irish) 3, 20, 57, 81,
    95, 161, 162, 178, 189, 207
industrialization 7, 84, 87, 90, 197, 199,
    208, 211
Ingold, Tim 7, 77, 87, 102, 115–16, 118,
    120–1, 141, 154, 209
inhabitants 7, 11, 18, 26, 27, 32, 59, 87, 114,
    127, 148, 159, 199
Innisfree 46, 62–4, 137
intelligentsia 164, 178, 184, 202
interconnections 14, 84, 94, 116, 119, 146,
    195, 200, 209, 211
interdisciplinarity 3, 5, 146, 211, 229
intertextuality 48, 78
intuition 86, 102, 115–16, 140, 209
invasions 16, 18, 38, 44, 58, 113
invocation 48, 49, 63, 75, 76, 137, 205,
    208, 209
Irish Literary Revival 3, 4, 10, 39, 43, 44,
    51, 52, 58, 72, 81, 82, 94–5, 100,
    102, 104, 106, 111, 114, 117, 146,
    149, 162–3, 164, 181, 183, 187, 189,
    193, 197, 208, 210, c211
    see also revivalist narratives
Irish scholarship *see* Irish Studies
Irish Studies 2, 42, 49, 207
Irishness 4–5, 8–11, 44, 45, 49, 52, 58, 70,
    71, 74, 78, 79, 94, 104, 106, 107,
    111, 128, 130, 137, 141, 147, 164,
    166, 169, 181, 184, 185–7, 195, 197,
    201, 207, 208, 209, 210–11

Joyce, James 78, 159, 161–3, 164, 166, 168,

Dubliners 78, 162, 168
Finnegan's Wake 78
Portrait of the Artist as a Young Man 162
Ulysses 78, 162
justice 11, 92, 199
see also ecojustice
juxtaposition 131, 133, 147, 171, 189, 191–3, 197

Kavanagh, Patrick 2, 10–11, 102, 104, 110, 111–41, 159, 161, 163–81, 186–8, 189, 190, 196, 200, 204, 209–10
A Poet's Country, Selected Prose 131, 165, 166, 169, 178–9
Collected Poems 169
Come Dance with Kitty Stobling and Other Poems 165, 179, 180
Great Hunger, The 102, 114, 125, 127–29, 133, 135
Green Fool, The 111–12, 121–23, 124, 128, 133, 135, 137, 181
Lough Derg 123–26, 128
Ploughman and Other Poems 111
Tarry Flynn 112, 114, 118, 128, 131–3, 135, 175, 181
Kinsella, Thomas 30, 32, 162
Knowledge 38, 47, 49, 50, 58, 68, 69, 86, 92–5, 99, 102–3, 115, 116, 118–19, 127, 137–8, 139, 146

labour 10, 85, 93, 100, 133, 139, 156–7, 204, 211
labourers 157, 198–9
land 3, 8, 9, 10, 11, 13, 15, 17–18, 19, 21, 23–9, 35, 41, 43, 44, 45, 50–2, 55–6, 58–60, 61, 62, 63, 65–6, 69, 72, 74–5, 76, 83–4, 87, 89, 90, 93, 94, 95, 102, 106–7, 115, 117, 121, 129, 134–5, 136, 137, 138, 140, 145, 148, 177, 186, 192, 195, 209

Land Acts 19, 51, 72
landmarks 95, 181, 204
land ethics 29, 138
landscapes 1–7, 9–10, 13, 16, 17, 18, 20, 23–30, 32, 35–6, 38, 41–6, 48–9, 52, 54–8, 61–8, 70, 72, 74–9, 82, 86, 90–1, 94–8, 100, 106, 107, 113–15, 117–118, 120–1, 126–7, 129, 136–8, 141, 144, 146, 151, 153–5, 157, 159, 162, 167, 171, 172, 175, 177, 180–1, 190, 192–4, 197,199, 200, 202, 204, 207–11
Le Fanu, Joseph Sheridan 53, 72, 148–9
Cock and Anchor, The 148, 149
House by the Churchyard, The 149
linen 156, 197–8
localities 3, 84, 89–90, 93–4, 118, 121, 123, 133, 135, 138, 177–80, 201, 209, 211
see also regions
luxury 153, 198

MacNeice, Louis Fredrick 2, 11, 159, 183, 185–205, 210–11
Autumn Journal 187, 188, 189, 199, 201, 204
Collected Poems 185
Out of the Picture 203
Zoo 186
management 20, 87, 92–3, 98, 145
marginalization 4, 11, 20–1, 81, 84, 95, 96, 101, 113, 122, 123, 146, 159, 187, 200, 210
masks 56, 107, 109–10, 204
mass production 190
materialism 92, 109, 110
Maturin, Thomas Charles 41, 53, 148
Women; or, Pour et Contre 148
medieval (period), the 9, 16–17, 30, 36, 39, 46, 113

Index 235

memory 15, 38, 46, 48, 75–7, 78, 102, 109, 115, 119, 121, 123, 126, 155, 159, 167–8, 172–3, 181, 196
metaphysical 9, 14, 62–3, 65, 76
metropolis 137, 157, 165, 166, 169, 172, 174, 178, 189, 191, 196
mindscapes 41, 46, 54, 56, 58, 62–5, 96, 208, 209
modernization 90, 105, 122, 157, 197
   modernism 110, 159, 162, 201
   modernity 106, 152, 157, 170, 171, 189–91, 205
Monaghan 34, 71, 111, 113, 116, 117, 121, 128, 135, 136, 137, 164, 177, 180, 181
monasteries 33, 37, 95
movement 11, 25, 41, 44, 88, 92–3, 95, 120, 140, 145, 158–9, 162, 163, 168, 187, 200, 202, 205, 210
multitude(s) 151, 154, 156, 163, 172, 173, 151, 154, 156, 163, 172, 173
mythologies 9, 47, 58, 69, 74, 77, 137

naming 15, 68, 70, 137, 176
narratives 2–4, 7, 8–11, 13, 23, 26, 28, 36, 41–2, 44, 45–6, 47, 48, 49–52, 59, 78, 81, 82, 84, 95, 98, 99–100, 104, 112, 116–17, 119, 121, 129, 141, 143, 146, 175, 187, 189, 207–8, 210
   revivalist narratives 10, 94, 100, 114, 141, 159, 201
nationalism 2–3, 5, 45, 70, 94, 95, 96, 98, 99, 104, 129, 130, 137, 150, 163, 184
nature 2–3, 5–8, 14, 15, 18–19, 24, 25, 27, 29, 32–4, 36–9, 41–7, 54–5, 57, 62–3, 73, 75–6, 91, 92, 93, 96, 101–2, 106, 113–14, 115, 133–4, 135, 136, 139, 141, 144–6, 157, 167, 168, 170, 177, 179–81, 192, 197, 199, 208, 210–11,
   see also environment, the
nature writing 34, 36, 41, 43, 44, 54, 144

North, the 4, 8, 11, 15, 35, 49, 64, 88, 91, 96, 101, 116, 123, 124, 127, 136, 139, 147, 164, 183–7, 189, 192–9, 205, 210
   see also Ulster
Northern Ireland 15, 88, 91, 187, 190, 197, 199
nostalgia 36, 39, 41, 44, 45, 53, 61, 76, 113, 129, 141, 147, 149–50, 168, 179, 181
novels 1, 42, 51, 53, 84, 95, 97–9, 103, 113, 116, 129, 139, 184

Liddiard, Anna 99
London 109, 122, 148, 152–3, 161, 163, 164, 165, 178, 196, 198

observation 91, 102, 128, 131, 133, 152, 154, 155, 158, 168, 174, 175, 189, 200
occult, the 53, 58, 62, 69
oral tradition (Irish) 34, 37
other 6, 14, 26, 31, 36, 37, 65
Owenson, Sydney (Lady Morgan) 41, 51, 95, 97, 99–100, 103
   O'Donnel: A National Tale 100
   Wild Irish Girl, The: A National Tale 99, 100

Paris 151–3, 155, 156, 157–8, 166, 169, 170, 174
parish 11, 90, 116, 119, 121, 123–4, 125, 126, 135, 136–7, 138, 164, 166, 177–80, 209
Partition, the 184, 185, 207, 210–11
patriotization 52, 58
   patriotism 66, 99
pastoral (mode), the 41, 55, 56, 83, 112–14, 147, 148, 153, 174, 179, 181, 188
   antipastoral 83, 114, 202
   Irish pastoral 113–14
   post-pastoral/urban pastoral 113, 147, 174, 177, 179

Index

pastoralism 82, 83, 113, 114, 144, 201
Patrick, St 3, 59, 60
Peasantry 50, 56, 58, 71–2, 79, 82, 95, 97–
104, 106–9, 111, 115, 120, 125, 127,
128–31, 133–5, 177, 195
Penal Code 50, 140
peripheries 59
personae 10, 11, 54–7, 58–9, 60, 62, 63,
64–5, 75, 76–7, 79, 104, 107,
109–10, 117, 120, 127, 134, 171, 173,
175, 204, 205
see also masks
phantasmagoria 79, 191
physicophobia 27
picturesque, the 41–3, 95, 97, 131, 141,
147–9, 150
pilgrimage 121, 124–5, 126
placelessness 49, 53, 61, 63, 64, 156
placenames 9, 15, 63, 68, 136–7, 179
plantation 18, 28, 35, 44, 51
ploughs 121–3, 130, 132,
Comhar 123
plurality 171, 183, 187, 193, 205
Poetics of dwelling 2, 111, 115, 116, 209
politics 8, 43, 144, 197
pollution 82, 87, 93, 146, 200, 201, 210
portrayals 3, 4, 8, 11, 25, 27, 33, 65, 94, 98,
99, 102, 104, 109, 110, 116, 120,
130, 131, 147–8, 162, 169, 170, 179,
196, 209, 210
see also representations
poverty 11, 19, 53, 75, 81, 82, 97–8, 89, 96,
97, 98, 100, 101, 124, 125, 139, 161,
194, 197, 199, 200, 208, 210
presencing see *Anwesen*
preservation 1, 20, 30, 34, 66, 82, 85,
91, 115
profit 24, 28, 83, 198, 199, 211
progress 8, 28, 81, 82, 91, 101, 199
provincialism 137, 166, 178
publishing 103, 147, 157, 163–4

raths 9, 30–3, 37, 47–8
rebellion 41, 49, 99
regions 3–4, 14–16, 20, 47, 49, 68, 74, 82,
85, 87, 88, 89, 92, 96, 97, 117, 184,
194, 209
regionalism 185, 186
repetitions 150, 175, 189, 197
representations 5, 8, 9–10, 14, 29, 42,
45–6, 51, 53–4, 57, 60, 61, 63–4,
71, 72, 73, 75, 82, 94, 96, 98, 99,
100, 103–4, 107–8, 129, 131, 136,
141, 146–7, 148, 159, 161, 163, 166,
167, 169, 173, 184, 190, 192–3, 194,
195, 197, 198, 200, 204, 205, 207,
208, 209–11
anxiety of representation 103, 211
misrepresentations 95, 128
Republic, of Ireland (the) 8, 15, 22, 88,
89, 90, 91, 92, 163, 207
rhetoric of compensation, the 51, 52,
58, 186
rootedness 54, 58, 74, 186
Romanticism 42, 45, 51, 95
Irish Romanticism 41, 42, 44–5
rurality 88, 89, 92, 94
see also countryside, the
Russell, George (AE) 70, 111, 147,
161, 164

scapeland 6
sceneries 54, 55, 60, 64, 75, 87, 178,
202, 205
sectarianism 42, 101, 184, 187, 198
sense of place 4, 8–11, 36, 44, 46, 49–51,
63, 65, 71, 72, 74–6, 78–9, 94,
114, 134–8, 140–1, 143–5, 149,
151, 158, 162, 163, 180, 183, 185, 187,
193, 201, 202, 208–10
Sheeran, Patrick 33, 46, 57, 62, 208
Sidhe 53, 64
see also faeries; *Tuatha Dé Danaan*

Index

sites 11, 32, 35, 47–8, 90, 92, 95, 97, 113, 124, 126, 147, 149, 151, 154, 161, 163, 164, 167–8, 171–2, 173, 179, 192, 203

Sligo 9, 20, 46, 63, 64, 96–7

soil 13, 25–6, 28–9, 58, 66, 76, 79, 82, 87, 106, 107, 119, 127–9, 135–6, 136, 137, 138, 181, 195, 209

see also clay

South, the 4, 49, 53, 59, 101, 186–7, 205

spectacle 157, 180

Spenser, Edmund 25, 26, 27–8, 29, 83, 201
Colin Clouts Come Home Againe 83
Faerie Queen, The 28, 83
Shepheardes Calender 83
View of the Present State of Ireland, A 26

stage Irishry 100, 103

standing-reserve 28, 29, 199

stasis 61, 114, 117, 162, 163, 209

stereotypes 10, 49, 97–8, 100, 103, 104, 115, 130, 163, 165, 197, 201, 208

streets 11, 97, 112, 117, 149–51, 154–5, 157–8, 162, 165, 167–70, 172–7, 179–81, 200, 202

Stuart, period 18, 71

subjugation 16, 26, 27, 83

sublime, the 41, 42, 43, 190, 193
urban sublime 190, 193

subversion 116, 129, 186, 187, 192, 197, 203, 210

supernatural, the 43, 45, 52–4, 56, 58, 61, 63–4, 79, 108, 113

sustainability 82, 85, 88–9, 91–4, 208

symbolism 6, 21, 41, 43–6, 54, 62, 65, 72–3, 107, 127, 134, 147, 161, 179, 209

Synge, John Millington 70, 73, 77, 95, 107, 165

Tara 31–2, 46–8, 68, 79, 208

taskscapes 120, 209

technology 6–7, 85, 187, 199, 202

temporality 85, 90, 114, 115, 120, 154, 167

Thirties generation, the (of poets) 185, 188

Thoor Ballylee 57, 65, 70, 73, 76, 77

Tír na nÓg 56, 59–60, 62–3, 65, 75

trains 11, 25, 189, 200–2, 204–5

trauma 36, 41, 49, 187

travelling 19, 32, 81, 91–2, 94, 104–5, 107, 132, 139, 164, 195–6, 208, 209, 210, 211, 212–3, 219, 222

travel writing 10, 187, 200, 205

tree veneration 16, 17

trees 21–5, 27–30, 36, 37, 42, 46, 51, 74, 76, 83–4, 121, 122, 125, 127, 134, 147–8, 196, 223, 226, 227, 230

topographical tradition, the 24, 25, 41, 46–9, 52–3, 58, 68, 74, 76, 78, 149, 195, 204, 205, 208–9

topography 46, 47, 52, 58, 74, 76, 149, 204, 208–209

topophilia 46–7, 49, 143

tourism 6, 20, 65, 81, 82, 85–6, 87, 90, 131, 195, 197, 200, 202–3

Tuatha Dé Danaan 46
see also faeries; *sidhe*; *Tír na nÓg*

Tudors, the 16, 18, 27, 34

Ulster 101, 113, 122, 136, 161, 164, 184–6, 193, 197, 198, 199, 210
see also North; Northern Ireland

unemployment 81, 82, 112, 124, 144, 200, 201

urbanization 7, 84, 105, 145, 154, 147, 208
urban sprawl 20, 84, 87, 207
urbanites 84, 86

vernacular, the (Gaelic) 94, 96, 102, 103, 108, 137, 139

violence 11, 42, 148–9, 184, 211

voices 10, 38, 82, 93, 100, 109, 125, 186, 211

238   *Index*

walking 123, 150–5, 158, 162, 167–8, 172–
   3, 179, 200
wanderings 45, 46, 54, 55, 56, 57, 58, 59–
   61, 64, 74, 75, 79, 108, 205
war(s) 35, 77, 125, 126, 139, 163, 165–6,
   178, 194
  First World War 20, 76
  Second World War 11, 20, 122, 124,
    125, 126, 139, 163–4, 165, 178,
    184, 185
West, the (Irish) 1, 2, 9, 17, 46, 58, 59, 64,
   96–7, 112, 195
wilderness 6, 7, 9, 10, 13, 16, 27–8, 31, 37,
   43, 45, 57, 63, 64, 82, 96, 144,
   146, 151, 154, 199, 207, 208
Williams, Raymond 151
woodlands *see* forests

Yeats, William Butler 2, 9, 41, 44–6,
   52, 53, 54, 55–9, 60, 61–5, 67–8,
   69–70, 73, 75, 76, 77–9, 95, 96,
   97, 100, 103–4, 106–9, 111, 127,
   131, 134, 147, 161, 165, 166, 186,
   187, 208
  Autobiographies 58, 68, 69, 110
  Cathleen Ni Houlihan 108
  Celtic Twilight, The 58, 109–10
  Collected Poems 54, 59
  Crossways 45, 54, 56
  Last Poems 77
  Mythologies 58
  Secret Rose, The 108, 110
  Shadowy Waters, The 67
  Stories of Red Hanrahan, The 108
  Vision, A 107, 187
  Wanderings of Oisin, The 46, 59, 62,
   63, 113

Reimagining Ireland

Series Editor: Dr Eamon Maher, Technological
University Dublin

The concepts of Ireland and 'Irishness' are in constant flux in the wake of an ever-increasing reappraisal of the notion of cultural and national specificity in a world assailed from all angles by the forces of globalisation and uniformity. Reimagining Ireland interrogates Ireland's past and present and suggests possibilities for the future by looking at Ireland's literature, culture and history and subjecting them to the most up-to-date critical appraisals associated with sociology, literary theory, historiography, political science and theology.

Some of the pertinent issues include, but are not confined to, Irish writing in English and Irish, Nationalism, Unionism, the Northern 'Troubles', the Peace Process, economic development in Ireland, the impact and decline of the Celtic Tiger, Irish spirituality, the rise and fall of organised religion, the visual arts, popular cultures, sport, Irish music and dance, emigration and the Irish diaspora, immigration and multiculturalism, marginalisation, globalisation, modernity/postmodernity and postcolonialism. The series publishes monographs, comparative studies, interdisciplinary projects, conference proceedings and edited books. Proposals should be sent either to Dr Eamon Maher at eamon.maher@ittdublin.ie or to ireland@peterlang.com.

Vol. 1   Eugene O'Brien: 'Kicking Bishop Brennan up the Arse': Negotiating
           Texts and Contexts in Contemporary Irish Studies
           ISBN 978-3-03911-539-6. 219 pages. 2009.

Vol. 2   James P.Byrne, Padraig Kirwan and Michael O'Sullivan
           (eds): Affecting Irishness: Negotiating Cultural Identity Within and
           Beyond the Nation
           ISBN 978-3-03911-830-4. 334 pages. 2009.

Vol. 3   Irene Lucchitti: The Islandman: The Hidden Life of Tomás O'Crohan
           ISBN 978-3-03911-837-3. 232 pages. 2009.

Vol. 4   Paddy Lyons and Alison O'Malley-Younger (eds): No Country for Old
           Men: Fresh Perspectives on Irish Literature
           ISBN 978-3-03911-841-0. 289 pages. 2009.

Vol. 5   Eamon Maher (ed.): Cultural Perspectives on Globalisation and Ireland
ISBN 978-3-03911-851-9. 256 pages. 2009.

Vol. 6   Lynn Brunet: 'A Course of Severe and Arduous Trials': Bacon, Beckett and Spurious Freemasonry in Early Twentieth-Century Ireland
ISBN 978-3-03911-854-0. 218 pages. 2009.

Vol. 7   Claire Lynch: Irish Autobiography: Stories of Self in the Narrative of a Nation
ISBN 978-3-03911-856-4. 234 pages. 2009.

Vol. 8   Victoria O'Brien: A History of Irish Ballet from 1927 to 1963
ISBN 978-3-03911-873-1. 208 pages. 2011.

Vol. 9   Irene Gilsenan Nordin and Elin Holmsten (eds): Liminal Borderlands in Irish Literature and Culture
ISBN 978-3-03911-859-5. 208 pages. 2009.

Vol. 10   Claire Nally: Envisioning Ireland: W. B. Yeats's Occult Nationalism
ISBN 978-3-03911-882-3. 320 pages. 2010.

Vol. 11   Raita Merivirta: The Gun and Irish Politics: Examining National History in Neil Jordan's *Michael Collins*
ISBN 978-3-03911-888-5. 202 pages. 2009.

Vol. 12   John Strachan and Alison O'Malley-Younger (eds): Ireland: Revolution and Evolution
ISBN 978-3-03911-881-6. 248 pages. 2010.

Vol. 13   Barbara Hughes: Between Literature and History: The Diaries and Memoirs of Mary Leadbeater and Dorothea Herbert
ISBN 978-3-03911-889-2. 255 pages. 2010.

Vol. 14   Edwina Keown and Carol Taaffe (eds): Irish Modernism: Origins, Contexts, Publics
ISBN 978-3-03911-894-6. 256 pages. 2010.

Vol. 15   John Walsh: Contests and Contexts: The Irish Language and Ireland's Socio-Economic Development
ISBN 978-3-03911-914-1. 492 pages. 2011.

Vol. 16   Zélie Asava: The Black Irish Onscreen: Representing Black and
           Mixed-Race Identities on Irish Film and Television
           ISBN 978-3-0343-0839-7. 213 pages. 2013.

Vol. 17   Susan Cahill and Eóin Flannery (eds): This Side of Brightness: Essays
           on the Fiction of Colum McCann
           ISBN 978-3-03911-935-6. 189 pages. 2012.

Vol. 18   Brian Arkins: The Thought of W. B. Yeats
           ISBN 978-3-03911-939-4. 204 pages. 2010.

Vol. 19   Maureen O'Connor: The Female and the Species: The Animal in Irish
           Women's Writing
           ISBN 978-3-03911-959-2. 203 pages. 2010.

Vol. 20   Rhona Trench: Bloody Living: The Loss of Selfhood in the Plays of
           Marina Carr
           ISBN 978-3-03911-964-6. 327 pages. 2010.

Vol. 21   Jeannine Woods: Visions of Empire and Other Imaginings: Cinema,
           Ireland and India, 1910–1962
           ISBN 978-3-03911-974-5. 230 pages. 2011.

Vol. 22   Neil O'Boyle: New Vocabularies, Old Ideas: Culture, Irishness and the
           Advertising Industry
           ISBN 978-3-03911-978-3. 233 pages. 2011.

Vol. 23   Dermot McCarthy: John McGahern and the Art of Memory
           ISBN 978-3-0343-0100-8. 344 pages. 2010.

Vol. 24   Francesca Benatti, Sean Ryder and Justin Tonra (eds): Thomas
           Moore: Texts, Contexts, Hypertexts
           ISBN 978-3-0343-0900-4. 220 pages. 2013.

Vol. 25   Sarah O'Connor: No Man's Land: Irish Women and the Cultural
           Present
           ISBN 978-3-0343-0111-4. 230 pages. 2011.

Vol. 26   Caroline Magennis: Sons of Ulster: Masculinities in the Contem-
           porary Northern Irish Novel
           ISBN 978-3-0343-0110-7. 192 pages. 2010.

Vol. 27   Dawn Duncan: Irish Myth, Lore and Legend on Film
            ISBN 978-3-0343-0140-4. 181 pages. 2013.

Vol. 28   Eamon Maher and Catherine Maignant (eds): Franco-Irish
            Connections in Space and Time: Peregrinations and Ruminations
            ISBN 978-3-0343-0870-0. 295 pages. 2012.

Vol. 29   Holly Maples: Culture War: Conflict, Commemoration and the
            Contemporary Abbey Theatre
            ISBN 978-3-0343-0137-4. 294 pages. 2011.

Vol. 30   Maureen O'Connor (ed.): Back to the Future of Irish
            Studies: Festschrift for Tadhg Foley
            ISBN 978-3-0343-0141-1. 359 pages. 2010.

Vol. 31   Eva Urban: Community Politics and the Peace Process in
            Contemporary Northern Irish Drama
            ISBN 978-3-0343-0143-5. 303 pages. 2011.

Vol. 32   Mairéad Conneely: Between Two Shores/*Idir Dhá Chladach*: Writing
            the Aran Islands, 1890–1980
            ISBN 978-3-0343-0144-2. 299 pages. 2011.

Vol. 33   Gerald Morgan and Gavin Hughes (eds): Southern Ireland and the
            Liberation of France: New Perspectives
            ISBN 978-3-0343-0190-9. 250 pages. 2011.

Vol. 34   Anne MacCarthy: Definitions of Irishness in the 'Library of
            Ireland' Literary Anthologies
            ISBN 978-3-0343-0194-7. 271 pages. 2012.

Vol. 35   Irene Lucchitti: Peig Sayers: In Her Own Write
            ISBN 978-3-0343-0253-1. Forthcoming.

Vol. 36   Eamon Maher and Eugene O'Brien (eds): Breaking the
            Mould: Literary Representations of Irish Catholicism
            ISBN 978-3-0343-0232-6. 249 pages. 2011.

Vol. 37   Mícheál Ó hAodha and John O'Callaghan (eds): Narratives of the
            Occluded Irish Diaspora: Subversive Voices
            ISBN 978-3-0343-0248-7. 227 pages. 2012.

Vol. 38 Willy Maley and Alison O'Malley-Younger (eds): Celtic
Connections: Irish–Scottish Relations and the Politics of Culture
ISBN 978-3-0343-0214-2. 247 pages. 2013.

Vol. 39 Sabine Egger and John McDonagh (eds): Polish–Irish Encounters in
the Old and New Europe
ISBN 978-3-0343-0253-1. 322 pages. 2011.

Vol. 40 Elke D'hoker, Raphaël Ingelbien and Hedwig Schwall (eds): Irish
Women Writers: New Critical Perspectives
ISBN 978-3-0343-0249-4. 318 pages. 2011.

Vol. 41 Peter James Harris: From Stage to Page: Critical Reception of Irish
Plays in the London Theatre, 1925–1996
ISBN 978-3-0343-0266-1. 311 pages. 2011.

Vol. 42 Hedda Friberg-Harnesk, Gerald Porter and Joakim Wrethed
(eds): Beyond Ireland: Encounters Across Cultures
ISBN 978-3-0343-0270-8. 342 pages. 2011.

Vol. 43 Irene Gilsenan Nordin and Carmen Zamorano Llena (eds): Urban
and Rural Landscapes in Modern Ireland: Language, Literature and
Culture
ISBN 978-3-0343-0279-1. 238 pages. 2012.

Vol. 44 Kathleen Costello-Sullivan: Mother/Country: Politics of the Personal
in the Fiction of Colm Tóibín
ISBN 978-3-0343-0753-6. 247 pages. 2012.

Vol. 45 Lesley Lelourec and Gráinne O'Keeffe-Vigneron (eds): Ireland and
Victims: Confronting the Past, Forging the Future
ISBN 978-3-0343-0792-5. 331 pages. 2012.

Vol. 46 Gerald Dawe, Darryl Jones and Nora Pelizzari (eds): Beautiful
Strangers: Ireland and the World of the 1950s
ISBN 978-3-0343-0801-4. 207 pages. 2013.

Vol. 47 Yvonne O'Keeffe and Claudia Reese (eds): New Voices, Inherited
Lines: Literary and Cultural Representations of the Irish Family
ISBN 978-3-0343-0799-4. 238 pages. 2013.

Vol. 48   Justin Carville (ed.): Visualizing Dublin: Visual Culture, Modernity
            and the Representation of Urban Space
            ISBN 978-3-0343-0802-1. 326 pages. 2014.

Vol. 49   Gerald Power and Ondřej Pilný (eds): Ireland and the Czech
            Lands: Contacts and Comparisons in History and Culture
            ISBN 978-3-0343-1701-6. 243 pages. 2014.

Vol. 50   Eoghan Smith: John Banville: Art and Authenticity
            ISBN 978-3-0343-0852-6. 199 pages. 2014.

Vol. 51   María Elena Jaime de Pablos and Mary Pierse (eds): George Moore
            and the Quirks of Human Nature
            ISBN 978-3-0343-1752-8. 283 pages. 2014.

Vol. 52   Aidan O'Malley and Eve Patten (eds): Ireland, West to East: Irish
            Cultural Connections with Central and Eastern Europe
            ISBN 978-3-0343-0913-4. 307 pages. 2014.

Vol. 53   Ruben Moi, Brynhildur Boyce and Charles I. Armstrong (eds): The
            Crossings of Art in Ireland
            ISBN 978-3-0343-0983-7. 319 pages. 2014.

Vol. 54   Sylvie Mikowski (ed.): Ireland and Popular Culture
            ISBN 978-3-0343-1717-7. 257 pages. 2014.

Vol. 55   Benjamin Keatinge and Mary Pierse (eds): France and Ireland in the
            Public Imagination
            ISBN 978-3-0343-1747-4. 279 pages. 2014.

Vol. 56   Raymond Mullen, Adam Bargroff and Jennifer Mullen (eds): John
            McGahern: Critical Essays
            ISBN 978-3-0343-1755-9. 253 pages. 2014.

Vol. 57   Máirtín Mac Con Iomaire and Eamon Maher (eds): 'Tickling the
            Palate': Gastronomy in Irish Literature and Culture
            ISBN 978-3-0343-1769-6. 253 pages. 2014.

Vol. 58   Heidi Hansson and James H. Murphy (eds): Fictions of the Irish
            Land War
            ISBN 978-3-0343-0999-8. 237 pages. 2014.

Vol. 59   Fiona McCann: A Poetics of Dissensus: Confronting Violence in
Contemporary Prose Writing from the North of Ireland
ISBN 978-3-0343-0979-0. 238 pages. 2014.

Vol. 60   Marguérite Corporaal, Christopher Cusack, Lindsay Janssen and
Ruud van den Beuken (eds): Global Legacies of the Great Irish
Famine: Transnational and Interdisciplinary Perspectives
ISBN 978-3-0343-0903-5. 357 pages. 2014.

Vol. 61   Katarzyna Ojrzyn'ska: 'Dancing As If Language No Longer
Existed': Dance in Contemporary Irish Drama
ISBN 978-3-0343-1813-6. 318 pages. 2015.

Vol. 62   Whitney Standlee: 'Power to Observe': Irish Women Novelists in
Britain, 1890–1916
ISBN 978-3-0343-1837-2. 288 pages. 2015.

Vol. 63   Elke D'hoker and Stephanie Eggermont (eds): The Irish Short
Story: Traditions and Trends
ISBN 978-3-0343-1753-5. 330 pages. 2015.

Vol. 64   Radvan Markus: Echoes of the Rebellion: The Year 1798 in Twentieth-
Century Irish Fiction and Drama
ISBN 978-3-0343-1832-7. 248 pages. 2015.

Vol. 65   B. Mairéad Pratschke: Visions of Ireland: Gael Linn's *Amharc Éireann*
Film Series, 1956–1964
ISBN 978-3-0343-1872-3. 301 pages. 2015.

Vol. 66   Una Hunt and Mary Pierse (eds): France and Ireland: Notes and
Narratives
ISBN 978-3-0343-1914-0. 272 pages. 2015.

Vol. 67   John Lynch and Katherina Dodou (eds): The Leaving of
Ireland: Migration and Belonging in Irish Literature and Film
ISBN 978-3-0343-1896-9. 313 pages. 2015.

Vol. 68   Anne Goarzin (ed.): New Critical Perspectives on Franco-Irish
Relations
ISBN 978-3-0343-1781-8. 271 pages. 2015.

Vol. 69   Michel Brunet, Fabienne Gaspari and Mary Pierse (eds): George
           Moore's Paris and His Ongoing French Connections
           ISBN 978-3-0343-1973-7. 279 pages. 2015.

Vol. 70   Carine Berbéri and Martine Pelletier (eds): Ireland: Authority
           and Crisis
           ISBN 978-3-0343-1939-3. 296 pages. 2015.

Vol. 71   David Doolin: Transnational Revolutionaries: The Fenian Invasion of
           Canada, 1866
           ISBN 978-3-0343-1922-5. 348 pages. 2016.

Vol. 72   Terry Phillips: Irish Literature and the First World War: Culture,
           Identity and Memory
           ISBN 978-3-0343-1969-0. 297 pages. 2015.

Vol. 73   Carmen Zamorano Llena and Billy Gray (eds): Authority and
           Wisdom in the New Ireland: Studies in Literature and Culture
           ISBN 978-3-0343-1833-4. 263 pages. 2016.

Vol. 74   Flore Coulouma (ed.): New Perspectives on Irish TV Series: Identity
           and Nostalgia on the Small Screen
           ISBN 978-3-0343-1977-5. 222 pages. 2016.

Vol. 75   Fergal Lenehan: Stereotypes, Ideology and Foreign
           Correspondents: German Media Representations of Ireland,
           1946–2010
           ISBN 978-3-0343-2222-5. 306 pages. 2016.

Vol. 76   Jarlath Killeen and Valeria Cavalli (eds): 'Inspiring a Mysterious
           Terror': 200 Years of Joseph Sheridan Le Fanu
           ISBN 978-3-0343-2223-2. 260 pages. 2016.

Vol. 77   Anne Karhio: 'Slight Return': Paul Muldoon's Poetics of Place
           ISBN 978-3-0343-1986-7. 272 pages. 2017.

Vol. 78   Margaret Eaton: Frank Confessions: Performance in the Life-Writings
           of Frank McCourt
           ISBN 978-1-906165-61-1. 294 pages. 2017.

Vol. 79 Marguérite Corporaal, Christopher Cusack and Ruud van den Beuken (eds): Irish Studies and the Dynamics of Memory: Transitions and Transformations
ISBN 978-3-0343-2236-2. 360 pages. 2017.

Vol. 80 Conor Caldwell and Eamon Byers (eds): New Crops, Old Fields: Reimagining Irish Folklore
ISBN 978-3-0343-1912-6. 200 pages. 2017.

Vol. 81 Sinéad Wall: Irish Diasporic Narratives in Argentina: A Reconsideration of Home, Identity and Belonging
ISBN 978-1-906165-66-6. 282 pages. 2017.

Vol. 82 Ute Anna Mittermaier: Images of Spain in Irish Literature, 1922–1975
ISBN 978-3-0343-1993-5. 386 pages. 2017.

Vol. 83 Lauren Clark: Consuming Irish Children: Advertising and the Art of Independence, 1860–1921
ISBN 978-3-0343-1989-8. 288 pages. 2017.

Vol. 84 Lisa FitzGerald: Re-Place: Irish Theatre Environments
ISBN 978-1-78707-359-3. 222 pages. 2017.

Vol. 85 Joseph Greenwood: 'Hear My Song': Irish Theatre and Popular Song in the 1950s and 1960s
ISBN 978-3-0343-1915-7. 320 pages. 2017.

Vol. 86 Nils Beese: Writing Slums: Dublin, Dirt and Literature
ISBN 978-1-78707-959-5. 250 pages. 2018.

Vol. 87 Barry Houlihan (ed.): Navigating Ireland's Theatre Archive: Theory, Practice, Performance
ISBN 978-1-78707-372-2. 306 pages. 2019.

Vol. 88 María Elena Jaime de Pablos (ed.): Giving Shape to the Moment: The Art of Mary O'Donnell: Poet, Novelist and Short Story Writer
ISBN 978-1-78874-403-4. 228 pages. 2018.

Vol. 89 Marguérite Corporaal and Peter Gray (eds): The Great Irish Famine and Social Class: Conflicts, Responsibilities, Representations
ISBN 978-1-78874-166-8. 330 pages. 2019.

Vol. 90 Patrick Speight: Irish-Argentine Identity in an Age of Political Challenge and Change, 1875–1983
ISBN 978-1-78874-417-1. 360 pages. 2020.

Vol. 91 Fionna Barber, Heidi Hansson, and Sara Dybris McQuaid (eds): Ireland and the North
ISBN 978-1-78874-289-4. 338 pages. 2019.

Vol. 92 Ruth Sheehy: The Life and Work of Richard King: Religion, Nationalism and Modernism
ISBN 978-1-78707-246-6. 482 pages. 2019.

Vol. 93 Brian Lucey, Eamon Maher and Eugene O'Brien (eds): Recalling the Celtic Tiger
ISBN 978-1-78997-286-3. 386 pages. 2019.

Vol. 94 Melania Terrazas Gallego (ed.): Trauma and Identity in Contemporary Irish Culture
ISBN 978-1-78997-557-4. 302 pages. 2020.

Vol. 95 Patricia Medcalf: Advertising the Black Stuff in Ireland 1959–1999: Increments of Change
ISBN 978-1-78997-345-7. 218 pages. 2020.

Vol. 96 Anne Goarzin and Maria Parsons (eds): New Cartographies, Nomadic Methologies: Contemporary Arts, Culture and Politics in Ireland
ISBN 978-1-78874-651-9. 204 pages. 2020.

Vol. 97 Hiroko Ikeda and Kazuo Yokouchi (eds): Irish Literature in the British Context and Beyond: New Perspectives from Kyoto
ISBN 978-1-78997-566-6. 250 pages. 2020.

Vol. 98 Catherine Nealy Judd: Travel Narratives of the Irish Famine: Politics, Tourism, and Scandal, 1845–1853
ISBN 978-1-80079-084-1. 468 pages. 2020.

Vol. 99 Lesley Lelourec and Gráinne O'Keeffe-Vigneron (eds): Northern Ireland after the Good Friday Agreement: Building a Shared Future from a Troubled Past?
ISBN 978-1-78997-746-2. 262 pages. 2021.

Vol. 100 Eamon Maher and Eugene O'Brien (eds): Reimagining Irish Studies for the Twenty-First Century
ISBN 978-1-80079-191-6. 384 pages. 2021.

Vol. 101 Nathalie Sebbane: Memorialising the Magdalene Laundries: From Story to History
ISBN 978-1-78707-589-4. 334 pages. 2021.

Vol. 102 Roz Goldie: A Dangerous Pursuit: The Anti-Sectarian Work of Counteract
ISBN 978-1-80079-187-9. 268 pages. 2021.

Vol. 103 Ann Wilson: The Picture Postcard: A New Window into Edwardian Ireland
ISBN 978-1-78874-079-1. 282 pages. 2021.

Vol. 104 Anna Charczun: Irish Lesbian Writing Across Time: A New Framework for Rethinking Love Between Women
ISBN 978-1-78997-864-3. 320 pages. 2022.

Vol. 105 Olivier Coquelin, Brigitte Bastiat and Frank Healy (eds): Northern Ireland: Challenges of Peace and Reconciliation Since the Good Friday Agreement
ISBN 978-1-78997-817-9. 298 pages. 2022.

Vol. 106 Jo Murphy-Lawless and Laury Oaks (eds): The Salley Gardens: Women, Sex, and Motherhood in Ireland
ISBN 978-1-80079-417-7. 338 pages. 2022.

Vol. 107 Mercedes del Campo: Voices from the Margins: Gender and the Everyday in Women's Pre- and Post-Agreement Troubles Short Fiction
ISBN 978-1-78874-330-3. 324 pages. 2022.

Vol. 108 Sean McGraw and Jonathan Tiernan: The Politics of Irish Primary Education: Reform in an Era of Secularisation
ISBN 978-1-80079-709-3. 532 pages. 2022.

Vol. 109   Gerald Dawe: Northern Windows/Southern Stars: Selected Early
Essays 1983–1994
ISBN 978-1-80079-652-2. 180 pages. 2022.

Vol. 110   John Fanning: The Mandarin, the Musician and the Mage:
T. K. Whitaker, Seán Ó Riada, Thomas Kinsella and the Lessons of
Ireland's Mid-Twentieth-Century Revival
ISBN 978-1-80079-599-0. 296 pages. 2022.

Vol. 111   Gerald Dawe: Dreaming of Home: Seven Irish Writers
ISBN 978-1-80079-655-3. 108 pages. 2022.

Vol. 112   John Walsh: One Hundred Years of Irish Language Policy, 1922–2022
ISBN 978-1-78997-892-6. 394 pages. 2022.

Vol. 113   Bertrand Cardin: Neil Jordan, Author and Screenwriter: The
Imagination of Transgression
ISBN 978-1-80079-923-3. XXX pages. 2023.

Vol. 114   David Clark: Dark Green: Irish Crime Fiction 1665–2000
ISBN 978-1-80079-826-7. 450 pages. 2022.

Vol. 115   Aida Rosende-Pérez and Rubén Jarazo-Álvarez (eds): The Cultural
Politics of In/Difference: Irish Texts and Contexts
ISBN 978-1-80079-727-7. 274 pages. 2022.

Vol. 116   Tara McConnell: "Honest Claret": The Social Meaning of Georgian
Ireland's Favourite Wine
ISBN 978-1-80079-790-1. 346 pages. 2022.

Vol. 117   M. Teresa Caneda-Cabrera (ed.): Telling Truths: Evelyn Conlon and
the Task of Writing
ISBN 978-1-80079-481-8. 228 pages. 2023.

Vol. 118   Alexandra Maclennan (ed.): The Irish Catholic Diaspora: Five
Centuries of Global Presence
ISBN 978-1-80079-516-7. 264 pages. 2023.

Vol. 119   Brian J. Murphy: Beyond Sustenance: An Exploration of Food and
Drink Culture in Ireland
ISBN 978-1-80079-956-1. 328 pages. 2023.

Vol. 120   Fintan Cullen (ed.): Ireland and the British Empire: Essays on Art and Visuality
ISBN 978-1-78874-299-3. 264 pages. 2023.

Vol. 121   Natalie Wynn and Zuleika Rodgers (eds): Reimagining the Jews of Ireland: Historiography, Identity and Representation
ISBN 978-1-80079-083-4. *Forthcoming.* 2023.

Vol. 122   Paul Butler: A Deep Well of Want: Visualising the World of John McGahern
ISBN 978-1-80079-810-6. 244 pages. 2023.

Vol. 123   Carlos Menéndez Otero: The Great Pretenders: Genre, Form, and Style in the Film Musicals of John Carney
ISBN 978-1-80374-135-2. 258 pages. 2023.

Vol. 124   Gerald Dawe: Politic Words: Writing Women | Writing History
ISBN 978-1-80374-259-5. 208 pages. 2023.

Vol. 125   Marjan Shokouhi: From Landscapes to Cityscapes: Towards a Poetics of Dwelling in Modern Irish Verse
ISBN 978-1-80079-870-0. 260 pages. 2023.

Vol. 126   Pat O'Connor: A 'proper' woman? One woman's story of success and failure in academia
ISBN 978-1-80374-305-9. *Forthcoming.* 2023.